The Literature of Jealousy
in the Age of Cervantes

The Literature of Jealousy in the Age of Cervantes

STEVEN WAGSCHAL

University of Missouri Press   Columbia and London

Copyright © 2006 by
The Curators of the University of Missouri
University of Missouri Press, Columbia, Missouri 65201
Printed and bound in the United States of America
All rights reserved
5 4 3 2 1   10 09 08 07 06

Library of Congress Cataloging-in-Publication Data

Wagschal, Steven, 1967–
The literature of jealousy in the age of Cervantes / Steven Wagschal.
        p. cm.
Summary: "Explores the theme of jealousy in early modern Spanish literature
through the works of Lope de Vega, Cervantes, and Góngora. Using the
philosophical frameworks of Vives, Descartes, Freud, and DeSousa, Wagschal
proposes that the theme of jealousy offered a means for working through
political and cultural problems involving power"—Provided by publisher.
Includes bibliographical references and index.
        ISBN-13: 978-0-8262-1696-0 (hard cover : alk. paper)
        ISBN-10: 0-8262-1696-X (hard cover : alk. paper)
    1. Spanish literature—Classical period, 1500–1700—History and criticism.
2. Jealousy in literature.   3. Cervantes Saavedra, Miguel de, 1547–1616—
Criticism and interpretation.   4. Vega, Lope de, 1562–1635—Criticism and
interpretation.   5. Góngora y Argote, Luis de, 1561–1627—Criticism and
interpretation.   6. Literature and society—Spain.   I. Title.
PG6066.W34 2007
860.9'353—dc22   2006   2006024598

⊗ This paper meets the requirements of the
American National Standard for Permanence of Paper
for Printed Library Materials, Z39.48, 1984.

Designer: Kristie Lee
Typesetter: Bookcomp, Inc.
Printer and binder: The Maple-Vail Book Manufacturing Group
Typefaces: Century Schoolbook and Caxton

*Publication of this book has been supported by a contribution from
the Program for Cultural Cooperation between Spain's Ministry of
Education and Culture and United States Universities.*

To Sandy,

> Of whom I have been jealous
> But who never gives me cause

Contents

Acknowledgments

The people whom I should thank for assistance in this project are many.

At Indiana University, grants from the Office of the Vice President for Research, the College Arts and Humanities Institute, and the West European Studies National Resource Center have afforded me extra time for research, without which finishing this book would have been more difficult.

Parts of Chapters 2, 6, and 7 are based on articles I published earlier, and I thank the publishers for permission to reproduce and modify this material: "A Woman Not Fit to Rule: The Gendering of Jealousy in Lope de Vega's *Arminda celosa*," *Bulletin of the Comediantes* 55:2 (2003): 81–94; "Writing on the Fractured 'I': Góngora's Iconographic Evocations of Vulcan, Venus and Mars," in *Writing for the Eyes in the Spanish Golden Age,* ed. Frederick A. de Armas (Lewisburg, PA: Bucknell University Press, 2004), 130–50; and "'Mas no cabrás allá': Góngora's Early Modern Representation of the Modern Sublime," *Hispanic Review* 70:2 (2002): 169–89, which is reprinted and modified by permission of the University of Pennsylvania Press.

All translations of primary texts as well as secondary materials from other languages are mine unless otherwise noted. The prose translations of verse are meant only as an aid to those who do not read the languages well enough to follow along without them.

Many friends and colleagues have read chapters or helped me think through certain ideas in this book, and I am very grateful for their efforts: Catherine Larson, Alejandro Mejías-López, Gina Herrmann, Melissa Dinverno, York Gunther, Elizabeth Amann, John Slater, Josep Sobrer, and Kathleen Myers. Other friends and relatives have offered different kinds of support, which I appreciate: Kabi Hartmann, Stephen Cooper, Michael Westlund, Frederick de Armas, Clancy Clements, Deborah Cohn, Consuelo López-Morillas, Irma Alarcón, Andrea Wohl, Eric Silverman, Harry Wagschal, Ruth Shapshay, and Stan Shapshay. I also wish to thank Rebecca Curtis, without whom I would be a different person, and Joseph Macaluso and Catherine Vallejo, for helping nourish my interest in Ibero-American fictional worlds early on.

Since this project developed out of work done at graduate school, I thank my dissertation director, Gonzalo Sobejano, for inspiration and encouragement, as well as the other committee members, Félix Martínez-Bonati, Patricia Grieve, Isaías Lerner, and Marcia Welles, for their most helpful criticisms and suggestions.

Clair Willcox and Jane Lago at the University of Missouri Press deserve my gratitude for their guidance through the final stages of this project. I would also like to thank the two anonymous readers whose suggestions helped improve the final manuscript.

Closer to home, I thank my daughters, Molly and Marlena, who have been very patient, knowing that there was no chance that we'd be getting a dog until this book was done. Now it's done.

I dedicate this book to Sandy Shapshay, to whom I am grateful for her love, patience, time, good humor, philosophical acumen, and other things, both more and less ethereal.

The Literature of Jealousy
in the Age of Cervantes

Introduction
Understanding Jealousies

> [N]othing is more deceptive than the laying down of general
> laws for our emotions. Their texture is so delicate and intricate
> that even the most cautious speculation can hardly pick out a
> single thread and follow it through all its interlacing.
>
> —G. E. Lessing, *Laocoön*

When Miguel de Cervantes described his writing in 1614, the author of *Don Quixote* explained that his favorite among his own poems was "El romance de los celos" (The Ballad of Jealousy). Jealousy
plays an important role in Cervantes's novels and novellas, one of the
most widely read of which is *El celoso extremeño* (The Jealous Old
Man from Extremadura). Cervantes's foremost literary rival, Félix
Lope de Vega, composed six dramas that contain the word *jealousy* in
the title. Scores more treat plots of love and intrigue in which people
suffer or are motivated to kill; in his poetic treatise of 1614, Lope de
Vega recommended the use of this theme to other dramatists, many
of whom, like Tirso de Molina, put his advice into practice in their
own plays, such as *Celosa de sí misma* (Jealous of Herself). Lope de
Vega's avowed enemy was Luis de Góngora, Spain's most important
early modern poet, who wrote many poems about jealousy. His most
accomplished work, from 1613, is a recasting of the classical myth
of Polyphemus, in which the Cyclops kills Galatea's lover out of jealousy.

My study asks why representations of jealousy abound in the literature of Spain's Golden Age. At this crucial period of Spanish history, why are the most important authors obsessively writing on
jealousy in poetry, prose fiction, and drama? What does the emotion
offer these writers, just as Spain is beginning its long decline from
the apex of European hegemony? In answering these questions, I

1

draw the conclusion that jealousy is a tool in their texts for working through a series of political and cultural problems involving power. Long misunderstood by literary critics as a simple plot device, jealousy, I argue, is a flexible, polyvalent designation that resists simple reduction.

The abundance and variety of representations of jealousy in early modern Spain range from the terrifying to the harmless, from monsters to air. Monsters were considered hostile, powerful beings of strange genesis who weighed heavily on the minds of those who feared them. Air was an intangible and innocuous substance of little force, yet one on which humans depended for life itself. Between these extremes, representations of jealousy were incredibly varied, frequently inconsistent, and even paradoxical. It was a tempest, thunder and lightning, but also fog, cloud, and air; a plague, rabies, poison, monster, but sometimes just lowly mud. It was noble but also hellish, caused blindness but lent visual acuity. It made one ill and it made one kill. Jealousy was life's worst torment, yet it dissipated in the sun like a fine dew.

This book examines these varied and contradictory representations, while illuminating the appeal that jealousy had for three of Hispanic literature's most renowned writers: Lope de Vega, Miguel de Cervantes, and Luis de Góngora. Jealousy flourished in early modern Spanish culture and society, and it served a central function in a large number of literary texts by these three authors of drama, prose, and poetry. Through an analysis of their works, I argue that jealousy is fundamental to understanding the aesthetics, epistemology, and morality of the time. Aesthetically, jealousy lends itself to Baroque tropes of predilection: hyperbole, paradox, and the proliferation of metaphors. Adding rivalry to a lyric love relationship, jealousy brings movement to a static situation, which is Heinrich Wölfflin's single most important criterion of Baroque art. Epistemologically, jealousy can be both a form of *engaño* (deceit) and, paradoxically, a path to *desengaño* (a concept roughly translatable as "disillusionment," but with other nuances). These two poles of Spanish Baroque epistemology are a major focus of seventeenth-century writing, both fictional and nonfictional. Literary texts problematize the ambiguity surrounding jealousy's double valence: characters may enter a state of deception precisely because of their jealousy; antithetically, they may find desengaño only once their suspicions are aroused. Concerning morality, jealousy opposes a notion of pure love and has been used pejoratively to evoke a negative, un-Christian worldview.

From a modern vantage point, jealousy also illuminates issues of race, class, and gender in early modern Spain. It functions as a metonymy for those the dominant elements of society deem morally bankrupt, be they Jews, Moors, or Protestants, that is, as a stand-in for the race or ethnicity of minorities. Relying on negative racial stereotypes of Jews and Moors, depictions of the jealous can be related to the period's obsession with blood purity, honor, and the converso-Morisco question. Regarding class and gender, representations of jealousy portray social strife between peasants and nobles, and between women and men. Depictions of rivals in love symbolically lend themselves to the interests of the rising absolutist regimes of Philip III and Philip IV, to the extent that absolutism aims at weakening bonds among people and classes, while strengthening those between monarch and vassal. Also, with respect to gender, some representations of jealousy make female characters look weak-willed and irrational, while others lend grandeur to male characters, thus reinforcing patriarchal hierarchies.[1]

This book responds to a dearth of scholarship on jealousy in Spanish literature that dates back centuries. In 1611, in his *Tesoro de la lengua española o castellana* (Treasure of the Castilian or Spanish Language), Sebastián de Covarrubias wrote that "Spanish and Italian poets have already written so much about jealousy that it seems preferable not to treat it here" (Los poetas españoles y italianos tienen escrito tanto de zelos, que me ha parecido no tratar yo aquí dellos). Modern literary criticism seems to have taken a cue from his enigmatic entry. This paramount theme of Spain's Golden Age has been obscured by studies fixated on honor and has received remarkably little critical attention.[2] There are only two, article-length

---

1. In describing the mockery of some female protagonists in Spanish drama, I find Rosemary Lloyd's critique of Stendhal's *De L'Amour* useful: "[A] woman who actively experiences so powerful an emotion is perceived as menacing and therefore must be ridiculed, not merely by the lover, but by the narrator himself" (*Closer and Closer Apart: Jealousy in Literature*, 9). In dramatic works, this often applies to the playwright's and other characters' attitudes toward jealous female subjects.

2. Louis Combet suggests, in his study on Cervantes, that jealousy is so personally disturbing that few scholars desire to investigate it: "[J]ealousy . . . is one of the key themes of his oeuvre and its omnipresence has always struck observers. Struck, yet also, at times, bothered" (*Cervantès ou les incertitudes du désir: Une approche psychostructurale de l'œuvre de Cervantès*, 324).

studies on the role of jealousy in the Spanish Golden Age, both on the theater, and in each the author makes sweeping generalizations about the emotion, treating it as a singular phenomenon. While Horst Baader asserts universals that cannot hold true given the actual representations that abound, Hymen Alpern concludes that the contradictions between competing conceptual claims on jealousy result in "gibberish." Alpern catalogs what I term "conceptual claims." He typically makes an assertion (for example, "jealousy . . . produces love"), followed by another that is largely incompatible (for example, "Jealousy destroys love"), thus promoting the mistaken notion that nothing systematic can be said about jealousy, that it is superficial and irrelevant. Contradicting this tendency, he attempts to reveal the emotion's constant features: it is "incompatible with reason," "a passion of violence" in which "blood must be shed," assertions that are simply not true when applied to all Golden Age drama.[3] Written in a very different vein, Baader's essay reflects an implicit Heideggerian orientation in which art is revelatory of Being, arguing that the presence of jealousy signals the general awakening of "self-consciousness" (*Selbstbewußtsein*).[4] For Baader, jealousy is always secondary to honor because the individual's emotions are always trumped by society's values in the Spanish Golden Age. Jealousy is relegated to the "private sphere," which is the exclusive domain of women, whose emotions have "no social meaning." In contrast, men live in the "public sphere," where their jealousy always serves the requirements of honor and never plays a motivational role. This distinction, for Baader, explains why there is no equivalent in Spain of Shakespeare's *Othello*. While revealing interesting tensions in some dramas, Baader's analysis is overly reductionist, not allowing for differences in accounts of jealousy beyond anatomical gender. Furthermore, his hypothesis contains a self-contradiction in that this turning inward to the self allegedly occurs in a society that continually draws one (that is, men) away from self-understanding.[5]

Other critics have made important contributions on the role of

3. Hymen Alpern, "Jealousy as a Dramatic Motive in the Spanish *comedia*," 277, 280–81.

4. I translate this multivalent word following Macquarrie and Robinson's English version of *Being and Time*, 2.6.435, 486, 566.

5. Horst Baader, "Eifersucht in der Spanischen *Comedia* des Goldenen Zeitalters."

jealousy in discrete works of a single author, especially on Cervantes. But such studies cannot address the importance of jealousy as a wider social, political, and artistic phenomenon. In contrast, this study is the first to analyze representations of the emotion across genres in texts by multiple authors.

Jealousies

Such a grand theme cannot possibly possess a unitary meaning throughout a broad corpus. By attending closely to the ways in which jealousy is represented in specific texts, I am able to show how it engages the ideological and formal makeup of these texts. In her book on jealousy in modern French narrative, Rosemary Lloyd has a similar intention in revealing the relationship between this theme and its modes of representation: "The richness and complexity of these meditations on jealousy, narrating and reading suggest the degree to which writers and thinkers have drawn on imagery and structures associated with jealousy in producing their literary and philosophical frameworks."[6] In part, I argue, jealousy has this power over ideology and form because it is not a unitary phenomenon with a static signification, but a polyvalent, shifting signifier whose presence exerts itself in a matrix of meaning.

Typical of literature on jealousy are the *conceptual claims* that explicitly attempt to define it; these are false if taken as the universals they pretend to be. All of the following cannot be true of jealousy if it is a unitary phenomenon, yet all have been proclaimed in early modern texts: "Jealousy is air," "there is no love without jealousy," "love is stronger than jealousy," "jealousy is more powerful than love," "jealousy destroys love." Linked to these conceptual claims are what I term *affective genealogies,* in which the poet or character makes jealousy a metaphorical progeny or progenitor of some other concept. For instance, the last tercet of Garcilaso de la Vega's Sonnet 31 reads,

> O jealous fear, whom do you resemble?
> Even envy herself, your own cruel mother,
> is terrified of the monster she hath borne!

6. Lloyd, *Closer and Closer Apart,* 15.

> (¡O celoso temor!, ¿a quién pareces?
> que aun la invidia, tu propia y fiera madre,
> se espanta en ver el monstruo que á parido.)[7]

Garcilaso explains not what jealousy is, but what it is worse than, as if the poet were afraid to define it, suggesting that the fear associated with many psychological accounts of jealousy has taken over the sonnet itself. If applied to particular states of affairs represented in literature, most of these conceptual claims have some validity, but as universals they are clearly mutually exclusive.[8] The critics who have dealt with the question have either sought to imitate art by asserting their own universals or, alternatively, declared that the contradictions between competing conceptual claims result in "gibberish," thus implying that nothing can be stated about such an unsystematic theme. But surely love is not nonsensical simply because there are many different kinds, as expressed throughout a large group of texts. Therefore, following an Aristotelian model of concepts, jealousy can be understood as multiple. As Aristotle claimed against Plato regarding the "good," the only way to understand it is to investigate the different kinds that exist, not to posit a "form."[9]

The problem of defining jealousy in particular (and emotions in general) has less to do with its inconsistency than with the fact that it refers to many phenomena. Indeed, for Descartes, the emotions are "indefinite" in number.[10] In the sixteenth and seventeenth centuries, followers of Thomistic philosophy located emotions within the sensitive soul, in the heart. Emotions, or passions, as they were usually called, were subdivided into two types, concupiscible and irascible, referring to whether love or hatred was aroused, respectively.[11]

---

7. Garcilaso de la Vega, *Obras completas con comentario,* 147. This sonnet follows a classical conception of the monster. As Marie-Hélène Huet points out in *Monstrous Imagination,* the original Aristotelian definition of *monster* is based on a lack of resemblance between parents and offspring (22).

8. In the language of philosophical logic, these conceptual claims are incompossible.

9. See Chapter 1 for an elaboration of Aristotle's idea in this regard.

10. René Descartes, *The Passions of the Soul.*

11. Lawrence Babb surveys a variety of French and English volumes, all followers of Aquinas's *Summa Theologica* (2.23.4), including La Primaudaye's *Academie* and Burton's *Anatomy of Melancholy* (Babb, *The Elizabethan Malady: A Study of Melancholia in English Literature from 1580 to 1642,* 4n9). In Spain, Juan Luis Vives followed Aquinas on this division.

Love inspired desire, while hatred caused aversion, which in turn led to other passions, such as joy or sorrow. As I have noted, literary representations of jealousy often conflict with each other. This is something attributable, at least in part, to the passion's being simultaneously concupiscible and irascible; that is, it is neither love nor hate, but a compound passion composed of antithetical elements. Thus, early moderns understood jealousy as inherently paradoxical.

Analyzing jealousy is complicated by the difficulty in specifying what the term refers to in the external world. For some early moderns, jealousy had a very limited definition, signifying only the irrational fear of a married man regarding his wife's chastity; for others, jealousy had a much broader scope. In the most important sixteenth-century European treatise on the emotions, *The Passions of the Soul* (book 3 of *De Anima et Vita* [On the Soul and on Life]), Juan Luis Vives classifies jealousy as a morally objectionable emotion with the capacity to transform humans into "most ferocious beasts."[12] Although Vives most often considers jealousy as something that a man feels toward his wife, he argues that any person can be jealous of just about anyone else.[13] Since it is often violent and powerful, jealousy is considered one of the disturbances or *perturbationes,* a subcategory made up of intense emotions.[14]

In the late twentieth and early twenty-first centuries, the very notions of what emotions are and how they are related to attitudes, feelings, rationality, and conceptuality are hot topics in psychology and philosophy of mind. In this introduction, I provide arguments from these fields that jealousy is not unitary, but a complex of distinct emotional experiences and feelings that may be in a situation

12. Carlos G. Noreña, *Juan Luis Vives and the Emotions,* 142. As Noreña points out, Vives relies on Aquinas's *Summa Theologica* while simultaneously ushering in a Renaissance approach to the emotions: "[T]he contrast between it [the *Summa*] and Vives' tract highlights the striking difference between the systemic rigidity of scholastic philosophy and the looser descriptive approach of Vives . . . [and] epitomizes the change from medieval to Renaissance patterns of thinking" (*Juan Luis Vives,* 161).

13. "[W]e alone want to enjoy that beauty. . . . We can therefore be jealous of our children, sisters, mothers, students, or people trusted to our care; not because we want to enjoy their beauty, but because we do not want others to enjoy it unfairly or improperly. . . . I usually have in mind one sex, but both should be included, since the turmoil of this disorder is no less and the eagerness to act upon it no less acute among women than among men" (Vives, *The Passions of the Soul* [1538], 85–87).

14. Noreña, *Juan Luis Vives,* 143.

of flux. I have sought to disentangle the phenomena as they relate to human experience in order first to ascertain what it is that authors seem to be referring to in their representations. If their work is mimetic, then what is it they are imitating? Further complicating matters, all of the authors refer not only to jealousy that obtains in actual human minds, but also to literary traditions of jealousy, sometimes as a self-conscious, allusive literary device, while at other times in an intertextual competition in which each author tries to achieve the most hyperbolic representation of the emotion. In these instances, the object of representation is no longer a feature of the human mind at all, but a rhetorical strategy.

Psychology and Moral Philosophy

Clinical psychology offers useful distinctions for understanding emotions in human beings. For Gary Hansen, jealousy is a *compound emotion* that results from the *situational labeling* of what he terms a *primary emotion,* such as suspicion or anger, with respect to the interpersonal, social context in which the primary emotion is experienced. Hansen explains, "Anger or fear *describe* the state. Jealousy *explains* the state."[15] From an intrapersonal perspective, W. Gerrod Parrott has examined case studies to posit a framework in which to understand the emotion. Like Hansen's *situational labeling of a primary emotion,* Parrott's distinctions depend on describing another emotion in a given situation. To explain differences in emotional response, Parrott emphasizes not the societal context, but the subject's focus, appealing to the notion of "attention." For instance, the primary emotional responses to "fait accompli jealousy" (a case of jealousy in which the jealous subject has irrefutable evidence of the lover's infidelity) vary with the lover's focus of attention: if it is on the "loss of the relationship," then the lover will feel "sadness"; if it is on the wrongdoing or betrayal of the beloved or rival, then the lover will feel "anger and hurt"; if it is on "one's own inadequacy," then depression will ensue; if it is on the "superiority of the rival," then the lover will feel "envy."[16] Thus, while Hansen's approach relies on

15. Gary L. Hansen, "Jealousy: Its Conceptualization, Measurement, and Integration with Family Stress Theory," 212, emphasis added. This notion is similar to Aquinas's view.
16. W. Gerrod Parrott, "The Emotional Experience of Envy and Jealousy," 20.

externalizing—referring to others' appraisals of the jealous person's conduct or belief—Parrott's is internalizing, informed by the jealous person's own inner thoughts and reactions to those thoughts.

Sigmund Freud's most important insight concerning jealousy is one that I refer to repeatedly in the chapters that follow. The psychoanalyst enunciated a mimetic process that playwrights such as Lope de Vega obviously intuited as well: that jealousy of the beloved can arise from a projection to the beloved's mind of the lover's own illicit desire for another person: "[T]hey let themselves be guided by their knowledge of the unconscious, and displace to the unconscious minds of others the attention which they have withdrawn from their own."[17] For Freud, these displacements are typically desires of matrimonial unfaithfulness. In sum, a jealous person can become jealous because of his or her own desires for people other than his or her own sexual partner.

As a psychological explanation of jealousy with philosophical ramifications, Jean-Paul Sartre makes use of Stendhal's and Proust's accounts of male jealousy as a "universal" experience of the desire to be God: "[Stendhal and Proust] have shown that love and jealousy can not be reduced to the strict desire of possessing a *particular* woman, but that these emotions aim at laying hold of the world in its entirety through the woman."[18] Sartre thus points to a metaphysical meaning of male jealousy.[19] Unfortunately, this is exclusively male, heterosexual jealousy. Sartre's ideas are unquestionably gendered and not readily applicable to those who are not heterosexual males, a problem shared by René Girard's *Deceit, Desire and the Novel: Self and Other in Literary Structure.* For Sartre, and for those who follow his study of the emotions, such as contemporary virtue-ethicist Gabrielle Taylor, jealousy is a vice, for it treats others as objects.[20]

17. Sigmund Freud, "Some Neurotic Mechanisms in Jealousy, Paranoia and Homosexuality," 226.

18. Jean-Paul Sartre, *Being and Nothingness: An Essay on Phenomenological Ontology,* 562.

19. Peggy Kamuf, elaborating on Jacques Derrida's thought in the introduction to her abridged English edition of his works, takes the notion of metaphysical jealousy even further, stating, in fictional first-personal Derrida, "In everything I talk about jealousy is at stake" (*A Derrida Reader: Between the Blinds,* xxi).

20. See Gabrielle Taylor, "Envy and Jealousy: Emotions and Vices." On treating others as objects, Roland Barthes agrees, in *A Lover's Discourse: Fragments,* and it is in this way that he explains the perceived negativity of jealousy. The

Such psychological or virtue-ethical assertions, while useful in ascribing motivation, as well as explaining and judging behavioral dispositions and beliefs, never explain what an emotion is. Nor can these approaches fully distinguish emotion from a feeling or an attitude. Not knowing what is being represented exacerbates the theoretical problems inherent in analyzing that which is represented. To wit, Parrott equivocates in the citation above as he conflates individual emotions with "depression," a condition comprising a whole range of emotions, feelings, and behaviors (for instance, loss of appetite, feelings of sadness or despair, attempts at suicide, to name a few that are listed in the most recent standard psychiatric manual, which includes "depression" as a psychiatric disorder).[21] By its very nature, the clinical literature studies elements of behavior and thought in isolated trials in the hope that these theses are provable, leaving aside grander theoretical questions (such as "What is a mind?" or "What is an emotion?"). Similarly, the fundamental inquiry of virtue ethics—that is, which dispositions to act and feel make a person good and which bad—seems not to question sufficiently what it is interrogating so that its level of analysis remains of the first order. Virtue ethics, moreover, may have limited applicability in literary studies, where the morality of characters is not usually a scholar's prime concern.

Philosophy of Mind

For more rigorous distinctions, formulated into a general theory, I turn now to the contemporary philosophy of mind. This field is primarily practiced in the analytic tradition, but it also attracts researchers who might more clearly be identified with the Continental one.[22] I rely in part on Ronald de Sousa's groundbreaking book *The Rationality of Emotion* (1988), an analytic work that demonstrates

---

deontological philosophy of Immanuel Kant coincides here with virtue ethics on this point as well: treating others as a possession is immoral.

21. American Psychiatric Association, *Diagnostic and Statistical Manual of Mental Disorders (DSM-IV TR)*, 345–428.

22. Some readers better acquainted with other fields may not be familiar with the broad divide in contemporary Western philosophy between analytic philosophers (who tend to be Anglo-American) and Continental philosophers (who tend to be non-UK Europeans). In broad strokes, analytic philosophy limits its inquiry to phenomena that can be studied with logical analysis, such as language and logic itself, while Continental philosophy extends its study to broad questions

not only that emotion and rationality are not necessarily mutually exclusive, but more importantly, that some rationality is dependent on emotional experience. The monster breathes air, too. The other philosopher on whose work I draw is Peter Goldie (*The Emotions: A Philosophical Exploration* [2000]), who might more aptly be categorized as belonging to the Continental tradition. Whereas texts such as de Sousa's concentrate on rationality, the more Continental studies, such as Goldie's, while treating rationality, also draw on accounts of emotion that are more readily adaptable to literary studies because they approach the subject from a phenomenological perspective, in the manner of Heidegger and the Existentialists, thus lending themselves to analyses of characters' feelings. Indeed, Goldie notes self-consciously that his remarks may sound obvious because of their "common sense" acceptance, and that they may seem odd only to someone deeply steeped in the analytic tradition, that is, someone like de Sousa.

The philosophy of mind provides the advantage of considering emotions in terms of their relationship to rationality, which is how they are often framed in literary texts. Indeed, Othello's passion is more often than not explicitly treated as irrational in literature—as provoking thoughts that do not correspond to intersubjective appraisals of reality—despite the fact that it may at times be grounded in justified belief of adultery or some other form of faithlessness on the part of a loved one. Even in these latter cases, jealousy is often imaged as irrational both by characters who experience it psychically and by those who observe it in others. For instance, in Lope de Vega's *Arminda celosa* (Jealous Arminda), discussed in Chapter 2, the female protagonist's emotion is repeatedly denigrated as a "fantasy of the mind" despite its empirical basis in her husband's philandering. The nature of irrationality is not questioned in such literary texts. Rather, irrationality is equated with any emotional experience, in an antithetical opposition between Reason and the Passions (qua emotions). But a contemporary philosophical analysis of emotions vis-à-vis rationality demonstrates that emotions may very well be consonant with what modern philosophers term *instrumental rationality,* which is a mental state that leads to the achievement of a desired

---

of existence and phenomenology. As an English philosopher, Peter Goldie challenges this division with his phenomenological perspective in the tradition of Heidegger and the Existentialists.

goal.[23] Such ideas counter the long-standing, misguided yet prominent dualism that was spawned in philosophical discourse by Plato and bolstered by Descartes in his early works. De Sousa explains, "A long tradition views all emotions as threats to rationality. . . . Many philosophers have espoused this view, exhorting Reason to conquer Passion." To counter the false dichotomy of reason versus passion, de Sousa analyzes the elements of rationality and emotion, and demonstrates that "reason and emotion are not natural antagonists."[24] His main interest is indeed how emotions fit into a theory of rationality. This view on reason and emotion has been bolstered by the research of contemporary neuroscientists such as Antonio Damasio, who has explored the topic in a book that draws on evidence from neurological scans, autopsies, and historical case studies to confirm that emotions are often an aid to reason, not a hindrance.[25]

For de Sousa, emotions are mental states that can be distinguished from moods, in that the latter lack a clear object (called a "target").[26] A *target* is the term used to describe the particular object of a belief, a desire, or an emotion: "Unlike most emotions proper, moods do not clearly have intentional objects [targets]. If I am sad (an emotion), my sadness must be directed *at* some loss which I view as its cause. If I feel listless (a mood), I can look for a cause, which might be low blood sugar; but I am not listless *at* low blood sugar or anything else." Jealousy is different from other emotions, such as sadness, because it takes (at least) two different targets: "The [logical] structure of jealousy, for example involves a number of different objects [targets] in different roles: the person one is jealous *of* plays an entirely different part in one's jealousy from that of the rival *because of whom* one is jealous."[27] I would add to this that jealousy may also be directed at

---

23. De Sousa uses the term *strategic rationality* (*The Rationality of Emotion*, 163–65) for this concept that originates in modern philosophy with Kant; but most philosophers (e.g., Robert Nozick, *The Nature of Rationality*, 133–35) call this "instrumental rationality" or "instrumental conception of practical rationality," terms I prefer because they better approximate the meaning of Kant's *Werkzeug* for "practical reasoning" in the *Critique of Practical Reason*.

24. De Sousa, *Rationality of Emotion*, 4, xv.

25. Antonio Damasio, *Descartes' Error: Emotion, Reason and the Human Brain*.

26. De Sousa also calls the "target" an "intentional object" in *Rationality of Emotion*. But in contemporary philosophy of mind, the phrase *intentional object* refers not to a particular object, but rather to the content of a sentence (i.e., the meaning of a sentence). For the sake of clarity, I use only de Sousa's term *target* when writing about a specific object.

27. De Sousa, *Rationality of Emotion*, 7, 75.

oneself, as a third target (for instance, see above for Parrott's notion that "depression ensues" when the attention is focused on "personal inadequacy").

Thus explaining the importance of the target to emotions, de Sousa goes on to clarify how this relates to rationality. The most important element of rationality is what de Sousa calls "the criterion of success": "[A]ny concept of rationality must be founded on a criterion of success. Success, in this sense, is defined as the attainment of the formal object of the state in question; for example, truth is the success of belief, good of want." Emotions have their own criteria of success, distinct from those of belief and desire, but unlike the criteria of success for these other elements of intentionality, there is "no such single formal object of emotions"; that is, for each emotion, the formal object relates to that specific emotion itself: "[W]hat determines the success of fear—what justifies it, if you like—is that its target be fearsome."[28] If a hiker in British Columbia feels fear upon sighting a grizzly bear, it could easily be argued that the fear is justified, that is, that the formal object of fear meets the criterion of success that the object be "fearsome," leading to an appraisal of rational fear. However, if the same hiker feels fear of the innocuous, common brown toad, the criterion would not be met. Adapting this to jealousy, then, the formal object of the emotion of jealousy is that the target be *jealousy-provoking*. For instance, if a woman knows that her boyfriend is always attracted to older, dark-haired women, then her jealousy will be rational whenever he is with such a woman.

The de Sousian analysis of the emotions demonstrates that emotions are intrinsically neither arational nor irrational. Like belief and desire, they lend themselves to rational analysis. Furthermore, as inseparable parts of intentionality, the success outcomes of the other elements may depend on the emotional response. That is, the experience of jealousy may lead to rational belief and desire. It may attune the senses to potential or actual threats (for example, to learn whether an amorous partner is engaged in behavior that is faithless to monogamy), helping both to attain secure knowledge (which is the success criterion for rational belief) and to fulfill one's desire (which is the success criterion for want), for instance, to put an end to philandering if it is occurring. Such is the case with *Jealous Arminda,* in

28. De Sousa, *Rationality of Emotion,* 142, 20, 20. In analytic terms, the *formal object* is a second-order appraisal of content; i.e., it refers not to the content itself, but to the conditions under which the truth value for that content would be satisfied.

which the protagonist's jealousy helps thwart her husband's future love affairs, thus aiding in fulfilling her desire to have him remain faithful. It is in this sense that jealousy may be *instrumentally rational.*

This model offers an explanation in terms of rationality as to why some forms of jealousy will be rational and others will not, depending on the success of the jealousy-provoking criterion. Indeed, at times, the emotion seems counterproductive and even pathological to the point of being deleterious to the jealous person, and in these cases, it is likely that the criterion of success is not met. Contemporary clinical psychology provides for descriptions of kinds of jealousy that are forms of paranoia. Additionally, there are numerous examples in literature of pathological jealousy, some of which will be explored in the chapters that follow, such as Cervantes's *Jealous Old Man from Extremadura,* who, irrationally, becomes jealous of his wife even before he has a specific bride in mind.

Somewhere in between a focus on "rational" and "pathological" jealousy lies the work of Peter Goldie. Although he admits that some forms of jealousy are clearly "rational" or "irrational" (even pathological), this philosopher argues that the focus of work such as de Sousa's is too limiting. Instead, Goldie seeks to understand the emotions in terms of their *intelligibility,* their *appropriateness* and *proportionality,* criteria that are much thinner than rationality.[29] Emotions can be understood without their being clearly rational or irrational. Notions like proportionality can be used to achieve a more nuanced view of a character. For example, Cervantes's Lauso, in "The Ballad of Jealousy," may have good reason to be jealous, making his jealousy *rational;* but that he dies from the experience is wholly *out of proportion.*[30] Along with these criteria are several others on which emotions should be analyzed. The most important, around which all of Goldie's other concepts coalesce, is the notion of *feeling towards:* "an essentially intentional psychological phenomenon with a special sort of emotionally laden content . . . which essentially involves feeling."[31] The concept of *feeling towards* captures that sense understood by every person who has ever experienced an emotion, that

29. De Sousa's rough equivalent for all of these nuanced terms is "reasonableness" (de Sousa, *Rationality of Emotion,* 5).

30. This is, indeed, one of the functions of Cervantes's poem: it parodies a hyperbolic instantiation of the emotion.

31. Peter Goldie, *The Emotions: A Philosophical Exploration,* 4.

an emotion carries with it both a *feeling* and a *personal perspective* or *point of view.* In a Heideggerian vein, Goldie argues that the experience of an emotion cannot be meaningfully represented by an impersonal report of the emotion, one that does not contain a point of view. Put in other words, if something arouses emotion it is because that something is important to someone. The emotion carries with it a *feeling* that is an inseparable part of the emotion. With respect to the contemporary philosophical debate on the emotions, both Goldie and de Sousa are "non-reductionists" (also known as "anti-reductionists") on the emotions because they hold that the feeling associated with an emotion cannot meaningfully be separated from its intentionality.[32] Emotions come with feelings that are their own separate kind of mental state, neither cognitive (relating to belief) nor motivational (relating to desire). The feeling attached to an emotion cannot simply be detached so that the other elements (that is, belief and desire) can be independently analyzed, after which the associated feeling can be added on post hoc.[33] Goldie disparagingly calls this reductionist tendency the "add-on view of emotion."[34]

For Goldie, emotions are "complex, episodic, dynamic, and structured." The first descriptor, "complex," brings to the fore that an emotion is not a singular phenomenon, but multiple. An emotion is composed of disparate elements: emotional experiences, perceptions, thoughts, feelings, bodily changes, dispositions. Emotions are *episodic* in that they come and go and come again, and *dynamic* in that emotional experiences vary with other factors, including past emotional experiences and others' reactions to them. Goldie draws attention to emotions' being in flux. When he contends that an emotion is *structured,* Goldie is situating emotion within a narrative of a person's life, where it belongs, along with a subject's point of view.

32. York Gunther discusses the terms of this debate in his essay "Emotion and Force" (279), in *Essays on Nonconceptual Content* (Cambridge, MA: MIT Press, 2003).

33. For instance, philosophers Martha C. Nussbaum in *Upheavals of Thought: The Intelligence of Emotions* (2001) and Bennett Helm in *Emotional Reason: Deliberation, Motivation, and the Nature of Value* (New York: Cambridge University Press, 2001) both (implicitly) conflate emotional experience with evaluative judgment. Although reductionism per se is not argued for, I infer that its allure to these philosophers qua scientists is the neat dissection of the emotions. If these are merely evaluative judgments, then one need not attend to anything else, say, for instance, the way they feel, their qualia.

34. Goldie, *The Emotions,* 4.

The meaning of the emotion is not some absolute that is divorced from a situation, but rather it is embedded in that situation, which, in literature, is usually how it is expressed, in a narrative structure. This structured element is clearly related to Goldie's overarching concept of *feeling towards,* which is a feeling *in* a particular set of circumstances. In arriving at these conclusions, Goldie both draws on literary fiction (in particular Proust's, among others) and provides an approach that is adaptable to analyzing an emotion as it unfolds in a narrative.[35]

Another of Goldie's distinctions that is useful for literary analysis is that between *emotions,* which are complex, and *emotional episodes,* which are discrete occurrences of emotion. In literary texts, the same word, *jealous,* is used to describe both a character who is experiencing an *emotional episode* and a character who has a disposition to be jealous all of the time, that is, to experience the *emotion* of jealousy. For instance, both the husband in *Los comendadores de Córdoba* (The Commanders of Cordoba, discussed in Chapter 1) and the husband in *The Jealous Old Man from Extremadura* (discussed in Chapter 4) are called "jealous" (*celoso*), but the former only becomes so when he learns of his wife's actual deception. He experiences an *emotional episode* of jealousy, whereas the latter suffers from jealousy as an *emotion,* described in the novella as an experience arising from a predisposition or character trait. Thus, Goldie's system makes the emotion a conglomerate of experiences over time in addition to the predisposition itself. In this, he is not far from Aristotle's ethics, where traits—or predispositions, for a more contemporary word—are developed over time.

Goldie provides the following example of an emotional episode, which is useful in demonstrating how jealousy is made up of diverse phenomena (although this is written in the second person, the reader senses that he speaks from his own experience):

> You are jealous because you think that she has run off with someone else. You cannot sleep: your heart and mind are racing all night. While you are getting dressed in the morning you cannot help imagining them together, talking and joking about you perhaps, and you are unable to keep your mind on anything else. On the way to work, you see another couple in the distance, one of whom looks just like her, and you practically

35. Ibid., 12–13.

faint, frozen to the spot in terror. Later in the day, you are pre-occupied with work for a while, and then suddenly, like a blow to the body, you see on your desk something of hers which triggers your feelings again, and you think 'If I'm not able to talk to her *now* then I don't know what I'll do'. The next minute your jealousy makes another turn, and you hope you never see her again; the telephone rings and the thought that it might be her fills you with dread. This complex of perceptions, thoughts, feelings, and bodily changes are dynamically related episodes of the same emotion—the same state of jealousy. And these elements fit in as part of a narrative of this part of your life, which will include not just these elements but also things which you do out of jealousy and your emotional expressions of jealousy . . . [and] all sorts of other aspects of your life on which your feelings of jealousy impinge . . . for example, your way of seeing things in general, your mood, and your character traits.[36]

Jealousy is many things in these texts because the term does not refer unproblematically to a single feeling, but rather to heterogeneous phenomena. Both clinical psychology and philosophy of mind offer distinctions and analytical tools for understanding the complexity of jealousy in early modern texts. Reciprocally, my study demonstrates that Lope de Vega, Cervantes, and Góngora represented jealousy in much the same way as de Sousa and Goldie understand it. The modern philosophical analysis of the emotions allows us to see jealousy in these early modern texts as a flexible, polyvalent designation that resists reduction.

Amorous Jealousy

For the sake of clarity, I have formulated a broad definition of *jealousy* and elaborated a series of terms that refer to some of its discrete incarnations (jealousies). My focus is on *amorous jealousy,* which I define in terms of its being a subjective experience: it corresponds to a group of emotions, feelings, thoughts, bodily changes, and attitudes that are experienced in relation to guarding the exclusivity of a relationship that one possesses from a rival and/or avenging the loss of that which was possessed. This complex is experienced in some proportion and with some level of appropriateness and intelligibility by a subject in the context of a love triangle, and is directed at the

36. Ibid., 14.

loved one and/or the self, and/or the rival, in which the rival may be real or imagined. It is distinguished from *amorous envy*—the desire to possess the love object of another—in that the context in which the lover finds herself allows her to feel a certain *right of possession* over the beloved, and hence the possibility of losing something.[37] Such a context is not always intersubjectively available and is largely dependent on the subject's individual appraisal, making such a distinction epistemologically troublesome at times (at least in theory).[38]

From a psychological perspective, the emotion as experienced in the early stages of jealousy (for example, suspicion) often changes over time (for instance, to anger), and yet modern West European languages refer to the experience, at least with respect to nouns, as one phenomenon (for instance, *jealousy, jalousie, gelosia, Eifersucht,* or *celos*). It is not necessary for all of the components (thoughts, feelings, and so forth) to obtain in order to signal the presence of jealousy. The experience, as seen through literary examples as well as philosophical theories and psychological studies, is not one phenomenon, but many. To wit, there is a difference between the emotion one might feel when one suspects that the beloved is unfaithful, the feeling that arises upon learning of real infidelity, and the attitude that might bring one to murder the beloved or to commit suicide. Yet one might say, "he killed himself out of jealousy," or "she murdered her husband because she was insanely jealous." Such assertions claim to have psychological validity in describing affective

37. *Amorous jealousy* is similar to what psychologists sometimes refer to as *romantic* or *sexual jealousy*. I believe that the adjective *romantic* would be confusing in this literary study because of the many etymologically related words referring to, among other things, the literary movement preceding nineteenth-century realism, the novels of chivalry, as well the special variety of octosyllabic verse in Spanish. Against the use of the term *sexual jealousy,* I concur with Parrott ("Emotional Experience of Envy and Jealousy") that it is too limiting and does not evoke the rich subtleties of "love" often associated with the emotion.

38. For the sake of illustration, I provide a hypothetical extreme-case scenario: Imagine an insane person who is "in love" with a man she saw on the subway, but to whom she has never spoken. She follows him around, finds out he's married, and plans to kill his wife, whom she interprets as interfering. According to a strict definition, she would be "envious," for she *has* no right to this man. But to label her "envious" fails to account for her "feeling towards." From her perspective, she is jealous, because she *knows* the man loves her, too. After all, he looked at her on the train. She also *knows* that the wife will try to destroy the relationship; this jealous person wants to protect the relationship she already possesses. In less exaggerated cases as well, there is often a conflict between "knowledge" and "belief." Thus, I have chosen to define *jealousy* in terms of the *subjective experience* of it, which acknowledges Goldie's phenomenological category of *feeling towards*.

experience, but with respect to actions, they are "labels" meant to explain a behavior.[39] As such, jealousy in certain contexts is not a feeling at all, but an interpretation of an action.

Following the line of reasoning suggested by Hansen's view, and later by Goldie's, that emotions are comprised of other *emotional episodes,* I offer the following terms that hone in on particular mental states as they are purportedly experienced in actual humans (human subjects of psychological and philosophical inquiry) and fictional constructs (literary characters and lyric voices):[40]

Suspicious jealousy relates to fears of losing the beloved, or to doubts regarding the actual possession of the beloved, which have not yet been confirmed by proof.

Evidential jealousy refers to the feelings experienced by the subject after *witnessing* an act of unfaithfulness by the beloved.

Fait accompli jealousy is a term I borrow from clinical psychology, describing the experience of the given fact—or the logical inference—that two people are involved in an amorous relationship (while this is similar to *evidential jealousy,* there is, however, no "witnessing" or "seeing" here).

Possessive jealousy (or *jealous guarding*) refers to that aspect of jealousy that seeks to possess the beloved fully, sometimes as a protective impulse and sometimes as an obsessively controlling one. The beloved's freedom is often limited by expressions of possessive jealousy, such as imprisonment and thought control.

Jealous sadness is the experience of sadness accompanying or following an experience of either *suspicious* or *fait accompli jealousy.*

Jealous anger, jealous rage, and *jealous fury* describe progressive degrees of the emotion of "anger" associated with the experience of "jealousy."

The terms that I have developed incorporate Goldie's notion of *feeling towards* and make explicit the personal perspective of jealousy. At the same time, they acknowledge de Sousa's insight that

39. This is what Hansen refers to in his essay "Jealousy" as *situational labeling* of a primary emotion. For Hansen, the emotion "anger" that one feels is explained by the subject's and observers' using societal cues or contexts.

40. In my usage, the terms *lover, beloved,* and *rival* are ungendered and represent functional roles; any of them can be played by a female or a male. Thus Arminda can be a lover, Antonio her beloved, and Octavia her rival. In *El castigo sin venganza,* when the duke kills his wife and son, he is the lover, Casandra is the beloved, and Federico is the rival.

jealousy is more complex than other emotions in that it takes multiple targets.

The first three chapters of this study treat dramas by Lope de Vega. In Chapter 1, I reread two of Lope de Vega's "honor plays," shifting the critical emphasis away from honor and toward knowledge. In *The Commanders of Cordoba* and *Peribáñez y el Comendador de Ocaña* (Peribáñez and the Commander of Ocaña), jealousy motivates the protagonists' change of epistemological state from duped to disillusioned (*engañado* to *desengañado*). I argue that the valence of jealousy is ambiguous, and that its representation in these texts functions to uphold the hierarchical political order of early modern Spain.

Turning the focus to differences in the way jealousy is used in female characterization, Chapter 2 examines two plays in which powerful women are the protagonists. In *Jealous Arminda* and *El perro del hortelano* (The Dog in the Manger), the representations of women's emotions propagate cultural stereotypes of their weakness and irrationality. I demonstrate how Lope de Vega stakes out a conservative position in the early modern political debates on the suitability of queens as rulers.

Chapter 3 contrasts jealousy as a trivialized emotion in *La discreta enamorada* (In Love but Discreet) with the hyperbolized passion of *El castigo sin venganza* (Punishment without Revenge). While the two plays are similar in theme and structure, the most fundamental difference between them is their generic distinction: *In Love but Discreet* belongs to the realm of comedy, while *Punishment without Revenge* is a tragic work. This chapter demonstrates that genre can make all the difference in how jealousy is represented.

The next two chapters concern the prose fiction of Miguel de Cervantes. Chapter 4 interprets his novella *The Jealous Old Man from Extremadura* as centering on the moral opposition between virtue and vice. This dichotomy has both theological and racial overtones, and it relies on negative stereotypes of Jews, which are brought to the fore when the text is analyzed from the point of view of jealousy. My reading engages the critical debate on Cervantes's position in Hapsburg Spain, in which I demonstrate good reason for critical caution in imagining him as a progressive liberal in the modern sense.

In Chapter 5, I first review the critical appraisals of jealousy in

Cervantes's work, which assert, unanimously, that jealousy is contrary to love and, as such, was considered a vice by the author. Through an analysis of the characterization and metafictional statements in his last novel, *Los trabajos de Persiles y Sigismunda* (The Trials of Persiles and Sigismunda), I add an important caveat to this widespread belief: that there are some forms of virtuous jealousy in this text, which is Cervantes's most complete investigation of moral love.

Key examples of Góngora's poetry are the focus of the last two chapters. Chapter 6 examines his use of mythology in "Qué de invidiosos montes levantados" (What of the tall envious mountains). Bringing to bear insights from psychoanalysis, I interpret important visual images associated with jealousy by comparing Góngora's poem to Renaissance Italian and Spanish poetry and to Renaissance Venetian painting. I conclude that Góngora uses mythological images of jealousy to portray the fractious nature of the self, as he forges a modern notion of the psyche.

In Chapter 7, I argue that the "girlish jealousy" portrayed in the poem "Las flores del romero" (The Rosemary Flowers) is an embodiment of ways in which jealousy illustrates a Renaissance Neoplatonic view of beauty. I then turn to the zenith of hyperbole in Góngora's treatment of jealousy in his sonnet "A los celos" (On Jealousy) and in his *Fábula de Polifemo y Galatea* (Fable of Polyphemus and Galatea). In these poems, Góngora illustrates the antithesis of beauty, the sublime, anticipating an important aspect of modern aesthetics.

One

Jealousy and Epistemology in Lope de Vega's "Honor Plays"

> **Jealousy, Don Rodrigo, is a chimera, given form by envy, air and shadows, so that the yet uncertain but constantly imagined consequence becomes a fearful phantom in the night. A hideous ghost that draws a man to madness, and a lie that takes the name of truth.**
>
> —Lope de Vega, *El caballero de Olmedo*
> (The Knight from Olmedo)

> **Such were the monstrous effects of this venomous Liquor, on the Bodies of those who bathed in it; that some who only washt their mouth and throat, became a more strange metamorphosis than the rest; for their tongues, which were of solid, and substantial flesh, turned into a fire, that the whole world was in danger of its flames; others into the wind, which seemed to breathe a spirit of falsity, and like bellows puffed men's brains full of the air of lies and flattery.**
>
> —Gracián, *El criticón* (The Critic)

Because of his originality, his influential poetic treatise, and his remarkable prolificacy,[1] Lope de Vega is in a strong sense synonymous with the *comedia*.[2] Thus a study of the uses and meanings of

---

1. As is well known, Lope was, for Cervantes, "el monstruo de la naturaleza" (prodigy of nature) ("Prólogo al lector" to *Ocho comedias y ocho entremeses nunca representados,* in Cervantes, *Los entremeses de Cervantes,* 93).
2. *Comedia* is the term used to describe the hybrid genre of tragedy and comedy that was highly in vogue from the late sixteenth through the seventeenth centuries. See Chapter 3 for further discussion of its generic qualities.

jealousy in his drama also sheds light on how it worked in the early Spanish Baroque. Numerous plays by Lope refer to jealousy in their titles: *Los celos de Rodamonte* (Rodamonte's Jealousy), *Amor secreto hasta los celos* (Secret Love until Jealousy), *La escolástica celosa* (The Jealous Student), *Arminda celosa* (Jealous Arminda), and *Más pueden celos que amor* (Jealousy Is Stronger than Love). Scores of others, such as *Belardo el furioso* (Belardo the Furious) and *El perro del hortelano* (The Dog in the Manger), explore the theme without mentioning it in the title. Comedias such as Tirso de Molina's *La celosa de sí misma* (Jealous of Herself) and Guillén de Castro's *La tragedia por los celos* (Tragedy through Jealousy) demonstrate a similar interest, on the part of Lope's contemporaries, in representing jealous suspicion, suffering, and revenge on the stage.

The frequent references to jealousy in connection with love in Lope's work demonstrate a major concern, what might even be called an obsession. Clearly, there is evidence to suggest that his interest is somewhat autobiographical. In his turbulent relationship with Elena Osorio and her family (in which she left him for another man), Lope found the *materia prima* for many of his writings, as Alan S. Trueblood's compelling study of the *Dorotea* has shown. However, there is an additional rationale for depicting jealousy as the public's own taste, according to Lope's stated view. In his *Arte nuevo de hacer comedias en este tiempo* (New Art of Writing Plays in This Time), the Fénix proclaims, "Cases of honor are better because they forcefully move all people" (Los casos de la honra son mejores / porque mueven con fuerza a toda gente).[3] Jealousy, as I will show, plays an important role in these "cases," because it frequently motivates the protagonists' change of mental state between the polar opposites of Spanish Baroque epistemology, that is, from *engaño* (deceit) to *desengaño* (disillusionment [roughly translated]).

Notwithstanding its ubiquitousness, jealousy has often been dismissed by critics of Spanish theater as a topic unworthy of study, apparently because of its characterization as a "lower passion." Indeed, the theme is subterfuged in attempts to defend a wholly rational, consistent, and unambiguous conceptualization of the "honor code" (which is "noble," "rational," and "right"), while imaging jealousy as necessarily irrational. In his influential book on Lope de

---

3. Lope de Vega, *Arte nuevo de hacer comedias,* lines 327–28.

Vega's "honor plays," for example, Donald Larson insists on the unitary negativity of jealousy and implies that it is unimportant to an understanding of these plays:

> The motivating emotion in *Othello* is jealousy, and, like all emotions capable of producing tragedy, it is regarded by Shakespeare as an ambivalent quality, at once heinous and ennobling. In the *comedia,* on the other hand, jealousy or more particularly, marital jealousy is thoroughly disesteemed—one need only recall titles like *Celos aún del aire matan* and *El mayor monstruo los celos* to be convinced of this—and if it enters into the honor play, it does so peripherally. The protagonist's vengeance is induced more or less exclusively by a desire to repair his damaged honor.[4]

In contrast to what Larson interprets as the "peripheral" irrelevance of the emotion, José María Díez Borque writes several pages on the complexity of the emotion and describes its victory over honor: "[O]n many occasions, Lope presents us with the triumph of jealousy over honor . . . and jealousy overcomes the virtue and honesty of the lady. . . . Jealousy makes the man stop being who he is [dejar ser quien es]." Furthermore, Matthew Stroud has argued that recognizing the husbands' irrationality leads to a better understanding of these comedias, in which there is no clear separation of honor and jealousy.[5] Hence, while some critics of the honor plays have tried to eliminate "irrational jealousy" from the equation, the playwrights did not.[6] My aim is not only to demonstrate in greater detail than Stroud or Díez Borque the irrational aspects of honor as it is conflated with jealousy, but also to describe and explain the rational side of jealousy, which is usually overlooked. Stroud's cogent attack on the rationality of honor misses the point that jealousy can be rational (what I refer to as *instrumentally rational*) and that reason is not necessarily opposed to passion. It is a common assumption for most critics that reason and the passions must be at odds with

4. Donald Larson, *The Honor Plays of Lope de Vega,* 3.
5. José María Díez Borque, *Sociología de la comedia española del siglo XVII,* 35; Matthew Stroud, *Fatal Union: A Pluralistic Approach to the Wife-Murder Comedias,* 131.
6. In the same vein as Larson, see also Ramón Menéndez Pidal, *De Cervantes a Lope de Vega,* 139–65, and Francisco Ruiz Ramón, *Historia del teatro español,* 142–44.

each other, because of the pervasive influence of Plato's *Republic* over the millennia. The Platonic dichotomy between the *true rulers,* who were guided by their *Reason,* and the *producers,* who were led by their *passions,* required the paternalism of the *philosopher-rulers.* In the seventeenth century, Descartes's mind-body dualism only exacerbated this problem.[7]

Against the reason/passion split, de Sousa's analytical treatment of the emotions demonstrates that they may be rational or irrational.[8] Furthermore, contemporary neurobiological evidence points to a more complex intermingling of emotions and rationality. Jealousy is not a unitary fact, as certain critics would have it, but a complex, contradictory group of phenomena that cannot be so easily brushed away. Such nuanced complexity is explored in the works of Golden Age dramaturges. In Chapter 2, I will investigate the rationality of jealousy in female characters; but first, in this chapter, I will examine elements of irrationality as they commingle with rationality in jealous husbands.

Though jealousy has had little pedigree in Spanish literary criticism, the study of desengaño is renowned there.[9] As I will show, jealousy is precisely the psychological locus of the epistemological bridge leading away from engaño and toward desengaño. Engaño is a major theme of the Renaissance, while a preoccupation with desengaño is one of the distinguishing characteristics of the Baroque, particularly in Spain, and hence the abundance of jealousy in many of these plays has a deeper meaning than questions of sexual fidelity or even honor.[10] At the same time, there are sociopolitical implications associated with the depiction of jealous men and women.

7. Alpern's assertion that jealousy is "a passion of violence" that is "incompatible with reason" is typical of this bias ("Jealousy as a Dramatic Motive," 280).

8. Another philosopher, Martha C. Nussbaum, offers a different philosophical argument for the rationality of some emotions, given the interrelationship between beliefs, desires, and feelings (*Poetic Justice,* 53–78).

9. For Bruce W. Wardropper, desengaño involves mastering knowledge of oneself and of the true nature of the temporal world. It is arrived at by "tearing off the crust of illusion and *engaño.*" Wardropper argues that Spain in the seventeenth century is the place where the concept was most "obsessively" repeated (Wardropper, *Siglos de Oro: Barroco,* 83). He provides the following important references on desengaño: Luis Rosales, *El sentimiento del desengaño en la poesía barroca* (Madrid: Cultura Hisp., 1966), and Hans Schulte, *El desengaño. Wort und Thema in den Spanischen Literatur des Goltenen Zeitalters* (Munich: Fink Verlag, 1969).

10. For Larson, the protagonist of an honor play acts in order to reclaim lost

Illustrative of this link between *celos* and engaño/desengaño are the two epigraphs to this chapter: in the first, from Lope's *Knight from Olmedo,* jealousy is a monstrous purveyor of "lies" and deception, made of "shadows" and "air"; the second is Gracián's description of engaño as a venom that causes its victims to speak "lies" as "air" and "shadow." Indeed, the metaphorical imagery is remarkably similar. What explains this correspondence? The fundamental element that has been overlooked in studies of engaño and desengaño is the other meaning of the word *engaño,* that is, as regarding acts of unfaithfulness in a love relationship (which are often the grounds, or the imagined grounds, for a subject's jealousy). Just as jealousy is not one phenomenon—as I elaborated in the Introduction—neither is engaño. The dual meaning of *engaño* in Spanish relates the amorous sphere (with respect to actions and thoughts that are faithless to the institution of marriage) and the epistemological sphere (corresponding to the subject's belief about a state of affairs that does or does not obtain in the world). In what follows, I explore this problematic in two of Lope de Vega's "honor plays," *Los comendadores de Córdoba* (The Commanders of Cordoba) and *Peribáñez y el comendador de Ocaña* (Peribáñez and the Commander of Ocaña).[11]

---

honor after an offense. (In this sense, honor, as a societal good worthy of reclaiming, should be considered an instrumentally rational goal.) This idea is founded on the work of Américo Castro (in *De la edad conflictiva*) on Golden Age honor: Castro contends that the obsession with honor originates in the medieval caste struggles between Jews, Muslims, and Christians, out of which honor became the dominant factor in the constructed Christian national identity. In these struggles, the Christians saw themselves as violent warriors in contrast to the Muslims, who distinguished themselves in the arts and artisanry, while the Jews were proud of their professional skills and wisdom. For Castro, honor has two manifestations, sometimes referred to as horizontal and vertical: (1) blood cleanliness (*limpieza de sangre*), which is blood without Jewish or Islamic taint; and (2) masculine strength (*hombría*), which helps achieve control over the world by force.

11. I have chosen these two plays not because they are the plays in which jealousy is most pronounced as a rationale for violent action, but rather because they are considered the paradigmatic honor plays in the first part of Larson's book. Spanish quotations are from *Los comendadores de Córdoba,* in *Obras escogidas,* 3rd ed., ed. Federico Carlos Sainz de Robles, and *Peribáñez y el comendador de Ocaña,* 14th ed., ed. Juan María Marín. Citations will be made parenthetically in the text by page number and by act and line number, respectively, using the abbreviations *CC* and *PCO.*

The Commanders of Cordoba

In *The Commanders of Cordoba* (ca. 1596–1598), the two meanings of the word *engaño* are evoked, and they coincide on the same
action, showing the basic epistemological component of jealousy as a
force of desengaño. Since the world of appearances is often deceptive,
a degree of skepticism is found to be wise and good.[12] It is only with
jealousy that the hero of the play finds desengaño.[13]

At the outset, the Veinticuatro (who is one of three Don Fernan-
dos in this play)[14] is characterized by a host of superlative male attributes: noble, religious, king-loving, bellicose, and honorable; he is,
apparently, a faultless man. Importantly, he is not jealous in Peter
Goldie's sense of experiencing the emotion as a trait (as opposed, for
instance, to the protagonist of Lope's *Belardo the Furious,* who at the
beginning of that play is already suspicious). The Veinticuatro's only
flaw is one for which he can hardly be faulted: he leaves for battle to
pay service to his king too often, leaving his wife alone to suffer from
ausencia (that is, the loneliness caused by the absence of the loved
one). Perhaps he is not jealous enough and trusts her too much.[15]
Or it may be that he is simply so good that he is not able to suspect
hidden sin in others.

While he is away serving Christendom and the historical King
Fernando (the Catholic king) in the decisive battle of 1492 to recap-

12. Later on in the seventeenth century, not only a degree, but rather a method
of hyperbolic doubt was held by Descartes, in his *Meditations,* to be the only one
that would guarantee certainty of any belief.

13. That desengaño is "good" has its basis in engaño (deceit) as "evil," which
relies on scripture: "The serpent beguiled me, and I did eat" (Genesis 3:13 [New
Revised Standard Version]); "And there was war in Heaven: Michael and his
angels fought against the dragon. . . . And the great dragon was cast out, that
old serpent, called the Devil and Satan, which deceiveth the whole world" (Rev-
elation 12:7–9 [NRSV]).

14. This character is called "the Veinticuatro" in the play because he was one
of the twenty-four Andalusian municipal leaders. The three characters called
Fernando are the Veinticuatro, the king of Spain (husband of Isabel la Católica),
and one of the two brothers known as the commanders of Cordoba.

15. As Teodoro states in Lope's *Jealous Arminda,* women should not be trusted:
"I have little faith in Florela, since she is, in effect, a woman" (Poco de Florela fío,
/ que es, en efecto, mujer, *Arminda celosa,* p. 700). *The Commanders of Cordoba*
can be read as a play trying to prove the misogynistic point that leaving women
with too much time alone and too few restrictions or barriers will lead to their
unfaithfulness, since, "in effect," they are women.

ture Granada (the last remnant of Islamic rule in Spain), his wife, Beatriz, is characterized as morally weak and even corrupt. Her time away from the Veinticuatro is described as a jealous absence (*ausencia celosa, CC,* 1239); she feels jealousy of the Veinticuatro, most likely—as Freud would later hypothesize—because she herself already has thoughts or desires of unfaithfulness, and she transposes her awareness of her own illicit desire to her husband's consciousness.

In the first scene in which she appears, Doña Beatriz is talking to her husband's niece, Doña Ana, her friend and confidante. They are comparing and rating the appearance of certain men they have just seen. Although the scene is playful, the women are characterized as lascivious, resulting in a sharp contrast with the virtuous Veinticuatro, whom the king has just praised in the previous scene (*CC,* 1238–39). Woman's sexual desire is portrayed as dangerous, as something to be quelled.

The two knight commanders of the play's title,[16] Jorge and Fernando, nephews of the bishop and cousins of Doña Beatriz, soon arrive and immediately fall in love with Beatriz and Ana, respectively, becoming the suitors (and soon, the lovers) of the ladies, during the Veinticuatro's patriotic absence. Hence, they too, and particularly the elder commander, Jorge, are characterized as morally corrupt. According to prevalent ideology of the time, good women would have resisted the advances of these men. Instead, the women's moral corruption is anticipated by their visual interest and then by their encouragement of the two male cousins. The persons who share most of the blame for the situation, therefore, are Beatriz and Ana.

Already in act 1, the female members of the Veinticuatro's household are being deceitful, feigning happiness and relief that the Veinticuatro has returned from the brave exploits in Granada for which the king has awarded him a beautiful ring. For example, the servant Esperanza (Hope), who has been carrying on with the commanders' servant (*lacayo*), tells him:

> Just seeing you, my Lord, my hope is enriched by your faith and favor.

16. Like the Veinticuatro, the two cousins are often referred to by their title. They are *comendadores,* characters that often receive a negative treatment in Lope's comedias, representing as they do a throwback to feudalistic forms of government that are contrary to monarchal efforts at increasing absolutism.

(Ya con verte, mi señor,
de tu esperanza y favor
está mi esperanza rica. *CC,* 1242)

Now that the Veinticuatro has returned, Doña Ana will no longer
be able to freely see her lover Don Fernando, yet she expresses not
her sadness, but rather the opposite:

ANA. I've been sad.
VEINTICUATRO. And now?
ANA. Infinitely happy.

(ANA. Triste he estado.
VEINTICUATRO. ¿Y ahora?
ANA. Alegre infinito. *CC,* 1242)

Perhaps worst of all is the deceptive speech of his own wife upon
his return:

If my pleasure and soul (which is in you) were granted leave, I
would jump through the window or along the corridor. Thanks
be to God, my Lord, that I now see your face: I want to embrace
you once more.

(Si el placer lugar me diera
y el alma, que en vos está,
por la ventana saltara
o por este corredor.
Gracias a Dios, mi señor,
que ya veo vuestra cara:
otro abrazo os quiero dar. *CC,* 1242)

In truth, however, she is pining away for Don Jorge, as she engages the rhetoric of engaño.[17] The Veinticuatro, not a suspiciously
jealous man by nature, has no reason to doubt the authenticity of
these shows of affection, but rather he praises—in his absence of
knowledge, of truth—the sanctity of marriage, and the sheer joy
of his Odyssean homecoming: "Oh, how good now to be home!" (¡Que

---

17. Another important deception is the double entendre in which Beatriz,
upon the Veinticuatro's second return, responds, "Muy *mala* sin vos he estado,"
which can be translated either as "I've been very *badly* without you" or as "I've
been very *bad* without you" (*CC,* 1257, emphasis added).

ya en mi casa me veo! *CC,* 1242) is his initial reaction upon setting foot in the home; later, his lengthier, more reflective exposition reveals the depths of his deception (engaño) to the audience and other characters who know better:

> Oh, how much joy I receive! Who belittles marriage? Who was that ignorant fool who spoke badly of matrimony? Is the contentment which I have before me found in any other state? . . . Look here at my family, my servants and my wife, bursting with pleasure.

> (¡Oh, cuánto gusto recibo!
> ¿Quién pone en casarse mengua?
> ¿Quién era aquel ignorante
> que habló mal del casamiento?
> ¿Tiene otro estado el contento
> que ahora tengo delante?
> . . . .
> Miren aquí mi familia,
> mis criados y mujer,
> reventando de placer. *CC,* 1243)

Unmistakably, the Veinticuatro lives in a terrible state of deception, that is, of engaño, with respect to the honor of his household and the conduct and attitudes of his wife, family, and servants. Ironically, his perception of the situation is precisely the opposite of the reality. Given the value placed on desengaño in the Baroque, it cannot be stressed enough how negative this man's life would have seemed to a contemporary audience. If he were suspiciously jealous (if he suffered from the emotion in Goldie's sense), most likely he would have been more hesitant to expound such nonsense—in his case—about the joys of marriage, until he was more certain that his wife had been faithful to him (his suspicious jealousy would have led him to investigate the situation, and he would thus have been less *engañado*). Thus, this play suggests that a lack of suspicious jealousy diminishes the possibility of attaining epistemological certainty.

According to the text, a flaw seems to arise in the ostensibly perfect Veinticuatro, given the fact that he does accept responsibility for his state of dishonor later. It is reasonable to consider as this flaw his lack of suspicious jealousy up to this point.[18] In addition to

18. In act 3, the Veinticuatro accepts full responsibility for the state of dishonor: "I, alone, am to blame" (Yo soy culpado solo, 1260). He had failed to rec-

calling for men's suspicious jealousy, the text reinforces the need to keep women more effectively cloistered, since when they are granted enough freedom to choose they are proven untrustworthy (this is in contradistinction to the example of the young girl in Cervantes's *Jealous Old Man from Extremadura,* treated in Chapter 4).

Since they know that they themselves are lying, his family, servants, and wife recognize his state of engaño and label it exactly such, among themselves:

> BEATRIZ. Who hears this and yet fears not; Doña Ana, how will this end?
> ANA. Come on, my Lady, do not fear; there are many *deceived ones* among Love's guilty.
>
> (BEATRIZ. ¿Quién esto escucha y no teme,
> Doña Ana, en qué ha de parar?
> ANA. Anda, señora, no temas;
> Que de aquestos *engañados*
> tiene amor muchos culpados. *CC,* 1243, emphasis added)

In fact, the deceived husband is so trusting that he once again departs to serve the king at the beginning of act 2. As he is leaving, he provides his wife with a symbol of his honor and love for her, the very ring the king had awarded him earlier. The meaning of honor, according to its code, becomes apparent in an important speech, set off as a sonnet. In it, the Veinticuatro enunciates his belief that his whole being—more than just his self-worth—is connected with his honor (which in turn relies on his wife's conduct):

> With [this ring] I pledge to you all my reputation, and with it I certify my love for you; the world is small compared to its value; silver is of vile worth, gold a dream. I hereby give you my being, my honor, my whole estate: this is my faith: with loyal decorum, here my noble blood is sculpted. Keep it well, for I give you in this token worth, reputation, ring, silver and gold, loyalty, faith, honor, estate, blood and life.
>
> (En él todo mi crédito os empeño,
> y en él todo mi amor os certifico;

---

ognize the subtle warnings that Rodrigo was sending him in his letters. Now he obviously feels that he should have done something else, earlier, to prevent such dishonor.

para su estimación el mundo es chico;
la plata es precio vil, el oro es sueño.
Yo os doy aquí mi ser, mi honor, mi hacienda:
esta es mi fe: con mi leal decoro,
aquí mi hidalga sangre está esculpida.
Guardadle bien, que os doy en esta prenda
valor, crédito, anillo, plata y oro
lealtad, fe, honor, hacienda, sangre y vida. *CC,* 1245–46)

This act of ring-giving and the Veinticuatro's ceremonious speech are symbolic of renewed wedding vows, in which he reaffirms his loyalty (*lealtad*). It is precisely this item, the ring, a symbol not only of her husband's honor but of his "love" (*amor*), that Doña Beatriz will foolishly give away as a token to her lover, Don Jorge. It is for this faithless act that the play ultimately deems her immoral and sentences her to death. In destroying his "being" (*ser*), she is, in a sense, killing him. It is from this passage that the full value of what is at stake for the Veinticuatro—and for the male subject at the time—becomes apparent, and based on this, the play attempts to justify the reprehensible acts of violence later committed by the man.

At the time of this second departure, Beatriz expresses her own jealousy once more, to which the husband responds that she does not know his love well, for he would never "cheat on" or "trick" her, that is, *hacer engaños:*

BEATRIZ. Who doubts that you are not going to see one of those queens who at court . . . ?
VEINTICUATRO. Don't speak of such women; you touch on my honor. For as long as you are alive—would that God protect you for a thousand years—would I, when away, *cheat on* you with the queens you speak of? How badly you know my *love*!

(BEATRIZ. ¿Quién duda que a ver no vais
alguna reina de aquellas
que en la corte . . . ?
VEINTICUATRO.   No habléis de ellas;
que en el honor me tocáis.
Yo, mientras vos me viváis,
que os me guarde Dios mil años,
¿haceros, ausente, *engaños,*
con las reinas que decís?
¡Qué mal mi *amor* conocéis! *CC,* 1245, emphasis added)

Thus the deceived man (*hombre engañado*)—in both the amorous and epistemological senses—to whom the term *engaño* had previously been applied explicitly, now employs the verb *engañar* (to deceive) in the amorous/sexual sense. The coincidence reflects the epistemological importance of jealousy: in the play his amorous jealousy could prevent his wife from cheating on him and protect his honor; the same jealousy could help him know the truth, that is, help him live *desengañado*.[19]

The many linguistic double entendres[20] in act 2 provide a greater rhetorical basis for my focus on the wordplay with *engañar,* which henceforth creates a link between the epistemological and the amorous in jealousy, associated through the common fear of engaño (in both senses). For instance, after the parting scene with the ring described above, but before the Veinticuatro's actual departure, his wife's cousins arrive for a very short visit and bid him farewell. The deceived husband describes the commanders in glowing terms, which serves not only as a further source of irony for the audience, but more. The statement

> I don't have any better friends. They are my relatives, and are
> so good that I am honored at their side.

> (No tengo amigos mayores.
> Son mis deudos, y tan buenos,
> que me honro de su lado.)

creates dramatic irony based on his state of utter deception. Indeed, the opposite of what he says is actually true. He continues,

---

19. At this point, the play uncovers another irony: the man who has reason to be jealous is not, while the woman who has no legitimate reason to be jealous is. It should be noted that Ana, in addition to Beatriz, expresses jealousy of her lover's affection, which, like Beatriz's jealousy, is viewed as negative.

20. These are often linked to the precept of "engañar con la verdad" (deceiving with the truth), which, at the time of this early play, had not yet been formulated as a normative rule by Lope in his *New Art of Writing Plays*. Interestingly, the semantic category of death is related to many of the incidents of "engañar con la verdad" in this comedia as a form of foreshadowing: Beatriz, Ana, Fernando, and Jorge all announce their own deaths, equivocally, in what they mean as hyperbolic metaphors of love's sufferings, but which are, in effect, quite accurate descriptions of their true forms of demise at the end of act 3: e.g., Beatriz says, "you will find me dead when you return" (me halleréis / ya muerta cuando volváis, *CC,* 34).

Youths in whom to have great hope: I am obliged to see to their safety. Would that, in such hands, my honor should always fall.

(Mozos de grande esperanza:
a su fianza me obligo.
En tales manos cayese
siempre mi honor. *CC,* 1246)

Although he is trying to imply that his cousins are worthy of having his honor "fall into their hands" (that is, that he trusts them to hold or carry his honor), the equivocal meaning points rather to the true state of affairs, of which he remains ignorant, that is, through the metonymical "hands" of the cousins, his honor is slipping out of his own hands ("would that . . . my honor should always fall") and metaphorically becoming debased on the ground. He also exclaims, "What gallant men, what gentlemen!" (¡Qué galanes, qué hidalgos . . . ! *CC,* 1246), ushering in a play on the word *galanes.* A few moments later, when husband and wife are alone again, Beatriz reiterates the Veinticuatro's previous praise of her cousins, stating, "They are gallant men" (Galanes son, *CC,* 1247), in what is now a subtle case of "deceiving with the truth" (*engañar con la verdad*).[21] The statement "They are gallant men" is true only equivocally, since *galán* commonly meant "suitor" or "lover" in the Golden Age, and the commanders are in fact the lovers of Beatriz and Ana.[22] The word *galán* is repeated later in act 2 with this latter meaning by the faithful servant Rodrigo, who—jealous of Esperanza's affection for the cousins' servant Galindo, and her rejection of him—reveals his knowledge of the wife's adultery and the state of dishonor in the home:

RODRIGO. Do you think that I don't know that Don Jorge . . .
ESPERANZA. Don Jorge what? What purpose does it serve for your contemptible understanding to forge a maze of intrigue?
RODRIGO. He is the lover of the Lady? I know all about what's going on, and that the honor of this house is crying because of its exile. . . .

21. It should be noted that two of Lope's prescriptive items in the *New Art of Writing Plays*—the tropological *engañar con la verdad* and the thematic *casos de la honra*—are linked through jealousy.
22. On the meanings of *galán,* see Sebastián de Covarrubias's *Tesoro de la lengua española o castellana* (1611).

(RODRIGO. ¿Piensas que yo no he sabido
que don Jorge . . .
ESPERANZA.   ¿Qué don Jorge?
¿Qué sirve que enredos forje
tu entendimiento abatido?
RODRIGO. ¿*Galán* es de mi señora?
Ya sé todo lo que pasa,
y que el honor de esta casa,
porque le destierran llora . . . *CC,* 1249, emphasis added)

It is, significantly, through Rodrigo's jealousy that the Veinticuatro later gains confirmation of his wife's adultery and of his own general state of dishonor, and hence Rodrigo's characterization of Jorge as *galán* prefigures the Veinticuatro's ultimate desengaño. The Veinticuatro's change of state from engañado to desengañado is paralleled by the iteration and reiteration of the word *galán,* with its two meanings.

Although the concept of honor is important in this comedia, the Veinticuatro does not act solely by some sense of damaged honor—as some critics would have it—but rather from his vengeful jealousy. Although all the different causes of dishonor are important, he does not feel neutral in some detached, "rational" way toward them. His feelings are embedded in a situation that is of the greatest importance to him. The content and ordering of his questions reveal his *feeling towards* the subject matter, not his objective, dispassionate stance. Indeed, the very first specific question in his inquiry to Rodrigo in act 3 is whether or not his wife "loves" (*querer*) her cousin. Second, it is whether the latter "enjoys" (*gozar*) her:

VEINTICUATRO. [I] alone am to blame; tell me Rodrigo, does
Doña Beatriz love her cousin?
RODRIGO. She loves him.
VEINTICUATRO. Does her cousin enjoy Doña Beatriz?
RODRIGO. He enjoys her.

(VEINTICUATRO. [Y]o soy culpado solo; di Rodrigo,
¿quiere doña Beatriz su primo?
RODRIGO.   Quiérele.
VEINTICUATRO. ¿Goza a doña Beatriz su primo?
RODRIGO.   Gózala.

                            CC, 1260)

Thus, it is a question of her rejection of him, that is, the fact that she actually loves someone else (of course, by doing so, she dishonors him) that hurts him terribly. According to the honor code, and the laws of the time, only the adultery was important: love was not a question; yet it is for the Veinticuatro, since he is now suffering from an emotional episode of jealousy. My claim here is bolstered by Lope's use, in the *Dorotea,* of Xenophon's idea that jealous rage and not honor or justice leads a husband to kill: says Julio, "Armenius told Cyrus that husbands, on discovering them with adulterers, did not murder their wives because of their part in the offense, but out of fury at their wives' having withdrawn love from them and attached it to someone else" (Díjole Armenio a Ciro que no mataban los maridos a sus mujeres, cuando las hallaban con los adúlteros, por la culpa de la ofensa, sino por la rabia de que les hubiesen quitado el amor y puéstole en otro). And in the *Dorotea,* yet another Fernando—the autobiographical Lope character—ultimately realizes that Julio's claim is correct.[23]

Like Orlando Furioso, Ariosto's antonomastic jealous madman, to whom he now compares himself explicitly, the Veinticuatro is certainly moved by the emotion of jealousy: "Today, in what way do I differ from Furious Orlando?" (Hoy, ¿en que me diferencio / de otro furioso Roldán? *CC,* 1263). When he first learns that Fernando is wearing the ring he gave his wife, he reacts with self-described jealous anger and jealous sadness: "Oh rabid fury! Oh jealous abyss! Woe is me! What will I do?" (¡Oh rabia! ¡Oh celoso abismo! / ¡Ay de mí, triste! ¿Qué haré? *CC,* 1254). He does not suffer from suspicious jealousy as an emotion, but as an emotional episode he experiences vengeful jealousy. Focusing not on his own fault, but on the wrongdoing of others, he now seeks revenge on all who seem to be involved in belittling him.[24]

23. Lope de Vega, *La Dorotea,* ed. E. S. Morby, 265, 410. The English quotation is from Alan S. Trueblood and Edwin Honig's translation of the novel (131). Morby's footnote to this passage gives the source as Xenophon's *Ciropedia* (3.1.29), a work known in English as the *Kyrou paideia: or, The Institution and Life of Cyrus the Great.* He also points out that the speaker in Xenophon's text is not actually "Armenio," but the Armenian king (*el rey armenio*).

24. Frederick de Armas contends that the Veinticuatro is merely feigning jealousy here ("La estructura mítica de *Los comendadores de Córdoba,*" 769). While de Armas's reading is compelling in many ways, I believe my highlighting of the Veinticuatro's love for Beatriz, as well as the connection between this Don Fernando and the character of the same name in the *Dorotea,* provide an adequate defense of my emphasis on his sincere experience of jealousy.

Admittedly, much of the rhetoric of this comedia has more to do with honor than with jealousy. Nevertheless, some of the ways in which this regaining of honor is expressed are typical of texts dealing more straightforwardly with jealousy: for example, in his first jealous fit, after finding out about the ring possessed by Don Jorge, the husband briefly describes his doubts (a typical expression of jealousy in drama):

> Woe is me! What am I thinking? How could he be wearing it if she did not give it to him? Thus the "when" is certain. She gave it to him, what am I doubting?

> (¡Ay de mí! ¿Qué estoy pensando?
> ¿Cómo aquéste la trujera,
> cuando ella no se la diera?
> Luego ya fue cierto el cuándo.
> Diósela, ¿qué estoy dudando? *CC,* 1255)

In addition, he describes his anger as "fury" (*furia*), a topos of jealousy poetry, and himself as "loco" (*CC,* 1255), the passionate state par excellence whether referring to love or jealousy.[25] Admittedly, a large part of his anger is due to his fear of public dishonor and the fact that he has already been dishonored in front of the king. However, a part of this dishonor is—like rivalry in general, of which jealousy can be a species—linked to comparisons of self-worth.

Honor is evidently a much more noble sentiment than jealousy (which some theological works describe as a sin and which poetry often calls "monster," "fury," and "love's enemy"). Hence, the play's discursive orientation toward the concept of honor serves to condone and even praise the Veinticuatro's behavior at the end of act 3. How else to justify such acts of vengeful violence, directed against some who must have been wholly unaware of the dishonor (that is, they must have been innocent), as is the case of Medrano, the servant of the Veinticuatro who, in act 1, returns as a war hero with his master and who is not seen or mentioned in reference to the dishonoring

25. On fury, see the sonnets by Sannazaro, Garcilaso, and Góngora treated in Chapter 7. Regarding the Veinticuatro's exclamation "Come on, I'm going mad!" (¡Ea, que me vuelvo loco! *CC,* 1255), madness is often associated with jealousy. Insanely jealous characters in the Italian poem *Orlando furioso,* by Ludovico Ariosto; *The Jealous Old Man from Extremadura,* by Cervantes; and *Belardo the Furious,* by Lope de Vega, are well-known examples. In *The Commanders of Cordoba,* Rodrigo is also called "loco" by Esperanza because of his jealousy.

of the loyal husband, yet whom the latter seeks out and murders during the mad rampage.[26] This play is not one of those jealousy works concerned directly with the epistemological problem of ascertaining truth from appearance. Unlike Shakespeare's *Othello* (1612), the paradigmatic case of such works, it is not a question of belief versus doubt, appearance versus evidence. The extent of the dishonor is explained to the Veinticuatro by Rodrigo. He never calls into question the veracity of what the servant tells him; he does not doubt for long that his wife gave Don Fernando the ring. It is taken as true, and, largely, it is true. The king is not interested in proofs either. It is enough that his own trustworthy servant, the Veinticuatro, relates the story to him, for him to proclaim this as "a renowned and notable deed . . . deserving of a prize" (Hecho famoso y notable . . . dino de premio, *CC,* 1266). The epistemological problem of this play is present only insofar as it describes the case of an *hombre engañado* who moves to a state of desengaño. The play purposefully moves away from jealousy and toward honor to distance itself from sin (that is, the sin of jealousy), yet the hyperbolic spectacle of the mad husband killing all the people and all the household pets—which Lope borrowed from Juan Rufo's ballad version[27]—was too awe-inspiring for Lope to resist including it.

However, no matter what discourse is created for the purposes of rationalization, revenge and cold-blooded murder are only easily pardoned when the rule of law is subordinated to absolutist decrees. Just as the play is not about epistemological uncertainty (in the sense of inquiring into the problems of proofs versus appearances), nor is it concerned with a concept of justice.[28] Even if the modern reader grudgingly accepts that, to some extent (given the precepts of the worldview that Spanish Christians seem to have held at this time), those directly involved in the adultery and dishonoring deserve death as punishment for their crime, there is no solid ground (given the knowledge the audience has of events in the play) to justify the killing of Medrano and the servant women, among others.[29]

26. Medrano is killed on page 1264.
27. Larson details this borrowing well (*Honor Plays of Lope de Vega,* 41).
28. Stroud, *Fatal Union,* 83–84.
29. The servant women and others are mentioned at the end of the play only in order to be slaughtered: "RODRIGO. Shall the servant women die? / VEINTICUATRO. Kill them!" (RODRIGO. ¿Morirán las dueñas? / VEINTICUATRO. ¡Dalas! *CC,* 1265).

Just because they did nothing to avenge the Veinticuatro's damaged honor, or to warn him—as he complains, does not mean that they did so with intent (they may very well have lacked knowledge) or that they should be held responsible for their actions or lack thereof. In contrast, Beatriz, Ana, Esperanza, Jorge, Fernando, and Galindo are all actively engaged in the betrayal.

Evidence for this position is that the raving mad, murderous Veinticuatro kills the dog, parrot, and monkey of the house, allegedly because they also "kept quiet" about his honor. Yet just because they said nothing does not mean that they were capable of voicing their opinions. It may seem trite to point out that a dog cannot speak, but it is important to recognize that to hold an animal responsible for not speaking is irrational, for it transgresses the rules of logic. On the dog's "fault," the Veinticuatro says, in a statement that was probably intended to create a greater sense of *admiratio* (amazement) in the audience,

> Kill him, because he was present for everything but held back his speech; and thus, since he knew about it, and, I confess, he told me nothing about what was going on, that is a clear sign that he was guilty!
>
> (¡Mátale, que a todo estuvo
> presente, y su hablar detuvo;
> y pues lo supo, y confieso
> que no me dijo el suceso,
> señal es que culpa tuvo! *CC,* 1264–65)

In this sense, the reaction of the Veinticuatro is not just *out of proportion,* but indeed irrational.[30] This irrational element in the thoughts and actions aroused by his experiencing jealousy complicate what seemed like the rational element in the cause of the jealousy; by de Sousa's standards, the emotion should be judged "rational" because the object (target) of the emotion—his wife's having an affair with another man—should surely be construed as "jealousy-provoking." The Veinticuatro's experience over time is an excellent example of what Goldie has called the "complex of an emotion," as it metamorphoses from rational to irrational.

---

30. If he really means that the dog can "hold back his speech," then he suffers from delusions, a notion that certainly does not jibe with a rational view of honor.

It is not a purely rational sense of honor that brings the Veinticuatro to mass murder, but rather the passion of vengeful jealousy. His acts are only "justifiable" or "just" in a society that accepts absolutist nominalism, that is, the word of the king as truth, and the willingness to concede to the king's saying that a particular case is "just." Likewise, getting jealous revenge is certainly not a Christian virtue, unless, in the absolutist logic, the king says so. Indeed, the Veinticuatro is strongly characterized as a good Christian, though jealousy is sometimes associated with Judaism through the Hebrew scriptures[31] and with Muslims through the institution of the harem, a sultan's space for enclosing women that prevents other men's sleeping with them. Moreover, the New Testament negates jealousy's value, associates it with Jews, and labels it antithetical to love.[32] As José Antonio Maravall has written, the Spanish kings after Carlos I tended toward absolutism and needed playwrights such as Lope to uphold and reinforce this hierarchical order, while attempting to whisk away power from others (titled nobility, lower nobility), in order to consolidate their power, creating closer relationships between monarch and subject.[33] In this vein, *The Commanders of Cordoba* demonstrates that the king's word is to be up-

31. An example is Exodus 20:3–5: "You shall not have any other gods before me. You will not make any image, nor any imitation of anything that is in heaven, nor down on the earth, nor in the waters below the earth. You will not incline yourself to these, nor will you honor them; because I am Jehova your God, Strong, Jealous, and I return the evil deeds of the parents on their children" (No tendrás dioses agenos delante de mi. No te harás imagen, ni ninguna semejança de cosa que esté arriba en el cielo, ni abaxo en la tierra, ni en las aguas debaxo de la tierra. No te inclinarás à ellas, ni las honrrarás: porque yo soy Iehova tu Dios, Fuerte, Zeloso, que visito la maldad de los padres sobre los hijos, *La Biblia* [1569], trans. Casiodoro de Reina). All of my biblical quotes in Spanish are from this edition of the Bible, translated by Reina from the original languages and published in Basel in 1569; translations into English are mine. It is interesting to note that Pedro Calderón also employed this jealousy-Jewish/love-Christian dichotomy, allegorically, in a few *auto sacramentales* in which "The Synagogue" (*La Sinagoga*) appears jealous of "The Church" (*La Iglesia*) because God has left Israel for the Catholic Church (that is, Jesus has). The Synagogue in these *autos* feels hate and vengeance, as might a woman whose husband has abandoned her for someone else (Juan Carlos Garrot, "Sinagoga abandonada: Celos a lo divino en algunos autos calderonianos").

32. For instance, in Acts 13:45, Luke notes, "And when the Jews saw the crowds of people, they became jealous" (Y cuando los judíos vieron las muchedumbres, se pusieron celosos).

33. José Antonio Maravall, *La cultura del Barroco: Análisis de una estructura histórica,* 91–96.

held no matter how gruesome the crime and how intuitively "un-just" it may be. The black-and-white depictions of the morality of the characters do make the king's ruling seem more palatable, but what about Medrano and the other innocent victims who are mur-dered? Just as the absolutist needs the playwright, it appears that Lope, accordingly, needs an absolutist in his play to pardon his hero, have a "happy" ending (in which the pardoned man is married off to the conveniently widowed Constanza[34]), and uphold the honor code despite its many contradictions.[35] Regardless of attempts to systematize this code, it is not a system, but rather a heterogeneous combination of beliefs, emotions, and postures. An analysis of the role of jealousy in *The Commanders of Cordoba* and other dramas shows the inherent tension in the code of honor and the passionate side of the dramatic honor-bound husbands.

Alongside the irrational element of vengeful jealousy, the rational value of jealousy is seen in its necessity for preventing the ills of adultery, and, in the play's misogynistic spirit, in quelling women's sexual desire. Had the Veinticuatro been suspicious, he would not have been so easily tricked. Thus, based on a counterfactual infer-ence, the play asserts that male suspicious jealousy is beneficial in preventing engaño. Overall, the play's attitude toward jealousy is largely positive, notwithstanding the traditional assertions to the contrary in the text.

Peribáñez and the Commander of Ocaña

Like *The Commanders of Cordoba, Peribáñez and the Comman-der of Ocaña* (1614)[36] is a comedia that asserts the necessity of male suspicious jealousy, this time by portraying a subject who is much

34. The audience and the protagonist, no doubt, expect greater "constancy" from this *Constanza ex machina* marriage. However, even in this, the ambiguity abounds, since from the example of "Esperanza" (Hope), Doña Beatriz's complicit slave girl, we learn that names too can be deceptive.

35. In Chapter 4, I read the novella *The Jealous Old Man from Extremadura* as a parody of this play, based on what Cervantes may have perceived as the un-Christian, jealous nature of the theatrical honor code.

36. The play was first published in 1614, but according to S. Griswold Morley and Courtney Bruerton, in *Cronología de las comedias de Lope de Vega,* it was written in 1609–1612. Juan María Marín argues that the actual date of compo-sition of the play may be anywhere from 1604 to 1613. See the introduction to his edition of *Peribáñez y el comendador de Ocaña* (40–45).

more suspicious than the Veinticuatro, and who ultimately meets a less disastrous fate. The two plays contain notable similarities, such as the depiction of an honorable man deceived by a commander; a trip away from his home for the sake of duty; his disillusionment with respect to the commander; a final departure, this time feigned; a secret return to witness the deception and gain vengeance through murder; and the final absolution of the man's deeds by the king. Donald Larson's comparison of the two as honor plays brings these similarities to the fore. However, his attempts to prove their fundamental sameness fails to notice some of the key divergences, among which are the protagonists' jealousy (which differ in kind and intensity) and the number of explicit references to the emotion (which is much higher in *Peribáñez*). As in *The Commanders of Cordoba,* jealousy has a double valence in this play, where it leads to even greater ambiguity.

The drama takes place during the historical reign of Enrique III (1379–1406) and treats the fictional tale of a peasant-noble love triangle involving the peasant Peribáñez; his wife, Casilda; and the Commander of Ocaña, a knight in the Order of Santiago.[37] The very first lines spoken by Peribáñez serve as a gentle warning to his bride on their wedding day of the dangers of jealousy. To the priest's remark "My niece has a good head on her shoulders" (Mi sobrina es muy sesuda), Peribáñez responds, "As long as she is not jealous, that remark will be proven true" (Sólo con no ser zelosa / Saca este pleito de duda, *PCO,* 1.19–20). She assures him, in return, that she will never be jealous as long as he gives her no reason to be.[38] "I will never make you jealous" (Por mí, no sabréis que son), he assures her. Thus, from the beginning of the play, jealousy is denigrated as something that is to be avoided. In the context of the wedding ceremony—"the day in which you two are one" (el día / en que sois uno los dos, *PCO,* 1.26–27)—jealousy is the enemy of love. However, along with these pejorative words, ambiguity pertaining to its value is introduced by Inés, who refers to jealousy's divine origin: "They say that heaven gave love this penchant" (Dizen que al amor los cielos / le dieron

37. See my introduction to *Peribáñez y el Comendador de Ocaña,* Cervantes and Company, no. 14 (Newark, DE: Cuesta European Masterpieces, 2004), xi–xiii.
38. "Don't ever give me a reason in life to be jealous" (No me des ocasión / que en mi vida tendré celos, *PCO,* 1.21–22).

esta pensión, *PCO,* 1.24–25). Hence, jealousy seems to have a positive value as well, since whatever the heavens have ordained is by definition good.[39]

Later in act 1, the newly wed couple is left alone, and Peribáñez makes similar admonishments anew to Casilda in the form of a didactic alphabet poem (*abecedario*), the last letter of which is reserved for jealousy (*zelos*):

> For Z, you must stop yourself from being jealous [*zelosa*], because that is something that could take our loving bliss away from you, Casilda.

> (Por la Z has de guardarte
> de ser zelosa; que es cosa
> que nuestra paz amorosa
> puede, Casilda, quitarte. *PCO,* 1.440–43)[40]

When, in act 2, Peribáñez is away in Toledo on a mission to have his brotherhood's saint repainted, Casilda worries of experiencing jealousy of the women he might meet there, and thus invites her cousin Inés to sleep at her home, so that she has less opportunity to feel it:

> . . . because sleeplessness is a door through which jealousy passes from love to fear; there is no more sleep, when jealousy finishes love off.

> (que los desvelos son puertas
> para que passen los zelos
> desde el amor al temor;
> y en començando a temer,
> no hay más dormir que poner
> con zelos remedio a amor. *PCO,* 2.349–54)

---

39. My argument that there is ambiguity vis-à-vis the valence of jealousy in this play is in contrast to other critics' references to the irrelevance and solely negative characterization of jealousy.

40. It is also noteworthy that "jealousy" receives a full stanza of *redondillas* (octosyllabic lines rhyming in the pattern *abba*), in comparison to most of the other letters and words, which are given a cursory treatment; for example, *H* for "honorable" (*honrada*) is mentioned in the same quartet as *G* and *I*: "The G, for grave, and H for honorable, and with the I, you will be illustrious, if my house is enlightened by you" (La G, grave, y para honrada / la H que con la I / te hará ilustre si de ti / queda mi casa ilustrada, *PCO,* 1.416–19).

Once again, jealous fear (*temor*) is the enemy of love. The fears referred to are mere suspicions, without any basis in external reality.[41]

> INÉS. Well, what reason does his going to Toledo give you [to be jealous]?
> CASILDA. Don't you see, Inés, that jealousy is air, and that it comes from anywhere!
> INÉS. The song I've always heard says it comes from Medina.
> CASILDA. And what about Toledo, couldn't they come from there?
> INÉS. Toledo does have many beautiful women!

> (INÉS. Pues, ¿qué ocasión puede darte
> en Toledo?
> CASILDA. Tú, ¿no ves
> que zelos es aire, Inés,
> que vienen de cualquier parte?
> INÉS. Que de Medina venía
> oí yo siempre cantar.
> CASILDA.Y Toledo, ¿no es lugar
> de adonde venir podría?
> INÉS. ¡Grandes hermosuras tiene! *PCO*, 2.355–63)

Thus, Casilda fears that her husband will be attracted to another beautiful woman, just as Beatriz imagined "queens" (*reinas*) whom the Veinticuatro visited. Yet unlike her counterpart in *The Commanders of Cordoba*, Peribáñez's wife knows that her jealous suspicions are not worth entertaining, and thus attempts to banish them from her mind, as a woman should—says this drama—lest she challenge her husband.

Ironically, although Casilda is the one who is repeatedly advised not to be jealous and who is aware of her own propensity toward it, Peribáñez is the character who has the most intense jealous episode in the play. However, while his experience is bound up with great turmoil, the emotion is extremely efficacious and leads him not only to an esteemed desengaño, but also to protect his wife and his honor, bringing about the "happy" and "just" ending. Viewed from this per-

---

41. Typical of the treatment of jealousy in many of Lope de Vega's plays, it is suggested here that virtuous women try not to feel jealous, while the play, as I will show, promotes the opposite for men. Peribáñez meets a much better end than the Veinticuatro in large part because he is much more jealous throughout the play. These are prescriptive gender roles for both affect and action.

spective, Peribáñez's jealousy is instrumentally rational, in the Kantian sense, as it was for the Veinticuatro.

Peribáñez first experiences an emotional episode of jealousy when he visits the painter with his friend Antón on his second trip to Toledo. The knight commander, having fallen off his horse and in love with Casilda upon awakening from unconsciousness, had followed the newlyweds on their earlier trip to Toledo. In his obsession, the commander had commissioned—unbeknownst to Casilda—a large portrait of her from a local painter, giving him instructions to paint her from afar, and the painter happens to be the same one that Peribáñez seeks out for the repainting of Ocaña's saint, San Roque.[42] Peribáñez first notices how beautiful the woman in the painting is, and he slowly becomes more and more agitated, as noted rhetorically by his terse, direct questions. Antón recognizes his friend's "burning jealousy" in an aside:

> Although I may be an ignorant fellow, [even I can see that] Casilda is the subject of that portrait, and poor Pedro [Peribáñez] is burning with jealousy.

> (Puesto que inorante soy
> Casilda es la retratada,
> y el pobre de Pedro [Peribáñez] está
> abrasándose de zelos. *PCO,* 2.641–44)

Peribáñez's experience of suspicious jealousy leads him to inquire about the circumstances of the painting, the subject, and the patron. His words betray the fact that he did at first suspect his wife's complicity in an affair, that is, that he doubted her virtue and chaste love. To the painter's remark that "she is unaware of this important man's love" (ella no sabe / el amor de hombre tan grave), he asks, "You mean, she doesn't know?" (Luego, ¿ella no es sabidora?) expressing surprise and relief at her innocence, which the painter emphasizes:

---

42. As one critic explains, membership in this guild to San Roque (Saint Roch) seems anachronistic "as devotion to the saint did not really begin in earnest until the mid- to late-fifteenth century, well after the action of the play supposedly took place" (James Burke, "The Ritual Frame of *Peribáñez,*" 15). I would argue that its inclusion here by Lope de Vega is intended (a) to provide a reason for a peasant to leave his town so that the action can be developed, and (b) to make the reason for his absence a praiseworthy one, as was the Veinticuatro's in *The Commanders of Cordoba.*

. . . on the contrary, because she is so faithful, so much effort
was needed to paint her portrait.

(antes, por ser tan fiel
tanto trabajo costó
el poderla retratar. *PCO,* 2.664–72)

Notwithstanding the painter's declaration, Peribáñez, now a suspiciously jealous man, still doubts his wife's constancy. In some way
it must be her fault, he thinks, as he blames the commander's attentions on her beauty, in the traditional manner of misogynistic
literature: "Cursed be the man of humble means, who seeks a beautiful wife, amen!" (¡Mal haya el humilde, amén, / que busca mujer
hermosa! *PCO,* 2.745–46), he says repeatedly.[43]

Assuming (correctly, this time) that the commander has tried to
seduce her in his absence, this jealous husband is very cautious upon
his return. He fears having to confront her: "Because a husband's
jealousy should not be made known" (Porque zelos de marido, / no se
han de dar a entender, *PCO,* 2.695–96).[44] That jealousy must remain
secret is a topos of the jealous-husband plays (by Lope and others),
which is associated with the popular etymology of the word *celos* in
Spanish, not just from *zelus* but from *celare* as well.[45]

Peribáñez desires to know more about what has happened, and
more about Casilda's complicity (of which he remains unsure), before
speaking to her.

Oh, woe is me. If Casilda is not guilty, then why do I avoid going
to see her?

(¡Triste yo! Si no es culpada
Casilda, ¿por qué rehúyo
el verla? . . . *PCO,* 2.828–30)

43. On misogyny in literature, see Monica Brzezinski Potkay and Regula
Meyer Evitt's *Minding the Body: Women and Literature in the Middle Ages,
800–1500* (New York: Twayne, 1997).

44. These lines are repeated almost verbatim at 2.743–44.

45. As opposed to the words for "jealousy" in the other romance tongues (except
Portuguese), all of which derive from the Latin *zelus* and begin with the phoneme
/g/—as in the French *jalousie*—the word for it in Spanish begins with *z* or *c*: *zelos*
or *celos*. This is explained popularly by the influence of the Latin word *celare*,
meaning "to conceal" (see Covarrubias's explanation in his *Tesoro*).

The inability to know with certainty, and the tremendous doubts in his mind, cause him such great woe in fact, that, far from thinking of murdering his wife (whom he certainly doubts) as in other honor plays, his thoughts turn depressively to his own death: "Oh heaven, I hate my life. Who wants to take it away from me?" (La vida, cielos, desamo. / ¿Quién me la quiere quitar? *PCO,* 2.866–67).

Luckily for him, the laborers of his farm who had overheard the whole attempted seduction and Casilda's valiant self-defense are busy singing her praises publicly: "The wife is virtuous, as she is beautiful and pretty" (La mujer es virtuosa / cuanto hermosa y cuanto linda, *PCO,* 2.872–73). Unlike Shakespeare's Othello, who is misled by the deceptive appearance of false evidence, Peribáñez is led to the truth by external evidence, guided by the emotion of jealousy. He was suspicious of her part in the matter, hence his change from woeful before the song to his state of relief a few moments later:

> I feel invigorated upon hearing this song because what that fellow has sung is the real truth of what must have happened in my absence. . . . Oh, how much he owes heaven, the man with a good wife.

> (Notable aliento he cobrado,
> con oír esta canción
> porque lo que éste ha cantado
> las mismas verdades son
> que en mi ausencia habrán passado.
> ¡Oh, cuánto le debe al cielo
> quien tiene buena mujer! *PCO,* 2.880–86)

Had he not been racked with jealousy, he would not have heard the enlightening song; without doubts, he might not have dallied in the fields and instead might have hurried straight home, perhaps to murder his innocent wife for the sake of honor. Having been jealous, his fears now rest assured. It is noteworthy that he specifically states that his wife is "a good wife" (buena mujer), drawing attention to her morality and thus implicitly admitting (to the audience and to himself) that he had doubted it. Peribáñez was suspiciously jealous but tried to hide this from all, including Antón and himself.

Certainly, Peribáñez is concerned with "honor" and "dishonor" in key places in the text, but it must be established that he is also, or rather primarily, motivated by jealousy (at first, the fear of losing his love). Critics who treat the text exclusively as an honor play are not taking the whole drama into consideration. Love, too, is an important element of the play, as seen in the idyllic description of the newlyweds' pure and true love life in act 1, a section that has attracted attention from critics.[46] It is this beautiful love—not just a conventional conception of honor—that is threatened by the commander's "mad love" and his myriad plots of deception (most notably at 3.124–25). And jealousy, first suspicious, of the epistemologically oriented discovery kind, and later of the vengeful variety, is meant to protect Peribáñez's love and is successful at this, through the confirmation of his suspicion, the protection of his wife, and ultimately, the murder of his rival.

Ambiguity arises around the concept of jealousy: it is ostensibly negative (something to be avoided, as in act 1's opening scene), but the action in *Peribáñez* reveals male suspicious and vengeful jealousy to be instrumentally rational in protecting love (a personal good) and establishing justice (a social good). If Peribáñez were concerned merely with honor, he could have returned home from the painter's after seeing the portrait, without inquiring about his wife's part in it. That she played any role, that her chastity was called into question was enough for him to murder her (according to some interpretations of the honor code, as epitomized by the actions of Don Gutierre in Pedro Calderón's *El médico de su honra* [The Doctor of His Honor]). If honor is the motivating factor of *Peribáñez and the Commander of Ocaña,* as Larson and others claim, it is only efficacious in bringing about justice and desengaño precisely because jealousy is a large element of this desire, not a separate, "irrelevant" one.

Like the Veinticuatro, Peribáñez moves from a state of engaño to a state of desengaño. However, whereas the Veinticuatro serves as a negative example of the lack of pre-adulterous suspicious jealousy, Peribáñez demonstrates the utility and merit of both suspicious jealousy and well-directed vengeful jealousy. As in *The Commanders of Cordoba,* but to a greater extent, it is the husband's jealousy that leads to his desengaño. Explicitly, jealousy is both condemned as an enemy of love and ephemeralized as air. However, the denouements of these comedias complicate and deconstruct these notions, uncovering, ironically, that jealousy was in fact necessary to motivate the

46. See Marín's comments in his edition of *Peribáñez* (40).

protagonists' change of state between the polar opposites of Spanish Baroque epistemology, that is, from engaño to desengaño.

Both plays, in defining male vengeful jealousy as necessary and in requiring a monarch to sanction violent behavior, are concerned with legitimizing societal power structures, at the level of familial patriarchy and in the realm of political governance. The plays thus confirm the dominance of the man in his home and strengthen the direct link between the vassal and *his* king. *Peribáñez* draws out the political dimensions even more specifically, as James Burke has argued, in that the drama creates a correspondence between the commander's just death and the historical regicide of Pedro I by his brother Enrique II—whose descendant, Philip III, was in power at the time the play was written—by having Enrique III (Enrique II's direct descendant) condone the commander's murder.[47] Lope's happy ending entails that men have to be jealous of their wives and they have to act on it, just as Pedro I had to be justly murdered by his brother in the fourteenth century in order for Spaniards of the seventeenth to reap the rewards of their current monarch's rule.

47. Burke, "The Ritual Frame of *Peribáñez*," 11–27.

Two
Women, Jealousy, and Power

> **It is important to keep in mind that one of the most important functions of ideology is to veil the overt power relations obtaining in society at a particular moment in history by making them appear to be part of the natural, eternal order of things.**
> **—Linda Nochlin, *Women, Art, and Power***

As noted in the previous chapter's study of *The Commanders of Cordoba,* after hearing her deceived husband speak, Beatriz whispers aside: "Who hears this and yet fears not . . . ?" (¿Quién esto escucha y no teme . . . ? *CC,* 1243). Her fear is justified and anticipates the Veinticuatro's revenge as he murders everyone in their home, including the monkey and the dog. In Spanish Golden Age comedias, characters frequently express terror toward the potential jealous outbursts of others. Similar scenes of justified fear foreshadow a violent male character's actions in many of Lope de Vega's dramas, including *Punishment without Revenge, The Knight from Olmedo,* and *La desdichada Estefanía* (Unfortunate Estefanía). And in some of Lope's dramas with a socially powerful, jealous female protagonist, others fear the violence the woman will inflict upon them, just as they do that of the men. In contrast, however, they have little reason to fear the woman's rage, for jealousy alone never brings these female protagonists to murder. Against the backdrop of murderous male jealousy, this chapter examines Lope's treatment of female jealousy in two plays with socially powerful females, *Arminda celosa* (Jealous Arminda) and *El perro del hortelano* (The Dog in the Manger). With respect to gender and power, the way in which jealousy is portrayed in these plays is significantly distinct.

Jealous Arminda (ca. 1608–1615)

The jealousy of Arminda in *Jealous Arminda,* like the jealousy of other women in comedias, is imaged as irrational—as a passion that provokes thoughts that do not correspond to intersubjective appraisals of reality—despite its grounding in justified belief of adultery. Nevertheless, it is, in fact, consonant with what modern philosophers call "instrumental rationality," a mental state leading to the achievement of a desired goal. I will demonstrate how, in thematizing as irrational a female ruler's rational jealousy, Lope stakes out a conservative position in the early modern debate on the suitability of women as rulers.

The claim I will defend here is that personal reasons such as jealousy are never sufficient for a woman to kill her husband in plays by Lope (while jealousy can be sufficient for a man to commit murder). Surely, female protagonists of high social rank do commit murder, as does, for instance, the female regent in Lope's *La reina Juana de Nápoles* (Queen Joan of Naples). However, Christopher Weimer's analysis of *Queen Joan* demonstrates that the queen does not commit tyrannicide because of some personal injury, but rather because her husband is an archvillain. He is a foreign, effeminate tyrant who attempts to subvert the monarchic order based on birthright, and who has egregiously offended the queen and her people with murder plots and general political malfeasance.[1] In contrast, I argue, when it comes to personal jealous rage, women in the Spanish comedia may threaten to kill, but they do not follow through on their threats, as do their male counterparts. This makes the women look weak-willed, as their actions conflict with their statements. In Lope's *Jealous Arminda,* the jealousy of the societally powerful protagonist, Queen Arminda, is feared by all, yet her anger never results in irreversible violence. Despite the many anti-jealousy diatribes in the play, Arminda's jealousy actually helps bring about a comic resolution. Yet Arminda remains ignorant of the discrepancy between the alleged "irrationality" of her jealousy and its true "rationality," which evokes a misguided dualism between passion and reason. After reading *Jealous Arminda* in this light, I explore a similar portrayal of female jealousy in *The Dog in the Manger.*

1. Christopher Weimer, "The Politics of Husband Murder: Gender, Supplementarity and Sacrifice in Lope de Vega's *La reina Juana de Nápoles*," 44–47.

Jealous Arminda begins in medias res as Queen Arminda has learned that Antonio, the king consort, is having an affair with one of her ladies, but she knows not with whom.[2] She accuses Octavia of the offense, as two servants hold daggers to the mistress's chest. Octavia denies the truthful accusation and instead blames innocent Florela. Teodoro (Florela's fiancé) defends Florela's honor against this baseless charge, calling Octavia a liar. This leads Octavia to concoct a story that sways the queen, who now declares that she will require proof of Florela's offense.

In act 2, Antonio's servant, Julio, helps resolve Octavia's quandary: he dupes Florela into meeting the king later that night, under the pretense that she will be meeting her fiancé, Teodoro. At that meeting, she calls the king "my king" (mi rey), as she has been told to, in a line that uses two of Lope's preferred devices: speaking equivocally (*hablar en equívoco*) and deceiving with the truth (*engañar con la verdad*). This ruse would have worked perfectly, except that Antonio's fear of Arminda's jealous wrath outweighs his confidence in the plan. He has Octavia kidnapped to save her from the queen's clutches, an impetuous plan that backfires, for it newly arouses Arminda's suspicions. Spurred on by her jealousy, Arminda realizes that Antonio is still in love with Octavia. As punishment, the queen strips Antonio of his kingly title, leaving him a duke as before their wedding.

In the third act, Julio concocts a new plan to ingratiate his master with Arminda and have the title restored. Antonio feigns attempting

---

2. References are to Emilio Cotarelo y Mori's 1916 edition of *Arminda celosa*, and they will be made parenthetically in the text by page number using the abbreviation *AC*. Cotarelo y Mori considers the play authentic: "[W]e attribute it, without hesitation, as one of Lope's, for various reasons including . . . the author cites it as his own in his *Pilgrim in His Own Land* of 1618, and also because Agustín Durán, in whose handwriting is the copy (the only one in existence), states that he made the copy from the handwritten original; nothing can be argued against such statements" (Cotarelo y Mori, Prólogo, *Obras de Lope de Vega Publicadas por la Real Academia Española*, 3:viiii). Lope's chronologists, Morley and Bruerton, list this play under "*comedias* of doubtful or uncertain authenticity," that is, not definitively as an authentic play by Lope, because of an anomaly regarding the date in which the manuscript says the action takes place: "[The play] [t]akes place in Madrid, in the year 10622 (*sic*)." The erroneous year is "the reason why the play is classified as doubtful. . . . There is nothing in its versification to contradict its attribution to Lope" (Morley and Bruerton, *Cronología*, 423). They date it between 1608 and 1615. As far as I am aware, there are no studies of *Jealous Arminda* other than mine.

suicide, draws blood from a harmless wound, and moves the queen to pity and forgiveness. Duped once more, Arminda has but one request as she restores the kingship: that Antonio agree to marry his mistress off to another king. The play ends as that wedding and Florela and Teodoro's are about to begin.

Throughout the play, Arminda's jealousy is wrongly blamed many times as the cause of everyone's problems, both by other characters and by Arminda herself. But she has good reason to be jealous. Given that the husband she adores loves another woman, the object of her jealousy is definitely "jealousy-provoking" and thus rational, according to de Sousa's criterion. Nevertheless, it is stated repeatedly that jealousy is a form of engaño, which leads one astray. As Arminda herself proclaims,

> . . . jealousy is a kind of fantasy in which the soul barely has faith in reason. The eyes are doubted, and the ears are disbelieved. All things touched and seen seem like false dreams.
>
> (. . . los celos son,
> una cierta fantasía
> en que apenas se confía
> el alma de la razón.
> Los ojos no hacen fe,
> ni se creen los oídos.
> Sueños parecen fingidos
> cuanto se toca y se ve. *AC,* 694)

Such "fantasies" are assumed to be irrational and in contradiction with real data of the senses. However, in Arminda's case, on the contrary, they represent not personal hallucination, but rather intersubjective reality. She believes that jealousy is creating a state of confusion in her mind as she proclaims apostrophically to jealousy (*celos*): "The more I investigate you, the more confusing I find you" (Más confusos vengo a hallaros / mientras más os averiguo, *AC,* 697). Arminda uses the term *celos* to refer to an irrational obfuscation of the senses, and not to the word's more common meaning as defined in the *Diccionario de Autoridades:* " . . . the suspicion, worry, and fear, that the beloved has changed, or is changing his or her feelings of affection or interest, and directing them towards another" (. . . la sospecha, inquietud, y rezelo, de que la persona amada haya mudado, ò mude su cariño, ò afición poniendola en otra). Hence, the character who most benefits from the effects of jealousy in the play is also the one who disparages it most frequently. There is a conflict in the text between the negative rhetorical description of jealousy, especially as it pertains to women, and its positive effects (in Arminda's case) as seen through the denouement. Arminda never notices this discrepancy between speech and action, that is, between what she says about jealousy, on the one hand, and what jealousy helps her achieve, on the other.

In fact, Arminda consistently portrays jealousy as an ill through the end of the final act, when she has had more than ample proof of her husband's faithlessness. The question of whether he is or is not having an affair is never thematized; the adultery is simply presupposed. Arminda is not a female Othello, a character who seeks to ascertain the guilt or innocence of a spouse. She never doubts the infidelity as her male counterparts commonly do in other comedias— as did, for instance, Peribáñez, when he asked the painter specific, targeted questions regarding Casilda's involvement; rather, the question for Arminda is not *whether* but *with whom* Antonio is committing adultery. Throughout *Jealous Arminda,* the eponymous character continues to blame her own jealousy, and hence herself, for her situation. Forgiving the philanderer, she denounces the evil emotion: "Oh, what jealousy has caused! Oh, would that God should blaspheme jealousy!" (¡Que esto celos han causado! / ¡Oh maldiga Dios los celos! *AC,* 708).

Jealousy is also portrayed negatively by other characters. It seems irrelevant to them whether or not the jealous woman has a right, based on firm epistemic grounds, to experience it. Indeed, Antonio's characterization of woman's jealousy constitutes a direct link to the misogynistic tradition:

> . . . it is easier to tame a snake than to assuage the jealousy of a woman.
>
> (. . . que más fácil es de hacer
> una víbora amansar
> que querer asegurar
> los celos de una mujer. *AC,* 698)

Clearly, one of the reasons that it will be difficult to "assuage" this particular woman is that she is well aware of her husband's deceit. Evoking the topos of "woman as dangerous serpent," Antonio relies on the literary and religious tradition of the condemnation of women to bolster his assertion (as well as to detract blame from his personal wrongdoing). Hence, Arminda suffers not only his adultery but also his unjustified maligning of her sex. Adultery is regarded by Julio—in his quest to restore the kingship to his master—not as a deadly sin, but rather as a "lowly weakness" (indigna flaqueza), in agreement with the double standard codified in Philip II's *Nueva recopilación de las leyes de España* (New Compilation of the Laws of Spain), which outlined, in 1569, the right of husbands to murder their adulterous wives, while, not surprisingly, failing to provide a corresponding right for women.[3]

Notwithstanding her belief in jealousy's irrationality, Arminda feels the power of the emotion throughout much of the play, has moments of lucidity, and does act upon it. In act 1, she experiences possessive jealousy and plans how she might disrupt Antonio's *amores* through murder. Unlike jealous-husband characters, who usually murder their wives and sometimes also the alleged lovers, Arminda's force is focused exclusively on her rival, whom she initially desires to identify properly and punish accordingly in order to satiate her vehement anger. In this regard, it is important to recall that in the play's opening scene, Arminda threatens to kill Octavia, not Antonio. She does not want to kill his living body in the real world, but only, symbolically, his love for his mistress. There are two daggers held to Octavia's chest; one is to kill Octavia, while the other is to kill the king's love within her beating heart: "I do not wish to murder the king, but only to kill him in your breast" (No quiero matar al Rey, / sino matarle en tu pecho, *AC,* 693). How unlike Lope's *Punishment without Revenge,* in which the duke exercises his full violent wrath on his son and wife through deliberate, premeditated execution. And how different from those plays by Lope in which the jealous husband actually murders his wife for mere *suspected* adultery, such as *El toledano vengado* (The Avenged Man from Toledo) and *Unfortunate Estefanía.* The fait-accompli jealousy of even an extremely powerful woman does not lead to the murder of her husband, whereas a man's mere suspicious jealousy can lead to a woman's murder, even if the man is not as societally powerful.

Arminda's allegedly terrible wrath is alluded to several times: Feliciano animalizes her diseased reaction ("The queen is rabid with jealousy" [La Reina de celos rabia, *AC,* 697]); Antonio describes her

---

3. Melveena McKendrick, *Woman and Society in the Spanish Drama of the Golden Age: A Study of the* Mujer Varonil, 15.

as a potentially fatal snake; the opening scene depicts Arminda's servants holding daggers to Octavia's chest; furthermore, Julio exclaims, in a manner similar to Beatriz in *The Commanders of Cordoba,*

> Woe is me! I'm fearful of the moment in which the storm of this jealousy falls upon my shoulders!
>
> (¡Ay de mí! ¡Que estoy temiendo,
> cuando a mis hombros decienda
> la tempestad destos celos! *AC,* 703)

Antonio, too, fears the effects of her violent rage on Octavia: "I see on your naked neck, the sword of her vengeance" (veo en tu cuello desnuda / la espada de su venganza, *AC,* 706). But contrary to the characters' expectations, Arminda never fulfills these threats of violence, even after she knows all about Antonio and Octavia, and has uncovered the gamut of lies they have told.

The queen has threatened from the first scene to have the adulteress's head, but when the adultery is confirmed for her, she instead only strips Antonio of his title. Therefore, by the middle of act 2, Arminda's jealousy is no longer as potent as it once seemed. In fact, she even permits Octavia to continue her love affair with Antonio (*AC,* 705). Far from a "rabid" animal to be feared, the queen seems virtuous, not killing off but marrying away her rival to a socially superior male. All the anticipated jealous revenge has dissipated like a fine dew. As she did in the case of Antonio's kingship, Arminda exercises her power through sociopolitical coercion and not brute force, as Octavia explains:

> She has acted like a queen—you, like a villain—because she has given me the most honorable punishment, that of giving me a husband, despite my offense against her.
>
> (Como Reina ha procedido,
> tú como vil, pues me ha dado,
> habiéndola yo ofendido,
> el castigo más honrado,
> que ha sido darme marido. *AC,* 710)

Akin to the labeling of women's justifiable (rational) jealousy as morally corrupt, the play misrepresents women as unworthy in other ways. Not only is innocent Arminda disparaged, but so too is poor Florela, having been framed by Octavia, Antonio, and Julio. Teodoro, witnessing the concocted scene, has no faith in Florela and assumes immediately that she has been unfaithful to him: "I have little faith in Florela, since she is, in effect, a woman" (Poco de Florela fío, / que es, en efecto, mujer, *AC,* 700).

When arguing with his fiancée about this, Teodoro refers to his "honorable jealousy" (celos honrosos, *AC,* 707) and declares that he will never marry her since doubt has been cast on her chastity. Florela is outraged by his obstinacy and refers to jealousy as "a contagious disease" (enfermedad que se pega, *AC,* 707). She is right, in this case, about jealousy. Although Arminda's is fait accompli and therefore fact-based jealousy, Teodoro's is suspicious and, in fact, contradicted by external reality. Nonetheless, these distinct phenomena receive the same negative characterization and label (*celos*) as if they were one and the same thing. It is paradoxical that Teodoro's jealousy is defended as "honorable" while Arminda's is maligned and medicalized, for hers is truly legitimate. The difference is, of course, that Teodoro is a man and Arminda a woman in a society in which female jealousy is generally scorned and male jealousy is condoned, a view upheld in sixteenth-century tracts on the education of women such as the one by Juan Luis Vives. In *De institutione feminae Cristianae* (The Education of a Christian Woman [1523]), Vives contends:

> Now I must say a word about female jealousy. If a woman suffers from . . . excessive and violent [jealousy] . . . I think she must be given medical treatment. Above all, a woman should bear in mind that her husband is master of the household, and not all things permitted to him are permitted to her; human laws do not require the same chastity of the man as they do of the woman. In all aspects of life, the man is freer than the woman.[4]

It would seem that, in terms of power, Arminda's role as wife trumps her position as ruler. Clearly, from his most important work on the emotions, *On the Passions of the Soul,* Vives understood that women and men both suffer from jealousy. Whereas *Passions* makes a descriptive claim, the position in *Education* is that women ought not to feel it, that is, it is a normative one.

4. Juan Luis Vives, *The Education of a Christian Woman,* 232 (2:6.79).

Earlier, when Teodoro protests Octavia's accusation against Florela and the implication that he is the go-between for the king, he
expresses utter disbelief that the queen would believe her over him,
that is, a woman over a man, evoking a common gender bias that
presupposes the moral superiority of men to women:

> Is this what I should expect from you? You let a *woman*—a lying,
> crazy, cruel enemy—convince you that you should believe her
> over a *man* who is so faithful?

> (¿Esto esperaba de ti?
> Una *mujer* tu enemiga,
> loca, fingida, cruel,
> ¿más que un *hombre* tan fiel
> a que la creas te obliga? *AC*, 694, emphasis added)

On Teodoro's behalf, his friend Aurelio shores up these assertions,
confirms the former's loyalty, and expresses his unfathomable surprise at the queen's anger toward her great servant:

> And if I saw fish who spoke and made the heavens mute, and
> beastly animals ruling over men; if a Moor kept his word or if a
> woman away from her beloved remained faithful, I could believe
> these things more than to see that you hate Teodoro.

> (Y si viera hablar los peces,
> que hicieron los cielos mudos,
> y los animales rudos
> ser de los hombres jueces;
> si guardar palabra un moro
> o firme ausente mujer,
> más lo creyera que ver
> que aborreces a Teodoro. *AC*, 694)

A faithful woman or a trustworthy Moor (like talking fish or animals ruling over humans) are impossibilities in Aurelio's worldview,
and yet, they are more credible than what he is now witnessing.
As the audience will soon learn, it is in fact Octavia, the woman,
who is lying, and Teodoro, the man, who is telling the truth, and
hence, through this setup, Lope de Vega implicitly reinforces Aurelio's stereotypes. The queen really ought not to trust women, for
a faithful woman, as Aurelio suggests, is indeed an impossibility

(Octavia confirms this). Ironically, however, Arminda should real-
ize that this position is painfully self-contradictory since she herself
is a trustworthy woman. But such soul-searching questions are not
enunciated in this comedia; the misogynistic outbursts remain on
the surface, expressed but not questioned.

Upon closer examination of the two love relationships (of the main
action and of the secondary plot, respectively), it becomes clear that
they are mirrored reflections of each other. Whereas Arminda is a
woman and rightly feels jealousy toward a philanderer, Teodoro is
a man who is unjustified in feeling jealousy toward his faithful fiancée. While Arminda doubts her secure knowledge and blames an
almost preternatural Jealousy for creating "fantasies" in her mind,
Teodoro blames Florela and relies—as does Antonio—on the misogynistic tradition.[5]

The fact that there is no bloodshed in this tale of jealousy and
adultery is of tremendous significance and is revealing of the relationship between power and gender in the Spanish comedia. All but
one of Lope's plays that depict a woman who is actually adulterous
end with her execution, with the exception of *El castigo del discreto*
(The Discreet Man's Punishment). Yet of all the plays in which men
are adulterous, not one of them is ever killed by his wife for adultery
alone. The reason for this disparity is that the women of the comedia
do not gain revenge through physical violence, no matter what their
stature of authority. As Weimer points out, "[W]hen women in the
comedia kill under virtually any circumstances, the fundamental *va-
ronilidad* [manliness] of homicide makes it a problematic and potentially subversive deed."[6] Although Arminda is no ordinary woman—
she is queen and lives in the public sphere par excellence—she is

5. Although Arminda originally accuses Octavia as well as Jealousy, this lady
eventually meets a rather fortunate end, given her crime, whereas Jealousy—
hence, Arminda herself—is the target of some of the queen's very last, scathing
words in the play. That a woman should be maligned for being jealous is supported in classical myth in Ovid's tale of Cephalus and Pocris, in which Pocris
is killed accidentally while spying on her husband. Whereas the tale is tragic in
Ovid, for Cephalus loves his wife and feels responsible for her jealousy, Stroud
shows that variations of this theme in the Renaissance and Baroque periods increase the level of blame on the woman and decrease the husband's responsibility
such that the stories become misogynistic mouthpieces intent on diminishing a
woman's right to question the authority of her husband, as in Calderón's version
of the tale (Stroud, *Fatal Union,* 53).
6. Weimer, "The Politics of Husband Murder," 32.

like many of her comedia sisters in that she is not meant to question accepted stereotypes about women's roles in society, but rather to reinforce them.[7] Along similar lines, adulterous women almost always pay the price for their transgressions, for, as Yvonne Yarbo-Bejarano elucidates in her book on Lope de Vega, "[t]he murder of the transgressive wife and the display of her corpse provide an 'exercise in terror,' making women aware of the unlimited power of men."[8] If Lope were to depict a vengefully jealous woman actually gaining bloody revenge—even if she were a queen—the "unlimited power of men" might be shown to have serious bounds.

In many respects, Arminda is like the female monarch of Greco-Roman mythology, Juno (Hera). Because of Jupiter's philandering, the queen of Olympos was constantly jealous, always trying with little success to thwart her husband's conquests. Julio draws an explicit comparison between the pairs Arminda-Antonio and Juno-Jupiter:

> Argos watches over with a hundred eyes; but a subtle Mercury overcomes a hundred or a hundred thousand. I will trick Florela.

> (Argos con cien ojos vela;
> pero a ciento y a cien mil
> vence un Mercurio sutil.
> Voy a engañar a Florela. *AC,* 698)

The writers of the Renaissance and Baroque frequently evoked the figure of Argos in hyperbolic comparisons with a jealous man's possessiveness; the metonymical relation to jealousy was eased by Argos's being male.[9] Lope's version, however, is more in line with the

---

7. A woman of lower rank would be sanctioned by her husband for expressing jealousy (e.g., the warnings to Casilda in Lope's *Peribáñez:* "For Z, you must stop yourself from being jealous [*zelosa*], because that is something that could take our loving bliss away from you, Casilda" [Por la Z has de guardarte / de ser zelosa; que es cosa / que nuestra paz amorosa / puede, Casilda, quitarte, *PCO,* 1.440–43]). In contrast, because of her rank, Arminda has the "right" to express her jealousy.

8. Yvonne Yarbo-Bejarano, *Feminism and the Honor Plays of Lope de Vega,* 8.

9. For instance, in Cervantes's *Jealous Old Man from Extremadura,* Carrizales is "the Argos of that which he loved well" (*Exemplary Stories,* trans. and ed. Lesley Lipson, 156) (el Argos de lo que bien quería [*Novelas ejemplares,* ed. Harry Sieber, 106]).

tale as told by Ovid in the *Metamorphoses*. Antonio's servant Julio compares himself to Jupiter's servant Mercury, who slew the hundred-eyed guard whom Juno had charged with keeping watch over Io (who had been transformed into a heifer). Through this metaphor, Queen Arminda is likened to the ever-jealous queen of the gods, and Antonio to the ever-philandering Jupiter. The conceit is an apt one: the real distribution of power in the play is perceived in this mythological allusion, which casts doubts on the queen's "absolute" power, in light of her husband, who, though not fully a king, is a man. By comparing Arminda to Juno—never a match for Jupiter—Lope realigns the power axis of the play, demonstrating that sexual difference, according to this social order, is indeed the single most significant criterion with respect to worldly power. Although Arminda certainly enjoys more power than most women in Spanish drama, hers, just like theirs, is limited by the strictures of patriarchy, implicitly inherited with the Greco-Roman model of the Olympian gods. Both a king and a queen are monarchs, and such social rank distinctions usually play the most fundamental role in questions of power (that is, a woman who is queen is not restricted by the same mores as ordinary women), but the text implies that a queen, though she might possess absolute power, *should not* wield it.[10] Tellingly, this is another example of the descriptive/normative (is/ought) distinction, which was implied by Vives in his comments on women's jealousy.

Since the king is an adulterer and Arminda's jealousy helps her resolve this problem, jealousy is, in many respects, a positive, instrumentally rational force in this comedia. Yet, the characterizations of the emotion are negative;[11] these seem inappropriate and contradict the positive value of jealousy (which leads Arminda toward her desengaño and thwarts the king's future unfaithfulness). While Arminda's jealousy is rational, she is irrational in blaming that which has helped her. At work is the misguided preconception that emotions themselves are always irrational, one that de Sousa has labeled the "Reason-Passion bias." De Sousa's analysis of the elements of rationality counters this bias, as he is able to demonstrate that

10. Perhaps Lope placed the action of the play far away in England (and not in Spain or Italy, the loci of most of his comedias) in order to avoid questioning the ordained values of the Spanish monarchic system.

11. All are negative except Teodoro's self-described "honorable jealousy," which is known to be irrational, contrary to fact, and less than "honorable" since it doubts Florela's virtue.

"reason and emotion are not natural antagonists."[12] There are two important elements that demonstrate the rationality of Arminda's jealousy: First, there is the emotion's target, which meets the "the criterion of success." For the success criterion to be met, the target of her emotion must be jealousy-provoking, which, as I have shown, it is. Furthermore, Arminda's experience of jealousy attunes her senses to the problems around her, helps her both secure knowledge (learn who is having an affair with her husband) and fulfill her desire (to put an end to his philandering). As it secures the truth conditions for both knowledge and desire, it is "instrumentally rational." In de Sousian terms, her belief, desire, and emotion all coincide on her intentionality that her husband no longer cheat, in direct contradiction of the reason-passion bias.

It is worth exploring a gender-specific level to this reason-passion dichotomy in the early modern period, brought to the fore by Theodora A. Jankowski: "Man, the thinker and doer, was often imaged as the representative of reason. Woman, the daughter of Eve, whose emotions led her astray, was often imaged as emotion or passion."[13] These two interrelated elements, that jealousy be conceived of as irrational within the text and that it be the principal characteristic of a female ruler, are paramount to my reading of the play.

By associating the female ruler with "irrational" emotion, Lope's comedia positions itself toward the conservative pole of the early modern debate concerning the suitability of women to govern. As Jankowski explains, sixteenth- and seventeenth-century political treatises often had little to say about women as rulers, since rulers were conceived of in masculine terms and the king envisioned as the paterfamilias of the society. When women are mentioned, for example, by Machiavelli in his *Discourses,* it is to warn against their rule since women are a potential source of disorder. Likewise, Thomas More, in his *Utopia,* glosses over the notion that women could rule, since they are "the weaker sex."[14] Erasmus, in his *Education of a Christian Prince,* endorses what de Sousa calls the "prejudiced" view of emotion, opposing reason with passion, and then draws the connection to what he perceived as male versus female characteristics:

12. De Sousa, *Rationality of Emotion,* xv.
13. Theodora A. Jankowski, *Women in Power in the Early Modern Drama,* 59.
14. Ibid., 56; Thomas More, *Utopia,* 40, quoted in Jankowski, *Women in Power,* 57.

"[T]he rule of a prince over his people is not different from that of the mind over the body. . . . But you cannot be a king unless reason completely controls you. . . . It is the mark of a tyrant—and womanish, too—to follow the unbridled will of your mind."[15] Erasmus does not seem to have a place for women rulers, since he "acclaims marriage as the natural state for woman," in which the wife "owe[s] [obedience] to the husband."[16]

The debate over the suitability of women as rulers sometimes found expression in extreme tracts against women, such as John Knox's *First Blast of the Trumpet against the Monstrous Regiment of Women* (1558), which espouses views similar to those of Erasmus on the "nature" of women as subjects of their husbands. On the other side of the debate are Sir Thomas Elyot, who justifies women's participation in civic life in his 1540 treatise *Defense of Good Women,* and Castiglione, in *Il Cortegiano,* who uses Isabel I of Spain as the supreme example of virtue and merit.[17]

Lope's *Jealous Arminda* depicts a queen who feels, thinks, and acts in a way befitting the gender-typing of her sex in the early modern period, not as a full sovereign and not as a man would. As Melveena McKendrick has written on Golden Age male dramaturges, "[O]ne cannot expect miracles, even of the great."[18] What is very interesting about *Jealous Arminda* is how the other characters in the play seem to act and speak as if the queen were indeed a jealous husband who would punish even the hint of sexual betrayal with murder; and yet, even though her words are at times consonant with their fears, her deeds are not. As she is a reigning monarch, a role envisioned as male, the wrath of her metaphorical "sword of vengeance" (espada de su venganza, *AC,* 706) is feared. But in her particular instantiation as a female monarch, Arminda's "sword" never emerges.[19]

15. Erasmus, *The Education of a Christian Prince,* 175, 189, 190, quoted in Jankowski, *Women in Power,* 59.

16. McKendrick, *Woman and Society,* 9. Nevertheless, as McKendrick points out, it should be recognized that Erasmus thought women capable of reason and acknowledged that they require education to that end, just as men do.

17. Margaret L. King and Albert Rabil Jr., "The Other Voice in Early Modern Europe: Introduction to the Series," xxv; Jankowski, *Women in Power,* 58.

18. McKendrick, *Woman and Society,* 334.

19. The sword is commonly considered a phallic symbol: "It is quite unmistakable that all weapons and tools are used as symbols for the male organ: e.g.,

The difference from the very few husband-murder plays is clear: the malevolence of Arminda's husband has no explicit political dimension. Antonio is neither a foreigner nor a tyrant, nor has he been egregiously abusive of the queen's subjects; in this play, jealousy is isolated.[20] Indeed, I know of no play by Lope in which a husband is ever killed by his wife for anything less than his attempting a politically unjustifiable murder. Such is the case of husband murder in *Queen Joan of Naples,* which, as Weimer shows, does not challenge patriarchal models of authority—despite Juana's murder of her husband—but rather enhances them, for the king in that play is not simply a philandering husband, but indeed one who needs to be killed for a host of other reasons. It is not for her own sense of revenge that Juana acts, but rather to protect the patrilineal order of monarchic birthright, an order that in itself is patriarchal and conservative.[21]

In contrast, when the offense is limited to adultery and the emotion to fait accompli jealousy, as in *Jealous Arminda,* queens who are offended only by their kings' personal actions do not try to murder their husbands. For instance, in Lope's *El animal de Hungría* (The Animal from Hungary), the queen runs away to live in the woods after the king seduces her sister; and in *La corona merecida* (A Well-Deserved Crown), the queen merely complies with the king's wishes to take the woman he fancies as her own "lady-in-waiting"

---

ploughshare, hammer, gun, revolver, dagger, sword, etc." (Sigmund Freud, *The Interpretation of Dreams,* chap. 6). The absence of a sword symbolizes the absence of a phallus.

20. That is, neither known adultery nor jealousy (in isolation or conjointly) will lead a female character to murder her husband in any play by Lope de Vega (that is, in logical terms, known adultery and jealousy are *not sufficient conditions* for husband murder). In contrast, known adultery will always lead to a wife's murder, and a husband's jealousy (in isolation) may also lead to a wife's murder (known adultery *is a sufficient condition* for the murder of a wife, but jealousy is not).

21. Weimer, "The Politics of Husband Murder," 49–50. Nonetheless, Weimer finds some progressive level to that play, which I do not find in *Jealous Arminda:* " . . . *La reina Juana de Nápoles* emphatically rejects the automatic equation of anatomical gender with the corresponding sociocultural roles prescribed and imposed by patriarchal ideology. . . . [T]he play's victorious protagonist is nevertheless a woman whose actions leave no doubt that her gender makes her neither unfit to govern nor incapable of demonstrating a ruling monarch's defining virtues. . . . [T]his comedia places her center-stage as an exemplary female sovereign" (50).

(*dama de honor*). A minor transgression by the husband—against a wife's feelings, against the sanctity of marriage—merely provokes the woman's (harmless) jealousy, and is ultimately condoned. In representing these roles for women, Lope upholds the paradigm of male privilege in early modern Europe, adduced by Margaret W. Ferguson, Maureen Quilligan, and Nancy J. Vickers: "[W]hile significant differences exist among women of various social classes, equally significant differences exist between men and women at all levels of society. . . . [B]iological differences between the sexes have, throughout human history, been translated by social institutions into codes of behavior and law that privilege men over women irrespective of class."[22]

The Dog in the Manger (ca. 1613–1615)

Jealous Arminda shares many characteristics with the better-known drama *The Dog in the Manger*.[23] The most important among these are the presence of a very jealous female protagonist; a primary and a secondary love triangle; various (unrealized) threats throughout each play of outbursts of tremendous violence, corresponding to the representation of jealousy as a powerful force; and a comic resolution.

However, there is no contradiction or ambiguity with respect to Diana's jealousy in *The Dog in the Manger,* as there was with Arminda's. Diana's is utterly irrational and moderately destructive.[24] She has no claim on the man for whom she feels love; rather, she steals him away from another woman, of lower social rank and power, her lady-in-waiting Marcela.

As in *Jealous Arminda,* the primary jealous triangle involves two women and one man, but in this case the man is not yet married, only

---

22. Margaret W. Ferguson, Maureen Quilligan, and Nancy J. Vickers, *Rewriting the Renaissance: The Discourses of Sexual Difference in Early Modern Europe,* xxi, quoted in Jankowski, *Women in Power,* 49n3.

23. References are to Mauro Armiño's 1996 edition of *El perro del hortelano,* and they will be made parenthetically in the text by act and line number using the abbreviation *PH*.

24. In this comedia, jealousy does not work toward engaño or desengaño; there is no instrumentally rational (positive) outcome for Diana's jealousy, as in the other plays studied above.

engaged; his "unfaithfulness" (which, unlike Antonio's in *Jealous Arminda,* is not adultery) is instigated by the more powerful woman, Diana. A brief analysis of this work with respect to the representation of jealousy will further shore up my claims regarding jealousy, power, and the portrayal of women in Lope's dramas.

After Diana, the Duchess of Belflor, hears a man leaving her palace one night, her honor is apparently offended. But the audience soon learns that it is in fact her pride that has suffered the greater wound, when she becomes aware that the mystery man was there to seduce not her, but one of her servants. She feels deprived, envies this other woman, and demands to know the identity of both the man, Teodoro, and the lucky lady, Marcela. This initial *envy* will lead to her *jealousy,* a likely affective occurrence in such situations noted by psychologist W. Gerrod Parrott.[25] At first glance, such a change from one emotion to another is not well explained by a "rationality approach" a la de Sousa.

Diana's love for Teodoro is purely triangular; save for her gender, she would seem an excellent example of René Girard's concept of "triangular desire," as elaborated in *Deceit, Desire and the Novel.*[26] It is, she realizes, completely "born of jealousy," reminiscent of Garcilaso's Sonnet 31, in which he describes the paradoxical relationship of jealousy born of love, but which also gives life to love: "Crude grandson who gives life to your father" (Crudo nieto que das vida al padre). Diana herself believes this love to be strange, that is, atypical, and indeed, it is a relatively unusual idea with respect to conceptual claims and affective genealogies of jealousy.[27] Hence the descriptors "marvelous" and "impossible" in the sonnet she has composed for Teodoro's benefit:

25. Parrott, "Emotional Experience of Envy and Jealousy," 20.

26. Girard's assumptions are gendered and apply, for him, to males only. My application of his terms to a female character goes beyond their intended scope. I use his terms as a common paradigm by which to compare male and female characters.

27. Garcilaso de la Vega, *Obras completas con comentario,* 147. It is a more common view in Spanish comedias that jealousy can be used to revive love, but not to inspire it ex nihilo; thus Aurora complains, in *Punishment without Revenge,* of her futile attempts to make Federico jealous (*darle celos*): "But I had the same effect as I would have had on a diamond; because jealousy imprints not where there is no love" (pero el mismo efeto hice / que en un diamante; que celos / donde no hay amor no imprimen" (Lope de Vega, *El castigo sin venganza,* ed. C. A. Jones, 3.2058–60).

. . . and the idea of being jealous before being in love is a marvelous idea that has been held to be impossible. [However,] my
love has sprung out of my jealousy.

(y primero que amar estar celosa
es invención de amor maravillosa
y que por imposible se ha tenido.
De los celos mi amor ha procedido. *PH,* 1.552–55)

Although she allegedly does not understand how this love born of
jealousy is possible, she is, in essence, a Girardian, desiring only that
which another desires. Her beloved and interlocutor in this scene,
Teodoro, agrees on the impossibility, insisting on the logical distinction between cause and effect, true to the tradition of Aristotelian
scholasticism (he is a schooled secretary):

[T]hus I confess that I do not understand how it could be that
love comes to be born of jealousy, since the former was always
its father. . . . so, my Lady, this jealousy was born of some beginning, and that beginning was love; because the cause is not
born from the effects, but rather the effects from the cause.

([M]as confieso que no entiendo
cómo puede ser que amor
venga a nacer de los celos,
pues que siempre fue su padre.
. . . .
mas ya esos celos, señora,
de algún principio nacieron,
y ése fue amor; que la causa
no nace de los efetos,
sino los efetos della. *PH,* 1.568–71, 579–83)

But he seems to be wrong. Indeed, she does not "love" without jealousy, an emotion she indulges in to further her "love" through aural,
visual, and imaginative voyeurism of Teodoro and Marcela. Before
the action of the play, Diana has no interest at all in her secretary.
Driving the plot of inquiry and discovery here is Anarda, who is herself jealous of Fabio's love for Marcela, and from whom Diana learns
of Marcela's lover.[28] When Diana grills Marcela on the details of her

28. In introducing another minor jealousy subplot here, one that drives the
action, Anarda's role is similar to Jorge's in *The Commanders of Cordoba.*

love affair, she is not at all content to know just the facts. She wants to know exactly what Teodoro tells her, and how he does so: "And what does he say to you?" (¿Y qué te dice? *PH,* 1.262), she inquires.

This vicarious excitement increases as Diana gets closer to the object of desire; the next day she asks Teodoro himself to tell her what he says to Marcela and what kind of poetry he recites to her. Diana desires to have these things told directly to her, and she uses her sociopolitical power over Teodoro (she is the duchess, he a secretary) to force him to say them, under the guise of their being said for Marcela. Diana needs mediation to experience her desire, a portrait that aligns her, *avant la lettre,* with one of Girard's key examples of "mediated desire," Molière's *Don Juan.* In the following passage, Don Juan reports his emotional reaction—which he calls "jealousy" (*jalousie*)—to the sight of the happy peasant couple:

> I have never seen two people more happy with one another or who shone so with their love. The obvious tenderness of their passion for one another moved me; I was struck to the heart and my love began through jealousy. Yes, I could not bear to see them so happy together; resentment aroused my desires and I foresaw great pleasure in being able to upset their understanding and break this engagement which offended my delicate feelings.[29]

Quite foreseeably, Diana's "love" wanes when she succeeds in attracting Teodoro's attentions, for she no longer feels envy or jealousy. She loses interest in him after she has conquered his resistance, just as Don Juan does in most versions of the legend. And her desire is sparked anew only by further jealousy, when she perceives that Teodoro is returning to Marcela: "With jealousy, love awakens" (Amor con celos despierta, *PH,* 2.1895).

The irrationality of this emotion is borne out in that she sways back and forth in her passion (inconstancy). As she attains and then rejects her beloved, repeatedly, Diana demonstrates a mind that is terribly uncertain of its instrumental goals, vacillating and unsteady in its own desires. In this, the similarity to Don Juan comes to an end, for he knows well what his desires are, does everything to ful-

29. Molière, *Don Juan and the Stone Guest,* quoted in Girard, *Deceit, Desire and the Novel,* 51.

fill them, and either chooses to ignore the consequences (as in the play by Tirso de Molina), miraculously escapes them (Zorrilla), or defiantly embraces them (Molière, Mozart-da Ponte).

Returning to Girard's theory, Diana's vacillation is wholly understandable, for when a subject finally possesses an object, there is a metaphysical sense of failure: "The disappointment is entirely metaphysical. The subject discovers that possession of the object has not changed his being—the expected metamorphosis has not taken place."[30] The play certainly points to the limitations of triangular desire, but seems to disagree with the views of the French theorist on the utter failure of triangular desire, since in the comical ending the duchess overcomes her problem of requiring mediation and proclaims her love—her love without jealousy—for Teodoro in the absence of her rival, Marcela, and marries him. Furthermore, this kind of "love spawned of jealousy alone" is "a marvelous occurrence" (*una maravilla*) in the play, something strange and certainly not the rule for all desire, as Girard's theory promises.

Using de Sousa's schema of intentionality, it is revealed how Diana's desire is irrational. The success criterion for her desire (want) is not met, since when she comes close to obtaining it, she no longer desires it. Nevertheless, although she acts in an irrational way, her emotional response is certainly intelligible.

As the play's title indicates, Diana is like the proverbial "dog in the manger" "who does not eat, nor let eat" (*que no come, ni deja comer*). Figuratively, she desires what others want, not for the merit of the possessed objects in themselves, but rather precisely and only because another desires them. As long as someone else wants Teodoro, so does she, and once she gets him, she no longer wants him. A fundamental difference between Diana's jealousy in this text and Girardian "triangular desire" is that, in the latter, the subject who experiences it is not fully aware of it; a host of subterfuged psychoanalytic processes kick in to keep this disturbing knowledge from conscious awareness. In the case of the duchess, however, not only is she aware of her strange jealousy—her inner psychological workings seem completely transparent to her—and its origins in the desire to be the object of Teodoro's love, but additionally, she does not try to hide this from others or herself, but in fact confesses it openly to many

---

30. Girard, *Deceit, Desire and the Novel*, 88.

characters. She is, hence, not only irrational but also emotionally incontinent.[31]

Before her ultimate commitment to marriage at the end of the play, Diana feels she cannot come right out and let her "love" for Teodoro be known, for she fears it will dishonor her, given that she is a titled noble and he, her servant. The conflict between passion and honor is apparent from the beginning. It is not that she waivers between choices (as the husbands of the so-called honor plays do when they are uncertain of how to act), but rather, passions affect her in the etymological sense, that is, she is *passive* to the effects of them (not actively choosing between honor and love). This woman does not know what she values: allegedly it is her honor, but conflicting with this is the fact that she is displeased to learn that she has not been (more) dishonored at the outset of the play since no outside man has actually ever entered her palace without permission (Teodoro belongs to the palace, since he is her servant); more importantly, he was looking not for her, but for a mere servant of hers (her honor allegedly endured the greatest threat when she believed that the intruder had come to try to seduce her).

Ultimately, this conflict is resolved with a trick: a false genealogy is created by Teodoro that demonstrates that he is the long-lost son of the powerful Count Ludovico. Notwithstanding this comic resolution, the ending is not really a happy one. The baser elements of life have overcome the better ones: the duchess is fickle, Teodoro is fickle, and any notion of "true love" is absent. For Mauro Armiño, the ending represents the subversion of the theme of honor, in that Diana willingly looks the other way when the "scheming trick" (*trapacería urdida*) of the false lineage is brought out and marries someone who is actually beneath her, hence undermining the very system of honor that protects her privilege as a noble. For Armiño, Diana is a "representantive" of the "patriarchal structure," which she brings to ruin.[32] While agreeing with Armiño on this last point, I would argue, however, that there is no real subversion of this honor system. For Diana is not just any noble character, but rather a woman,

31. Such emotional incontinence is usually a characteristic of female characters in Lope's plays. The men, following courtly notions of love and jealousy as well as the honor code, generally try to hide their feelings from other characters when possible (e.g., as Peribáñez does in the painter's studio).

32. Mauro Armiño, introduction to *El perro del hortelano*, by Lope de Vega, 31–32.

a jealous woman. The only reason that the play can end this way is precisely because the duchess is female. This comedia does not teach its society's audience to question the values of the honor code, but, like *Jealous Arminda,* it only instructs them in the ideological lesson that women are not fit to rule and that they should not be entrusted to contain their own irrational appetites or to protect the established system of honor. In a speech reminiscent of Arminda's complaints about jealousy, Diana herself says as much:

> Oh jealousy! To what limits does your perfidy extend? You are a bad lawyer for a woman, because you've never taken a vow that you can keep for one day, on your honor.

> (¡Oh celos! ¿Qué no hará vuestra porfía?
> Malos letrados sois con las mujeres,
> pues jamás os pidieron pareceres
> que pudiese el honor guardarse un día. *PH,* 2.2124–27)

As in the case of Arminda as serpent, womanhood is dehumanized in this drama through the continual comparison of Diana to a dog. Whereas jealous men are sometimes terrible—for example, Herod in Calderón's *Jealousy, the Greatest Monster*—they are usually heralded as upholding their honor and depicted as heroes in drama, in scenarios that conflate honor and jealousy (for instance, *The Commanders of Cordoba*). Jealous women, on the other hand, are demeaned and likened to lower animals, regardless of whether the emotion they experience is rational or irrational.

By contrasting the play's primary symbolism, that of the dog in the manger, with the other explicit symbolic association in this play, that of Teodoro with the well-known mythological figures Phaeton and Icarus, the gender bias becomes clear. Whereas the woman is belittled by comparison to an irrational dog who is worthy of mockery, the man who aspires to worldly wealth over true love is repeatedly equated (certainly, with a tinge of irony) with two tragic figures known for literally reaching too high. Yet in the end, Teodoro succeeds in his endeavor—his is the least tragic of all outcomes—and he is rewarded for his fickleness with a duchy, as well as an illustrious, if false, lineage, one that will yield a very real and valuable inheritance in addition to a title from the otherwise heir-less Count Ludovico. Ultimately, the denouement reveals the inadequacy of Diana and Teodoro's symbolic models, and yet the characters remain framed by them. Diana is the dog (*perro*) who somehow learns to eat of the garden (*huerto*); at the end of the play, one could now say "she eats and does not let eat." In contrast, Teodoro is a triumphant Phaeton who has had the strength and endurance to hold the reins, a happy Icarus who has flown to the sun and lived to tell the world; through mythological symbolism, Teodoro successfully transgresses the bounds imposed upon humans, as he literally ennobles himself with verbal sleight of hand.[33]

In addition to an animalizing jealousy, the duchess is "loca" as well (which squares well with her previously described irrationality), a typical label of the jealous man or woman: says Teodoro, "you're insane with an amorous desire" (está loca / de un amoroso deseo, *PH,* 2.2268–69); also, he describes "the most important ladies" (las mujeres principales) as "furies" (furias, *PH,* 2.2249). Like Arminda and other mad jealous characters, the duchess threatens great violence. And at two key points, she thinks it might be better to kill Teodoro than to love him, since she is conflicted between honor (sometimes believing that she cannot marry a lesser man) and love (a passion inspired by jealousy): "Would it not be better to kill him?" (¿No será mejor matarle? *PH,* 1.1129), she asks; and later, she threatens Teodoro, "I will order that you be killed immediately" (Haré yo que os maten luego, *PH,* 2.2219).

Diana's "mad jealousy" does lead her to some severe actions, in contrast to the less irrational Arminda. Recalling the queen's action, one way Diana separates the lovers is by incarcerating Marcela (under the ruse that no premarital relations can take place without offending her honor), after she walks in on them as they are embracing each other, in an instance of evidential jealousy. Later, she does in fact strike Teodoro (*dar bofetones*), an expression of jealous anger (*PH,* 2.221–22). Then, vacillating shortly after this, and once again in love, she gives him money to appease him so that he will forgive her. After that, she threatens to kill him, as mentioned earlier.

Of course, she never kills him. Her violence, though greater than Arminda's, is severely limited. Teodoro is never seriously injured nor

33. Hayden Duncan-Irvin has linked Diana to the mythological goddess of the same name; however, apart from the character's name, this symbolic association is subtle and only implicit, that is, distinct from the overt canine imagery and the explicit mythological comparison of Teodoro to Icarus and Phaethon (Duncan-Irvin, "Three Faces of Diana, Two Facets of Honor: Myth and the Honor Code in Lope de Vega's *El perro del hortelano.*")

killed, as her jealousy threatens. There is no representation in the comedias of the grandiose jealous revenge that male characters perform in other plays, nor of the kind that jealous female characters have played elsewhere in literature, such as in Euripides' *Medea*. As Rosemary Lloyd notes regarding Stendhal, "[A] woman who actively experiences so powerful an emotion is perceived as menacing," which would help to explain why a highly patriarchal culture would not want to represent it in its total ferocity.[34]

The other important female character in the comedia is Marcela, whom Teodoro ultimately forsakes (as he is lured away by Diana, easily swayed by her wealth, nobility, and beauty). Teodoro tells her that their relationship is over, that they should be just friends now. Her love threatened, she experiences emotional episodes associated with the loss of a love object, first jealous sadness when she thinks solely about her loss, and then jealous revenge when she considers the offenders. However, this is not the kind of revenge available to Peribáñez (murder) or even to Diana (incarceration of her enemy, a slap on the face, threats of murder), but one more appropriate for her gender in conjunction with her social position. The only option for revenge that occurs to Marcela is to make Teodoro jealous (which, by some lyrical reports, is life's worst torment):

> However, I will be avenged, I'm not so ignorant that I don't know the trick of making another suffer.

> (Mas yo me veré vengada
> ni soy tan necia que ignoro
> las tretas de hacer pesar. *PH,* 2.1522–24)

Indeed, when Teodoro swears to Marcela that he loves only her, the worst revenge he can imagine to have inflicted on himself—if he is swearing in vain—is the experience of jealousy:

> Marcela, today my love is also founded anew, and if I ever forget you, let heaven punish me by having me see you in the arms of Fabio.

> (Hoy de nuevo fundo,
> Marcela, mi amor también,

---

34. Lloyd, *Closer and Closer Apart,* 9.

y si te olvidare, digo
que me dé el cielo en castigo
el verte en brazos de Fabio. *PH,* 2.1961–65)

The distinction between possible jealous outcomes for male versus female characters is made clear through the juxtaposition of the jealous male characters' reactions, on the one hand, and the powerful and powerless jealous female characters', on the other.

In sum, the jealousies of Queen Arminda and Duchess Diana were disparaged and feared by other characters in these two plays, a reaction that is similar to the terror felt toward the Veinticuatro in *The Commanders of Cordoba.* But these characters need not have feared: such jealous women never killed anyone, unlike their male counterparts in similar situations in Lope's plays (like the Veinticuatro, Peribáñez, the Duke of Ferrara in *Punishment without Revenge,* Castro in *Unfortunate Estefanía,* and Rodrigo in *The Knight from Olmedo,* among others). Rather, the women were made to look foolish for their jealousy, whether it was rationally justified (Arminda) or not (Diana), because they were female characters in the national drama of a society that feared depictions of violent, strong, and independent women. In this way, jealousy served to support the established hegemonic order, not only along class lines but in terms of gender as well. These representations of women's jealousy propagated cultural stereotypes of women's weakness and especially their irrationality, and tended toward the conservative side of the early modern political debates on the suitability of queens as rulers. In the false dichotomy between reason and passion accepted in these dramas, the women did not seem fit to rule since they themselves were ruled by emotion.

Three
Representing Dramatic Jealousy: From Comic to Tragic

> **If we resist our passions it is more from their weakness than from our strength.**
>
> —**La Rochefoucauld,** *Maxims*

The early modern Spanish national drama—the comedia—is generally considered a mixed genre. Neither tragic nor comic, it combines elements of both in greater or lesser degree in any given play.[1] Most of Lope de Vega's hundreds of dramas fall into this hybrid category. Nevertheless, a few may be classified at the extreme poles of the tragic-comic binary. In such atypical works, the portrayal of jealousy in figurative terms and the conceptual claims made about the emotion vary with respect to genre. As Rosalie Colie describes them, genres are "tiny subcultures with their own habits, habitats, and structures of ideas as well as their own forms."[2] When texts from each of these two main subcultures are set against each other, it becomes clear why the imagery of jealousy in comedias (qua tragicomedies) is so often paradoxical. Indeed, it is precisely because symbolic imagery and rhetorical devices of a certain kind are found in comedy, while those of a different kind are found in tragedy. Thus, in a mixed genre, based on the combination of the two, images and rhetoric typical of both are encountered, in disharmony.[3]

---

1. Thus, critics avoid translating the term *comedia* as "comedy," and instead often leave the term in its original Spanish, as I have done.

2. Rosalie L. Colie, *The Resources of Kind: Genre-Theory in the Renaissance,* 116.

3. This is one reason that I will explore in this chapter. There are other reasons that imagery of jealousy is paradoxical (as I suggested in the Introduction), which are elaborated in many of the other chapters, the most important of which is that jealousy is often imaged as irrational.

By appealing to the concept of genre, I account for what can be broadly conceived of as rhetorical differences in the representation of jealousy in an analysis of two comedias, first, Lope's comedy *La discreta enamorada* (In Love but Discreet),[4] and then, his tragedy *El castigo sin venganza* (Punishment without Revenge). Whereas in the former the power of jealousy is so minimal that it barely resembles the emotion of the same name studied in earlier chapters, in the latter—one of Lope's few real tragedies—for both males and females, the representation moves beyond even the most powerful jealousy studied thus far.

In Love but Discreet (ca. 1604–1608)

Jealousy in *In Love but Discreet* is so ludicrous that the treatment almost seems to be a satire of jealousy and of plays treating it. Significantly, this text corresponds to a characterization of those who are below us, according to Aristotle's notion of comedy, which is, "an imitation of men worse than the average; worse, however, not as regards any and every sort of fault, but only as regards one particular kind, the Ridiculous, which is a species of the Ugly." It is the base morality of the characters that corresponds to their ugliness. In this vein, *In Love but Discreet* contains a plot typical of what Northrop Frye calls "low mimetic comedy": "New Comedy normally presents an erotic intrigue between a young man and a young woman which is blocked by some kind of opposition, usually paternal, and resolved by a twist in the plot which is the comic form of Aristotle's 'discovery.' . . . The chief distinction between high and low mimetic comedy, however, is that the resolution of the latter more frequently involves a social promotion." This comic drama also contains elements of farcical slapstick—inherited from the *commedia dell'arte,* whose relationship with this drama has been studied by Nancy L. D'Antuono—the principal intention of which is to bring the spectators to laughter. More specifically, the play laughs at jealousy, something that recalls Otis Green's comment that "[t]he greater the esteem in which certain mores are held, the more pleasurable is the relief provided by the act of parodying them."[5] What in most other

4. Although commonly known in English by the title *In Love but Discreet,* the literal translation of this title would be "The Clever Woman in Love."
5. Aristotle, *Poetics,* 1459; Northrop Frye, *Anatomy of Criticism: Four Essays,* 44–45; Nancy L. D'Antuono, "Lope de Vega y la *commedia dell'arte:* Temas y

texts is a hyperbolized, paradoxical, awesomely powerful emotion is preposterous in this play. The grand passion of *The Commanders of Cordoba* and *Peribáñez and the Commander of Ocaña*, the somewhat frightening emotion in *Jealous Arminda* and *The Dog in the Manger*—even despite the societal bias against representations of truly fearsome females—is now debased to the lowest degree.

In Love but Discreet explores a series of six interconnected love triangles, all involving jealousy, centering on Fenisa's love for Lucindo, the boy next door.[6] In the first act, Fenisa's love from afar for Lucindo (who has never seen her) is spurred on by her uncharacteristically mild evidential jealousy,[7] when she witnesses an argument between him and Gerarda in which the latter is expressing her possessive jealousy and jealous anger because he has uttered a compliment to a passing woman on the street. Meanwhile, Doristeo arrives, also possessively jealous (because he has heard that Gerarda was with another man): "I am burning up" (Estoyme abrasando).[8] The fire that is burning Doristeo up ushers in an Ovidian leitmotif in the comedia. Gerarda, still angry, pretends that she is not interested in Lucindo, and walks off with Doristeo, who quickly forgives her and whose own jealousy immediately subsides. In doing this, Gerarda purposefully tries to make Lucindo jealous, with the intent of both making him suffer and increasing his love, implicitly following Ovid's advice in *The Art of Love,* which is offered by the Latin poet in a Homeric simile:

Just as a fire, growing frail as its forces gradually abate, itself lies hid, while the cinders grow grey on the surface of the fire;

---

figuras"; Otis Green, *Spain and the Western Tradition: The Castilian Mind in Literature from "El Cid" to Calderón,* quoted in Melveena McKendrick, "Celebration or Subversion?: *Los comendadores de Córdoba* Reconsidered," 353.

6. The six triangles are the following: (1) Fenisa-Lucindo-Gerarda; (2) Lucindo-Gerarda-Doristeo; (3) Fenisa-captain-Belisa; (4) Gerarda-Lucindo-Estefanía (Hernando); (5) captain-Fenisa-Lucindo; (6) Belisa-Lucindo-Fenisa. Some of these involve fictitious rivals, as in the case of Estefanía (who is actually the servant Hernando cross-dressing). Nonetheless, from the point of view of the jealous lover, fictitious rival or not, jealousy is aroused.

7. That is, her evidential jealousy is uncharacteristically mild in comparison to Lope's other comedias and most other literature involving fait accompli and evidential jealousy.

8. Lope de Vega, *La discreta enamorada,* 1.2. Subsequent citations will be made parenthetically in the text by act and scene number using the abbreviation *DE.*

but add sulphur, and it finds its extinguished flames, and the light that once was there returns—so when hearts grow torpid in dull repose and freedom from all care, sharp goads must call forth love. See that she has fears about you, and fire anew her cooling thoughts.[9]

Not unexpectedly, Gerarda's plan works. Having his jealousy aroused, Lucindo introduces in these opening scenes some of the typical topoi of literary jealousy when he speaks to his servant Hernando of being blinded ("Jealousy, why have you blinded me? [Celos, ¿por qué me cegáis?]) and of feeling crazed ("I am out of my wits with jealousy" [celos me tienen sin mí, *DE*, 1.4]).

In act 1, scene 5, the derogatory characterization of jealousy begins. The stature of jealousy is lowered from the heights of the gigantic and the demonic in other comedias, right down to the dirty ground:

Jealousy is a treacherous floor, so slippery that it can make even the strongest fall into the mud of love.

(Celos es suelo traidor
resbaladizo, de suerte
que hará caer al más fuerte
en los lodos del amor. *DE*, 1.5)

This emotion is seemingly strong, as suggested by the metaphor "it can make even the strongest fall," which contains an implied pun not on Ovid, but on another Latin poet, Virgil, who coined the phrase "Love conquers all" (omnia vincit amor) in Eclogue 10. Lope's pun suggests a new conceit in which *jealousy conquers all*. However, the adjective *slippery* and the metaphorical "mud of love" in which one would roll also recall slapstick elements of the *commedia dell'arte*, with the difference that such actions in this comedia are only alluded to and not performed on stage. The evidential jealousy that Lucindo feels is provoked by Gerarda, who has purposefully lashed out with

---

9. Ovid, *The Art of Love,* 97. Additionally, there is a similarity to the second of Andreas Capellanus's "rules of love," which requires jealousy of lovers: "He who is not jealous cannot love." These are rules "which the King of Love is said to have proclaimed with his own mouth and to have given in writing to all lovers" (Capellanus, *The Art of Courtly Love,* 184, 177). I will discuss the alleged necessity of jealousy in Chapter 5.

vengeance, not in any grandiose manner, but merely by making her lover jealous (as did the otherwise powerless Marcela in *The Dog in the Manger*).

Lope then introduces another topos of the jealous lover: that he wishes to see, or what Rosemary Lloyd has called the "compulsion to spy."[10] Says Lucindo, "I will drink with my eyes" (voy a beber por los ojos, *DE,* 1.5). This synesthetic metaphor is part of a larger conceit in which the dialogue itself seems to backslide down to the mud on the ground: "I've tasted the pepper of jealousy; I will drink with my eyes" (Diome pimienta de celos; / voy a beber por los ojos). This characterization of jealousy as a spicy irritant that provokes an easily sated thirst again smacks of physical humor. Furthermore, to explain the devotion to Gerarda that his jealousy has provoked, Lucindo exclaims, "I am a simple, faithful fish after the bait of that rod" (Ya soy pez simple y fiel / del cebo de aquella caña, *DE,* 1.5). He understands her game of triangular desire and his place in it, but cannot resist the bait, in an animalizing metaphor in which he belittles himself through comparison to such a simple, innocuous creature (at least Arminda was a viper, and Diana a barking dog). Later, in act 2, scene 3, this banalization of jealousy through animalization reaches its nadir: Lucindo recites, in his sonnet, "Oh, jealousy! With reason you've been called the mosquitoes of love" (¡Oh celos!, con razón os han llamado / mosquitos del amor). Like pepper, mosquitoes are only mildly annoying, and are easily destroyed with a slap of the hand.[11] Furthermore, after Lucindo realizes his plan to drink "with [his] eyes," he elaborates on his voyeurism and the qualities of his jealousy using the traditional image of drinking poison in what amounts to a horrendous piece of lyric poetry:[12]

HERNANDO. . . . . [S]he'll recognize you.
LUCINDO. Is she in his embrace?
HERNANDO. And how!
LUCINDO. I drink jealousy with my eyes and my soul begins to

10. Lloyd, *Closer and Closer Apart,* 10.

11. In Lope's sui generis work *La Dorotea,* a similar comparison is made between jealousy and a rather undignified insect, the flea, in a couple of lines of a poem "to a certain flea" (a cierta pulga), which Julio recites as comic relief: "You are like jealousy, for you bite and go wherever you please" (Como los celos eres, / Que picas y te vas por donde quieres, *La Dorotea,* ed. E. S. Morby, 377–78).

12. I will consider the metaphor of jealousy as poison in detail in Chapter 7.

burn. Oh poison that weakens life with your offenses; the eyes are the cup from which the soul drinks you up; if only I had never come here!

(HERNANDO. . . . que te podrá conocer.
LUCINDO. ¿Está en su regazo?
HERNANDO.   ¡Y cómo!
LUCINDO. Celos por los ojos tomo,
y el alma comienza a arder,
¡oh veneno, que desalmas
la vida con tus enojos,
siendo la copa los ojos
donde le beben las almas,
nunca yo viniera acá! *DE*, 2.2)

Certainly, even the monstrously talented Lope, who had such a keen sense of good verse, must have worked hard to make these *redondillas* sound awful, in a comic effort to portray stylistically Lucindo's banal, petty jealousy. In Colie's terms, these verses would be the "forms" of this particular generic "subculture." The *redondillas* call attention to themselves as lyric by the use of vocabulary frequently used in love poetry, for instance, "jealousy" (*celos*), "soul" (*alma*), "burn" (*arder*), "poison" (*veneno*), and "life" (*vida*). Having done this, the poetry is then incessantly bad: for instance, the locution "the eyes" (los ojos) is repeated in this short passage but not used in any antithetical sense, as is customary for exact repetition; instead of clearly developing a conceit, the repetition explains an obvious metaphor (as if it needed to be explained, the locution "I drink with my eyes" is elaborated with the clarification "the eyes are the cup" [siendo la copa los ojos]). Furthermore, the poem displays very little syntactical and phonological variety. For instance, three consecutive lines all begin with paroxytones (*palabras llanas*) with adverbial meaning: the words *siendo* (gerund of *to be*), *donde* (where), and *nunca* (never) seem to stultify the poem. Additionally, the sentence ends on the inelegant word *acá* (here), an oxytone (*palabra aguda*) with a rhyme totally out of place in the context of the passage.[13] The ridiculousness of Lucindo's passion relates clearly to its aesthetic expression.

13. It will rhyme with the lines to follow. My point here is not that it doesn't rhyme with anything, but that it doesn't rhyme with anything else in his speech.

A similar parody of love lyric, with clear formal deviations, is found at the end of act 2. Replete with many Petrarchan topoi, Lucindo's hendecasyllables sound even more ridiculous than his earlier octosyllabic verse:

> If you consider Tantalus in the water, you will see that I take him as an emblem: because if that fellow never touches neither fruit nor water, I saw her mouth and I never reached her mouth. . . . As the snow of her hand neared, it touched fire, because my soul—which despite abundant water, became a volcano of love—jumped out of my mouth. What will you tell me when I arrive at her mouth?

> (Si a Tántalo en el agua consideras,
> verás que ya le tengo por divisa;
> porque si aquél ni fruta ni agua toca,
> yo vi su boca y no llegué a su boca.
> . . . Templó el fuego
> arrimando la nieve de su mano,
> porque salió a la boca el alma luego,
> hecha un volcán de amor, por agua en vano.
> ¿Qué me dirás cuando a la boca llego? *DE,* 2.19)

Succinctly and humorously, Hernando replies to this: "Did you bite [her mouth]?" (¿Mordístela?). In the base rhetorical portrayal here, a few key elements should be especially noted: the repetition of the locution "su boca" twice within the same line, compounded by the phrase "a la boca" repeated twice in subsequent lines; the prosaic-sounding verbs in the preterit; and Hernando's farcical questioning. Such uses of lyric poetry in *In Love but Discreet* compare in theme but contrast radically in treatment with many of Lope de Vega's love poems, among which stands out Sonnet 56, "Que eternamente las cuarenta y nueve" (That the forty-nine eternally), which I will use to contrast further the comical nature of the awful-sounding verse. In the serious sonnet, Lope crystallizes the intense suffering accompanying the experience of evidential jealousy, precisely the kind Lucindo is referring to with the phrase "I drink with my eyes." In the

---

That is, the speech itself is out of sync with the rhyme scheme; I call this "rhyme enjambment," wherein the rhyme scheme begins a new stanza in disjunction with the ending of the syntactical sentence.

quatrains and in the first tercet, Lope describes in the third person
five of the worst punishments of Greek mythology, in two lines each:

> That the forty-nine eternally attempt to dry Lake Averno; that
> Tantalus never drinks the liquid from the water or eats the ap-
> ple from the tree; that Ixion forever suffers the course that his
> wheel moves on its axles; that Sisyphus, crying in hell, carries
> the rock up the hill; that Prometheus pays for the mad idea
> of stealing the divine flame in the Caucasus, which binds his
> arms. . . .

> (Que eternamente las cuarenta y nueve
> pretendan agotar el lago Averno;
> que Tántalo del agua y árbol tierno
> nunca el cristal ni las manzanas pruebe;
>   que sufra el curso que los ejes mueve
> de su rueda Ixión, por tiempo eterno;
> que Sísifo, llorando en el infierno,
> el duro canto por el monte lleve;
>   que pague Prometeo el loco aviso
> de ser ladrón de la divina llama
> en el Caucaso, que sus brazos liga . . .)[14]

There is the eternal suffering of the "forty-nine," metonymy for the
Danaids (the forty-nine daughters of King Danaus, who were condemned to fill bottomless containers); Tantalus, who suffered hunger
and thirst, while the remedy of these lay just beyond reach; Ixion, condemned forever to roll inside the spinning wheel; Sisyphus,
forced to raise the giant boulder only to watch it fall again; and
Prometheus, made to endure his liver being eaten by an eagle every

14. This sonnet appears in Lope's *Los palacios de Galiona* (José Manuel Blecua, ed., *Obras poéticas de Lope de Vega,* 56n), a comedia that Morley and Bruerton date between 1597 and 1602 in their *Cronología;* it was also published in
his *Rimas* (1602). This sonnet was one among a dozen by Lope that Giambattista Marino imitated very closely in his *Rime* in 1602, and in the later edition
of this work known as *La Lira,* published in 1614 (Dámaso Alonso, *En torno a
Lope: Marino, Cervantes, Benavente, Góngora, Los Cardenios,* 31–33). Marino's
version of Sonnet 56 is his Sonnet 62, "Alla gelosia" (To Jealousy), in *Poesie varie.*
Although mostly a translation, there are some minor differences in treatment,
most important of which is that the woman lies in the man's arms in Marino's
poem ("to see his beloved lying in the arms of another man" [la sua amata amica
/ veder giacersi ad altro amante in braccio, 13–14]) whereas the rival is emphatically in the woman's arms in Lope's sonnet (en brazos de su dama).

day.[15] In the last tercet, the poet switches to a personal register and declares,

> These are great torments, indeed; but it is far worse for a man to see another lover in the arms of his lady; he who has seen this can say so.

> (terribles penas son, mas de improviso
> ver otro amante en brazos de su dama,
> si son mayores, quien lo vio lo diga.)

The overwhelming hyperbole makes evidential jealousy one of the most horrible, painful punishments imaginable, aroused by actually seeing the beloved holding the rival in her arms (what the Veinticuatro comes home to in *The Commanders of Cordoba* and what Aurora witnesses in the mirror in *Punishment without Revenge,* as discussed later in this chapter). The antithesis between the lofty mythological subject matter of the first eleven lines and the straightforward declaration of the second tercet underscores the utter simplicity and apparent truth-value of the personal experience. This juxtaposition makes the statement seem like revealed truth—laid bare of artifice—as in Longinus's account of the sublime, or what, in reference to the last line of Quevedo's Sonnet 485, Gonzalo Sobejano has called "a true saying . . . a few true words."[16] The verb *to see (ver),* emphasizing the visual, is of the utmost importance here. The horror of what is seen provokes the emotion (implying that evidential jealousy is worse than suspicious jealousy, which can only be

---

15. Four of these five punishments are all from the same section of the *Metamorphoses* (4.778–802). In book 4, Ovid describes Juno's descent into the Underworld, where she meets the sufferers of five horrible punishments; the only one of these five that Lope does not repeat is that of Tythius. Lope replaces Tythius's story with that of Prometheus, which is recounted in 1.68–88. In his version of Lope's Sonnet 56, Marino exchanges this diversity of crime and suffering in order—it seems to me—to maintain sexual homogeneity among the mythological characters, as he replaces the reference to the Danaids with one to Tythius, making all of the sufferers male. In this, Marino seems to rely on the traditional bias of the age (which is still seen in Stendhal in the nineteenth century, as Lloyd demonstrates): that which understood women's jealousy as less abominable than men's, and hence less useful when hyperbolizing, in a society that feared the menace of powerful women. In this sonnet, Lope seems more progressive about women than he usually does.

16. Gonzalo Sobejano, "'Reinos del espanto': Garcilaso, Góngora, Quevedo y otros," 267.

imagined). Judging from comparable scenes of evidential jealousy in highly autobiographical writings (like Lope's *Belardo the Furious* and especially the *Dorotea*), it can be assumed that this lyrical poem is an imitation of life as well. When considered in light of these lyrical heights (with such carefully chosen images and exceptionally constructed hendecasyllables), the satirical quality of *In Love but Discreet*'s treatment of jealousy, with its bad, stilted verse, becomes clear.

Much of the drama concerns the play on Virgil and Ovid, that jealousy conquers all and should be used to arouse love; almost all of the characters do, in some way, fall victim to it. In act 1, scene 6, Fenisa devises a way to meet the man she loves and make him fall in love with her. Part of the problem she must overcome is that her mother, Belisa, is overprotective (she is called "jealous" [*celosa*] because she guards her daughter from others). Fenisa complains that she will never marry because her mother's guarding does not grant her any possibility to meet a man. Typically in a comedia daughters have only fathers (their mothers are almost always deceased), making this play somewhat unusual.[17] In *In Love but Discreet,* which reverses the customary order of so many literary conventions, it is Fenisa's mother who plays this paternal role of protection, metonymically related to jealous guarding. In arguing for greater maternal lenience, Fenisa raises her mother's own life as an example to explain that she too had first to meet a man in order to marry and have a child. In turn, Belisa claims that she was blessed with a husband because heaven saw her virtue, implying that the same will happen for Fenisa if she simply waits virtuously. To this, the daughter retorts irreverently: "Thus, why were you jealous of my father, who rests in heaven?" (Pues, ¿cómo fuiste celosa / de mi padre, que Dios haya? *DE,* 1.6). Responding truthfully to this painful question, Belisa admits that she suffered from fait accompli jealousy aroused by her late husband's philandering:

> . . . there was no jewel or fine dress, or silver in our home, nor any other thing, that he would not give away to some lady.

> (. . . no había joya o saya,
> plata en casa, ni otra cosa,
> que no diese a cierta dama. *DE,* 1.6)

17. Amy Williamsen-Cerón, "The Comic Function of Two Mothers: Belisa and Angela."

Belisa's earlier assertion, that her husband was "heaven sent," breaks to pieces. Additionally, that Belisa was jealous of her husband at a time before the action in the play further ridicules the supposed sanctity of marriage and points out the emptiness of honorable appearances, while establishing once again that *jealousy conquers all.* Belisa, too, had fallen into the mud that is jealousy.

Complicating matters, not Lucindo, but his father, the captain, arrives, asking for the hand of Fenisa. Since Belisa has misled herself into believing that he is coming to ask for *her* hand, this first provokes in her a tinge of jealousy; but the widow is indeed pleased to marry her daughter off to a wealthy, if much older, man. Fenisa slyly accepts the proposal to become engaged to the captain, but only to further her amorous intentions with his son, the man she really loves.

Lucindo is the character whose ups and downs of jealousy in all its variation and complexity best exemplify Goldie's notion of the structured, dynamic nature of emotional experience. With his interest in Gerarda aroused more than ever, Lucindo becomes enraged when, in evidential jealousy, he spies her in the arms of Doristeo. Certainly, Gerarda has no interest in Doristeo, something that she admits only to herself:

> He's jealous; let him suffer; I know what a man wants when he's disdained and forgotten. To incite him even further, I want to speak with Doristeo, whom I've never ever loved.
>
> (Celoso está; desespere;
> que por desdenes y olvido
> yo sé lo que un hombre quiere.
> Mas para picarle más,
> quiero hablar con Doristeo,
> a quien no quise jamás. *DE,* 1.10)

She is fanning the Ovidian flames of jealousy. But Lucindo does not know this is a trick; his jealous anger increases to the point at which he thinks of murder, which at first glance seems typical of other comedias: "How is it possible that I haven't yet taken out my sword, when I've been jabbed so many times!" (¿Qué no he sacado la espada, / haciéndome tantos tiros? *DE,* 1.11). However, quite differently from the comedia husbands, Lucindo never seriously considers shedding blood. Leaving his rhetorical question unanswered, he decides instead to make use of the same retribution that Gerarda inflicted upon him, a kind of revenge that is typical of females in Spanish drama who are not societally powerful (for example, it is Marcela's revenge of choice in *The Dog in the Manger,* but not Diana's):

> Well, by God, then I'll have to make you jealous, to see if with jealousy [*celos*] I can oblige you to love me, since the heavens [*cielos*] do not wish that I can oblige you by loving you!

> (Pues ¡vive Dios, que he de darte
> celos, por ver si con celos
> puedo a quererme obligarte,
> ya que no quieren los cielos
> que pueda amando obligarte! *DE,* 1.11)

In this passage, love and jealousy are opposed; jealousy is linked with human action, whereas love is aligned with heaven. Lucindo's utterance offers no explanation as to why he fails to pull out his sword, and hence his earlier remark seems like a hollow exaggeration, much like the dissipating threats of Arminda, whose "sword of vengeance" never materializes. Whereas the jealousy of the societally powerless female characters does not seem very different from that of similar females in other comedias, it is male jealousy that is the locus of difference in *In Love but Discreet,* for generic reasons. Here, the genre requires what I call "weak male jealousy"; at the same time, this type of emotional experience defines Lucindo's character and likens him to women.[18]

Lucindo has been manipulated by Gerarda. But she will pay the price for deviousness, as Lucindo cleverly reverses the situation. Instead of having Lucindo appear before Gerarda with another woman, Lope introduces another farcical crowd-pleaser, the cross-dressing man. As Laurie L. Urraro has noted, this transvestism is designed to provoke laughter.[19] Hernando, the servant, is ordered to dress up as "Estefanía" (a fictional love interest of Lucindo's) in a scenario

18. In "Eifersucht in der Spanischen *Comedia,*" Horst Baader affirms differences in male vs. female jealousy, but does not account for "weak male jealousy" in the comedia. All male jealousy for Baader is part of the public sphere, and hence is subordinate to honor. According to Hymen Alpern's scheme, Teodoro would have to kill Gerarda because "blood must be shed" (Alpern, "Jealousy as a Dramatic Motive," 281).

19. Laurie L. Urraro, "El travestismo y sus aportaciones cómicas en dos comedias del Siglo de Oro."

that leads to a series of interesting jokes and puns and, ultimately, to Gerarda's becoming overcome with jealousy. In act 2, scene 6, this leads her to the murderous thought "I must kill her" (matarla tengo) and then to an attempt at violence (against her rival, not her beloved, just as in *Jealous Arminda*), both of which are rendered ridiculous because they are aimed at a man in women's clothing and also because the attempted murder is ineffectual, merely leaving Hernando lightly bruised. There is a disparity between the brutal intention of Gerarda's action—described in the stage directions as "she charges [*embiste*] at Estefanía"—and its result. At the same time that Lope's desired effect is comedy, this degradation of Gerarda's action seems once more to shore up Lloyd's assertion, mentioned above, that expressions of female power must be ridiculed in a highly patriarchal society, in order for women not to pose a threat to men's power. Indeed, the drama suggests that Gerarda is foolish to act like a charging bull ("embiste"), an imitation of a powerful male animal and symbol of male sexuality.

At the same time, the power of jealousy over Gerarda's heart is exaggerated to such an extent that it is ridiculous: whereas she was in the arms of another man just moments ago, now she is on her knees begging Lucindo to come home with her; but he does not go. His vengeful jealousy now successfully infects her. As was Lucindo earlier, Gerarda is completely aware of her psychological swings, and she expresses the power of triangular desire over her in this way: "When you love me less, Lucindo, I love you more" (Cuando tú me quieres menos, / Lucindo, te quiero más, *DE*, 2.9), a feeling that has much in common with Diana's desire in *The Dog in the Manger.* Gerarda's jealousy has been reawakened by Lucindo's jealousy. This leads to a conceptual claim that lies implicit in this play: it is not love that is born of jealousy, but jealousy itself.

Returning to the other main subplot, the captain is presented as suspiciously jealous because of the insecurities he feels about being engaged to a much younger woman (Fenisa). Typical of the suspiciously jealous lover, he expresses his doubts to the audience (for him these are doubts, but the audience knows they refer to epistemological certainties):

Who doubts that he seems superior to her, and that she is grieved by seeing that she is condemned to my age where she will suffer without pleasure? . . . Now I'm beginning to get jealous.

(¿Quién duda que le parezca
mejor, y que le dé pena
ver que a mi edad se condena
donde sin gusto padezca? . . .
Ya comienzo a estar celoso. *DE,* 2.14)

Also typically, the captain shows a heightened awareness of detail that is not irrelevant to the facts at hand. The result is dramatic irony based on the lack of disparity between what he says and what is true, given the fact that he is presented as *suspicious* (he doubts and worries, for he has no real knowledge, but he is right to worry about such things). As part of the ruse created by Fenisa to have some contact with her real lover right under the noses of their unwitting parents, Lucindo kisses the hand of his "future mother" and exclaims "that I kiss this beautiful hand" (que os bese esa hermosa mano), to which the captain angrily replies, commenting on the adjective:

> What a superfluous courtesy. It was enough to say "hand"; why does he say *"beautiful"*?

> (¡Qué superflua cortesía!
> La mano basta decir;
> ¿para qué es decir *hermosa*? *DE,* 2.15, emphasis added)

Additionally, the captain thinks his son is overdressed for the occasion of being blessed by his "future mother": "You look ready for dancing . . . ready and *gallant*" (Para danzar eras bueno . . . Eres cierto y *galán, DE,* 2.15, emphasis added), which recalls the use of the word *galán* in *The Commanders of Cordoba,* with its double meaning.

Moved by his jealous fears and possessiveness, the captain plans to send his son away to battle, imitating the biblical motif often used by powerful men in literature to rid themselves of a subordinate but legitimate rival, in order to seduce the latter's wife.[20] The captain threatens violence when he learns that Lucindo actually is interested in his young fiancée: he says he feels "cólera" (a grandiloquent

---

20. This motif is found in the biblical story of King David and Uriah's wife (2 Samuel 11:1–27), Apuleius's *Golden Ass,* and Boccaccio's *Decameron.* The commander in *Peribáñez and the Commander of Ocaña* tried to use this ploy as well, knighting Pedro and then sending him off to battle.

term for anger) and that he will soon be a "león" (an animal metaphor implying greater ferocity than his son's "mosquito," discussed above). To avoid Lucindo's being sent off to Portugal, Fenisa involves her mother, whose jealousy over the captain was self-directed. Knowing that Belisa's self-esteem has been wounded by the fact that the captain chose her over her mother, Fenisa concocts yet another fiction to counterbalance the old man–young woman relationship, in which Lucindo is in love with Belisa, hoping, thus, that her mother might sway the captain from his intent to send the young man away. In the play, this dressing up of the young man's desire is akin to the transvestism, meant to seem preposterous and provoke laughter.

Finally, it is Fenisa's turn to be jealous: in act 3, Gerarda returns, with her own ruse to break up Fenisa and Lucindo, right at the moment when the two lovers are about to elope.[21] She makes Fenisa jealous, telling her that she is actually the fictional Estefanía and that Lucindo has been courting the two women simultaneously. Ironically, the title's "clever woman" (*la discreta*) begins to fall for her own type of trap, but Hernando quickly comes to the rescue, confessing to her his role as cross-dresser. Thus Fenisa's jealousy is short-lived, but it nonetheless has the effect of spurring on her love (or lust, in this case) such that she wants to consummate it as soon as possible: "But now jealousy has moved her; today your desires will be satisfied" (Mas los celos la han picado; / hoy se cumplen tus deseos, *DE,* 3.16). Just as it did for Gerarda and Lucindo in act 1, jealousy increases Fenisa's desire, in accordance with Ovid's ideal. Previously imaged as "mud," jealousy in the play is again associated with that which is least heavenly; now it is a spur to sex.

Thus Fenisa devises that she and Lucindo will not elope, but simply enjoy each other's bodies in the house (and henceforth declare themselves married according to the popular but disallowed custom), and do so while duping their respective parents into having sex with

21. Rather inauspiciously, Lucindo refers to their elopement this way: "I want to make you the Proserpine of this burning Pluto" (te quiero hacer Proserpina / deste abrasado Plutón, *DE,* 3.9). Such mythological imagery does not foreshadow any violence or death, as it might in other texts, but rather serves a humorous effect based on the juxtaposition of the god of the dead's violent passion as he erupts from the ground in the story of the rape of Persephone, with the known superficiality of Lucindo's passion (mosquito, pepper, etc.). The image is also incongruous because Lucindo and Fenisa are the same age. If anyone in this fictional world should be compared to Pluto—young Persephone's much older uncle—it should be the captain.

each other. The two couples slip off to bed, Lucindo and Fenisa knowingly, and Belisa and the captain both happily tricked into thinking that their mates are half their age.

Gerarda and Doristeo (who is now in love with Fenisa, too) are jealously spying on Belisa's house. Desiring to break up the amours of the couples inside, they simply yell "fire" (*fuego*). Once again Lope is "deceiving with the truth," because at the end of act 3, there is, indeed, a metaphorical fire in the house, no longer the fire of jealousy of which Doristeo complained at the beginning of act 1, but the result of all that added Ovidian sulphur: the smoldering sexual passion between Lucindo and Fenisa. Hearing the alarming words, the two couples run out of the house, the younger one ecstatic and the older one dispirited at being duped.

Thus the comic ending is achieved: the happy lovers are married and neither of the primary antagonists to their relationship can muster up enough strength to oppose them, or counteract their happiness. Not the father, who would have the right to punish his disobedient son, and who, as a jealous lover—whose betrothal has been violated—would normally be racked with violent thoughts (as is Rodrigo in *The Knight from Olmedo*).[22] Nor, for her part, Gerarda, who was so furious moments earlier that she feigned a blaze, but who now wishes the lovers well after seeing them together in love (normally a cause of terrible evidential jealousy). Both the captain and Gerarda had threatened monstrous violence, but now their jealousy seems to dissipate like so much air, a contradiction alluded to earlier by Hernando,

> Does it not offend you that a thing so easily blown by the slightest wind is a powerful enemy that can knock you down?
>
> (¿No te afrentas que una cosa
> que a todo viento blandea,
> para derribarte sea
> enemiga poderosa? *DE,* 1.5)

In Love but Discreet employs many of the commonplaces associated elsewhere with jealousy: revenge, suspiciousness, doubt, blindness, voyeurism, and suffering. However, these seem to have passed

---

22. Again, that Fenisa has a mother and not a father—who at this point could become angry—is yet another indicator of the reversal of order in this play.

beyond what can be designated by the term *topoi,* and should rather be called clichés. Slippery and dirty, while having the quality of the itch associated with pepper and the mildly irritating bite of the mosquito, jealousy is demeaned to its lowest, most trivial essence in this comedy that also debases the power of love, while portraying characters worse than ourselves who are successful in their endeavors and climbing in social status. The eponymous "clever woman in love" (*La discreta enamorada*) lies to everyone and becomes engaged to a man in whom she has no interest, only as a ruse, but ultimately is rewarded by marrying the man she wants. As a woman in early modern Spain, her *estado* (social standing) is now superior to what it was. While exhibiting throughout many elements of farcical slapstick, the play finishes with a comic resolution in which the lovers have overcome obstacles in order to marry. Moreover, the final scene of ridicule for the unhappy parents points to the play's additional ambition of producing a more Nietzschean emotion, that of happiness due to the suffering of the wretched.[23]

Punishment without Revenge (1631)

In Love but Discreet contains similarities in theme and structure to one of Lope de Vega's most acclaimed dramas, *Punishment without Revenge,* which was written about twenty-five years later. The most obvious of these is that both works depict a relationship between an older man and a younger woman who falls in love with the man's son; additionally, in both cases, the son is sought after by another woman, who attempts to destroy the relationship between the two lovers. In both cases, a love triangle is invoked involving a young man and a woman who is, in some way, considered his mother.

However, there are tremendous differences between the two. For instance, the young couple in the comedy are both unmarried, while Casandra in *Punishment without Revenge* is the Duke of Ferrara's wife; also, in the later play, the characters' social status is much

---

23. See, for instance, Friedrich Nietzsche: "To see others suffer does one good, to make others suffer even more: this is a hard saying but an ancient, mighty, human, all-too-human principle to which even the apes might subscribe; for it has been said that in devising bizarre cruelties they anticipate man and are, as it were, his 'prelude.' Without cruelty there is no festival: thus the longest and most ancient part of human history teaches—and in punishment there is so much that is *festive!*" (Nietzsche, *On the Genealogy of Morals,* 6:67).

higher. But the treatment and the denouement are what distinguish the two most of all, for *Punishment without Revenge* is a tragic work, containing many elements of Aristotelian tragedy, with little in it of the world of comedy. It is to this different generic "subculture" that the treatment of jealousy responds.

Punishment without Revenge was written at the end of Lope de Vega's life, and it is fitting that the dramaturge once more characterized jealousy, an emotion that he appears to have experienced first-hand during most of his life, as something grandiose.[24] In dire opposition to *In Love but Discreet,* this tragic work represents jealousy as a force that drives its sufferers to desperate acts, and jealousy is intrinsically linked to its tragic denouement in several ways.[25]

Jealousy drives the action of *Punishment,* as it does in the comic play. The duke's philandering, with which act 1 opens, is the jealousy-provoking target of Casandra's rational jealousy, which in turn leads to her desire for revenge. She hates being "the scorn of a lord" (desprecio de un señor)[26] and complains that

> In one month, I only saw him in my arms for one night, and afterwards on many others I saw him on which he did not wish to see me.

24. According to his letters, Lope experienced jealousy intensely. In a letter to the Duke of Sessa in 1617, he complained, "I'm dying of successor jealousy" (me muero de çelos de suçessor), commenting on the end of his relationship with Marta de Nevares (Lope de Vega, *Epistolario,* 3:141, quoted in Alan S. Trueblood, *Experience and Artistic Expression in Lope de Vega: The Making of "La Dorotea,"* 314; translations mine). In another letter, from 1614, he reflected on the "insane passion" of jealousy: "[T]hus I did not want that which I loved to think, see, speak with anyone else but me, and this jealousy was such an insane passion in me that I became jealous of even myself: because if she favored me greatly, then I imagined that she was faking, or that I could be someone else, or that I resembled in the present something else which at a past time, she used to like or which used to give her pleasure" (assí no quería que lo que yo amaba pensase, viesse, hablasse con otro que conmigo, y eran estos çelos tan desatinada pasión en mí, que llegaua a tenerlos de mí mismo: porque si me favorecían mucho, ymaginaua que lo fingían, o que yo podía ser otro, o parecerme entonces a alguna cosa que le agradaua o de que en otro tiempo había tenido gusto, *Epistolario,* 3:141, quoted in Trueblood, *Experience and Artistic Expression,* 314). His most autobiographical work, the *Dorotea,* relates the fictionalized story of his breakup with Elena Osorio and is riddled with representations of jealousy.

25. As it is well known, its full plot need not be reiterated here.

26. Lope de Vega, *El castigo sin venganza,* ed. C. A. Jones, 2.1002. Subsequent citations from this edition will be made parenthetically in the text by act and line number using the abbreviation *CSV.*

(Sola una noche le vi
en mis brazos en un mes
y muchas le vi después
que no quiso verme a mí. *CSV,* 2.1034–37)

Her choice of images ("night," "in my arms") and her emphasis on the verb *to see* (*ver*), which is repeated three times, link this speech with Lope's lyric Sonnet 56, mentioned earlier. In her fait accompli jealousy, Casandra is imagining the duke in the arms of another (*en brazos de otra*).

Considering the duke's role in the tragedy, his philandering is thus his hamartia, the fatal error that leads to the love relationship between his son, Federico, and his wife and ultimately to his perceived need to kill them both (indeed, there is a scene of recognition—an anagnorisis—wherein he admits that he has only himself to blame [*CSV,* 3.2516–19]).[27] Federico's love for Casandra causes Aurora, the duke's niece, to experience terrible jealousy, which she describes to Ricardo, the duke's servant, using metaphorical animal imagery:

[A]nd since jealousy is a lynx that penetrates walls, I came to see the cause.

([Y] como celos son linces
que las paredes penetran,
a saber la causa vine. *CSV,* 3.2064–66)[28]

Like *In Love but Discreet,* this play refers to many of the topoi of jealousy, including voyeurism, vengeance, and suffering. But the characteristics of these have little to do with those in the comic treatment of the theme. This is exemplified in the choice of animal used as an image of jealousy. The lynx, known for its intelligence, cunning, speed, and ferocity, is a more dignified symbol than the mosquito of

27. There is certainly no consensus among critics of this play that the duke is a tragic figure. T. E. May maintains that "Lope's Duke is a bachelor to begin with, is vicious, tyrannical and pompous, undergoes a conversion in which it is impossible to believe . . . and kills his wife and son by a trick that cannot be condoned" (May, *Wit of the Golden Age: Essays on Spanish Literature,* 154); however, David Kossof argues for just such a conversion: "[H]e serves the Pope heroically in war and returns home determined to observe a code of morality worthy of his state's leadership" (David Kossof, ed., *El castigo sin venganza,* 29).

28. It was commonly believed that the lynx could see through walls.

In Love but Discreet (and the dog of *The Dog in the Manger*). It should be noted that suspicious jealousy has a positive effect for Aurora, leading to her desengaño, just as it was instrumentally rational for the husbands studied in Chapter 1.

Because of her jealousy, Aurora quietly spies on the lovers and sees them:

> . . . I looked and saw a horrible thing: in the glass of a mirror I saw the count [Federico] measuring Casandra's roses with his lips.

> (miré y vi ¡caso terrible!
> en el cristal de un espejo,
> que el Conde las rosas mide
> de Casandra con los labios. *CSV,* 3.2073–76)

In stark contrast to the result predicted by Ovid, and to the characters who burn with jealousy as it becomes love, this evidential jealousy completely rids Aurora of any love for Federico. In this case, jealousy conquers love. However, it does not appease the jealous anger Aurora feels for having been scorned.

Although the play leaves the question unresolved, Aurora's jealousy is most likely the major factor in the duke's later desengaño, for she is the likely author of the anonymous note to the duke regarding the illicit love between Federico and Casandra (the audience knows that Aurora is a firsthand witness of their kissing). Like Tristan and Isolde, Federico and Casandra cannot help themselves in their illicit love for one other, a love to which they stoically resign themselves as they give in to their passion (*CSV,* 2.2026–30). When the duke comes home from battle after his absence of four months, Casandra asks Federico, "What should we do?" (¿Qué habemos de hacer?), to which Federico replies, "Die!" (¡Morir! *CSV,* 3.2265–66). The fear expressed in this exchange mirrors that which the characters felt in *The Commanders of Cordoba.*

All of the main characters in the play are overcome by jealousy. Casandra's jealousy of Federico's proposed marriage to Aurora—a betrothal he plans to hide the fact that he and his stepmother have been having an affair—is so tremendous that she would rather give the duke reason to be suspicious by voicing her disapproval of the wedding (and thus cause her death "a thousand times," as well as that of Federico) than to see her beloved marry another woman: "Let the duke kill me a thousand times, but you're not going to marry" (Quíteme el Duque mil vidas / pero no te has de casar, *CSV,* 3.2287–88). Unlike Lucindo's hollow, merely rhetorical threats, these imagined thoughts of being murdered will be tragically realized.

Casandra's jealousy is ultimately a death wish. With respect to the defiant thoughts it arouses and the actions it motivates, hers is perhaps the most powerful jealousy experienced by any woman in Lope de Vega's comedias.[29] However, while playing a role in one's own death is certainly a manifestation of some power, it does not compare with the effective power required to kill others, one that the duke exhibits when he has his wife and son executed according to his calculated, secret plan.

Federico is jealous of his own place in life and covetous of his father's title when he is first introduced in act 1. Federico's actions and words are very competitive, a most obvious example of which is his Oedipal sleeping with his father's wife. Federico is jealous about protecting what he has long since viewed as his own, as he expresses fear early on that his stepmother's future, legitimate children will inherit his father's dukedom (a fact that the duke uses to justify his son's murder when, ironically, Federico's fear is no longer true). A more veiled reference of his desire to take the father's place is the phrase he utters to the marquis, while holding Casandra for the first time after having helped her find her way: "Sir Marquis, I wanted to be a Jupiter at that moment" (Señor marqués, yo quisiera / ser un Júpiter entonces, *CSV,* 1.561–62). Since his father is the most powerful figure depicted in this hierarchical society, to be Jupiter is to be the duke.[30] He later admits this to Batín: "Although it is impossible, I have become envious of him" (Con ser imposible, llego / a estar envidioso dél, *CSV,* 1.987–88).

The duke's jealousy is typical of the jealous husband, though his predicament—having adultery occur between his son and his wife—is perhaps the worst imaginable offense to him. Although not a suspicious man by nature, he has an overwhelming emotional episode of

29. In Spanish literature, perhaps only Guillén de Castro's *La tragedia por los celos* depicts a woman whose jealousy is fiercer than Casandra's.

30. The allusion could also be interpreted as positing Federico as Jupiter and the duke as Saturn, Jupiter's father, who is killed by his son with the help of the mother. The use of mythological comparison to describe the power relations of the play recalls the same in *Jealous Arminda,* where Arminda was likened to Juno and Antonio to Jupiter (see Chapter 2).

jealousy when he is alerted to the situation by the anonymous letter, which he starts off by doubting: "You lie, this cannot be" (Mentís, que no puede ser, *CSV,* 3.2498). But he vacillates and quickly starts to believe its veracity: "There is no evil that does not fit in human weakness" (que no hay maldad que no quepa / en las flaquezas humanas, *CSV,* 3.2504–5). The duke seems jealous of his unique place in the world, of his very self, and resents that the count is taking his place, as a usurping copy that replaces the original.[31] These are not irrational fears, for Federico is envious of his father and has tried to take his place (for example, the Jupiter statement above). As is typical of the jealousy of powerful, offended men, the duke's leads to violence and the death of the offenders, with the special exception here that the revenge element should not be made public, which explains the conceit of the play's title.[32] The duke's jealous fury at his son is so powerful that it obliterates his strong paternal love, just as Aurora's love was destroyed by her evidential jealousy from what she saw in the mirror. Earlier, Federico had been his "sun" (as reported by Batín): "[Y]ou are the sun of his eyes, and four months of eclipse have left him impatient" (eres el sol de sus ojos / y cuatro meses de eclipse / le han tenido sin paciencia, *CSV,* 3.2152–54), a hyperbolic metaphor reminiscent of those used by lovers regarding their beloveds in the Petrarchan tradition. But now he wishes the sun dead.[33] The power of his jealous revenge is predicted by the marquis, metaphorically, when he speaks with Aurora about what heaven may cause:

> . . . if heaven does not first punish his liberties and strike them down with lightning as the infamous giants they are.

> (si no es primero el cielo
> sus libertades castigue
> y por gigantes de infamia
> con vivos rayos fulmine. *CSV,* 3.2131–34)

31. Casandra tells the duke that "he [Federico] has been a portrait of you" (retrato vuestro ha sido, *CSV,* 3.2656).

32. The duke tricks Federico into murdering Casandra by sending him in to kill an alleged assassin who is attacking her in the dark; after Federico unwittingly murders her, the duke then calls for the guards to kill his son.

33. Moreover, it is a sublime desire to wish death upon the sun. This idea recalls Góngora's sonnet "Ya besando unas manos cristalinas" (Already kissing two crystalline hands), in which the lyric voice calls on Jupiter to strike down the sun. See Chapter 7, n. 43.

In this reference to the battle of the gods and the Titans, the duke is once more implicitly compared to lightning-throwing Jupiter. Additionally, this passage echoes the final line of the penultimate stanza of Góngora's *Polifemo* (1613), which describes the Cyclops's violent jealous reaction: "a blasting trumpet warns of the thunderbolt" (previene rayo fulminante trompa).[34] As my study of the *Polifemo* in Chapter 7 will show, the enormity of the Cyclops's jealousy is fathomed, like the duke's, by its ability to overwhelm and annihilate tremendous feelings of love. In describing such destruction due to affective experience, Lope de Vega reshapes the Virgilian topos, combining it with Ovid, into the conceptual claim that "jealousy conquers all."

In contrast to Peribáñez and the Veinticuatro, each of whom needed a monarch to justify his acts of violence, the duke provides his own justification for destroying those who would disobey his authority, those who would treat him as anything less than Jupiter, anything less than an absolute power. The cruelty of his actions, in a state of affairs that is largely his own fault, paints a picture of a world that would benefit from the wisdom of a true leader, of an absolute king. *Punishment without Revenge* thus justifies the hegemony of Spain's rulers over its internal and external borders, by suggesting—like *Peribáñez* and *Fuenteovejuna*—that nobles can't be trusted to govern justly.

While the two plays analyzed in this chapter are similar in theme and structure, fundamental differences lie in their symbolic and rhetorical dimensions, which vary with their respective genres. The trivialized emotion of *In Love but Discreet* is at odds with the hyperbolized passion of *Punishment without Revenge*. The contrasting of these two plays—with each falling squarely into the generic category of comic or tragic—helps explain why the hybrid comedia often contains contradictory imagery and conceptual claims pertaining to jealousy.

---

34. Góngora, *The Fable of Polyphemus and Galatea,* in *Renaissance and Baroque Poetry of Spain,* trans. and ed. Elías L. Rivers; Góngora, *Fábula de Polifemo y Galatea,* ed. Alexander A. Parker, 61.8.

Four

Religion, Race, and Ethnicity in Cervantes's *Jealous Old Man from Extremadura*

For jealousy arouses a husband's fury, and he shows no restraint when he takes revenge.

—Proverbs 6:34

Most of Cervantes's works—like those of Lope de Vega—are riddled with jealous characters and situations, and the emotion figures as a principal theme in many, including *The Jealous Old Man from Extremadura, El viejo celoso* (The Old Jealous Man), *La casa de los celos* (The House of Jealousy), *El juez de los divorcios* (The Divorce Judge), "The Ballad of Jealousy," *The Galatea,* and *The Trials of Persiles and Sigismunda.*[1] In a unitary vein, jealousy in Cervantes generally proves a hazardous if not fatal obstacle to love. I will examine one exception to this tendency, the *Persiles,* in Chapter 5, where I will argue that Cervantes allows for a singular, benign kind of jealousy in love (a caveat that has gone largely unnoticed by critics). Before that, however, in this chapter I explore symbolic connotations of jealousy in *The Jealous Old Man from Extremadura* as they pertain to questions of religion, race, and ethnicity.

The Jealous Old Man from Extremadura (1613)

The Jealous Old Man from Extremadura is Cervantes's most intense examination of the jealous husband, a novella in which he

---

1. Américo Castro maintains that the frequency and prominence of the theme of jealousy in Cervantes's texts is "a sign of his concern with the theme" (signo de su preocupación por el tema, *El pensamiento de Cervantes,* 384).

depicts a kind of jealousy that is unequivocally negative and contrary to love, through which the author condemns the emotion as an irrational, grotesque, and destructive force. The novella is in Cervantes's collection *Novelas ejemplares* (Exemplary Stories), and whereas other critics have found the allegorical exemplarity of this novella in its condemnation of solipsism or as a defense of the freedom of choice, I argue for a complementary reading in which it embodies a religio-aesthetic allegory.[2] After providing a short synopsis of the novella, I will examine briefly the protagonist's pathological psychology. Then, I will outline how the protagonist is stereotypically and anti-Semitically characterized as a Jewish converso, both physically and morally (while this is never made explicit). After grounding these assertions of his Jewishness, I will draw textual parallels between his words and deeds and those of Jews and Jehovah in the Hebrew scriptures (Old Testament), especially in the Pentateuch. These Semitic references can be read as representing the Other, that which is racially, ethnically, or morally non-Christian. In this light, I interpret the novella's negative exemplary function: the Semitic associations are used to parody the popular jealous-husband plots of the Spanish comedia, and in particular, Lope de Vega's *Commanders of Cordoba,* so as to critique the honor code these plays embody.

The Jealous Old Man from Extremadura narrates the story of Carrizales, a man of extremes who hails from Extremadura. The novella begins with a short description of him as a depraved young man who, having squandered his inheritance, wanders off to the New World in search of fortune. His life is marked by several reversals of fortune that remind the reader of his "extreme" origins: from rich to poor to rich, and from inexperienced to licentious to abstemious. After the initial exposition of his life, he is presented as an

---

2. The collection's title asserts exemplarity, an exemplarity present in the novella tradition from its origins in the medieval exempla collections and in Italian and Spanish novella collections, such as those of Boccaccio and Pérez de Montalbán. Cervantes specifically refers, in the prologue to *Exemplary Stories,* to a moral teaching behind each story: "I have called them 'exemplary,' and on close examination you will see that there is not one from which you cannot extract some profitable example" (*Exemplary Stories,* trans. and ed. Lesley Lipson, 4). However, there is no clear consensus on the reason for this novella's exemplarity. Ruth El Saffar discusses the main character's solipsism in *Novel to Romance: A Study of Cervantes' "Novelas ejemplares,"* 40–45, and Alban K. Forcione reads the novella as centering on the freedom of choice in *Cervantes and the Humanist Vision: A Study of Four Exemplary Novels,* 31–92. My reading is indebted to Forcione's allegorical Christian interpretation, although with major distinctions.

old man who has returned to Spain with desires that seem simple: to marry, to have an heir, to die in peace. But the very thought of marriage provokes in him an incredible, visceral emotional reaction.[3] As it turns out, he is "the most jealous man in the world." (This text is also Cervantes's "entry" in the competition for the greatest hyperbole of jealousy.) Recovering from this experience, Carrizales decides never to marry. But (reminiscent of his earlier extreme peripeteia) one day he spies "a girl . . . of about thirteen or fourteen years of age" in a window and falls instantly in love.[4] Unable to resist his desire to marry, he nonetheless wishes to avoid future jealous fits. To this end, he schemes that the girl, Leonora, shall never have the desire nor the opportunity to betray him sexually. Thus, his plan is to placate his terrible pangs of jealousy before they have a chance to occur.

The girl's impoverished parents, having received considerable financial incentives, agree to his terms, by which they will rarely be able to see their daughter, for she will be kept in his house under double lock and key. No men shall ever be allowed in. He purchases slaves, among them a eunuch, and hires servants to care for him and her, all of whom must also observe the most severe restrictions. Leonora seems happy in this situation for about a year, according to the narrator; it appears that Carrizales's plan is working. Leonora knows of little other than the jealous old man. But a young rogue named Loaysa learns of her beauty and the conditions under which she is guarded, and his interest is piqued. He gains access to the house by first seducing the eunuch slave with music and the *dueña* who acts as Leonora's governess with promises of sexual favors. After helping to get Loaysa into the house by applying a soporific ointment to her husband, Leonora winds up in bed with the young man.[5] When the old man wakes up and searches for his wife, who is missing from

3. In today's psychiatric terms, his reaction might be termed a "panic attack."
4. Miguel de Cervantes, *The Jealous Old Man from Extremadura,* in *Exemplary Stories,* trans. and ed. Lesley Lipson, 152 (both quotes). Unless otherwise specified, all English translations are from Lipson. All citations of the novella in Spanish are from Harry Sieber's edition of *Novelas ejemplares,* 99–135. Subsequent citations will be made parenthetically in the text by page number using the abbreviations *ES* and *NE*. Lipson's *Exemplary Stories* is a widely available translation of Cervantes's novellas; on occasion, for reasons of interpretation, I point out a discrepancy between how I interpret the Spanish text and Lipson's choice of renderings.
5. In the version of this story that was published in the *Novelas ejemplares* (Madrid, 1613)—the one studied in this chapter—Leonora ultimately refuses his sexual advances. She struggles with Loaysa for hours in bed, resisting him, and in this way, they both fall asleep, exhausted. This ending contrasts with that of

their bed, he finds her sleeping in the arms of another man. Thinking suddenly of his honor, he heads back to his room for his dagger, but is overcome by emotion and ends up in a supine state in yet another extreme reversal. On his deathbed Carrizales forgives Leonora for what he thinks she has done, and blames his own jealousy for his problems. He then expires, after which Leonora enters a convent and Loaysa leaves town and heads for the New World.

Eponymously hyperbolic, the protagonist is pathological by early modern as well as modern standards. Gustavo Illades Aguiar argues that the character should be considered a "virtual patient" because his affliction is classifiable according to the writings of Francisco de Villalobos, a medical doctor whose ideas were widely disseminated and influential on both Juan Luis Vives and Huarte de San Juan, and hence accessible to Cervantes, who was familiar with the latter's work, as Mauricio de Iriarte, Otis Green, and others have shown. For Illades Aguiar, it is a faulty imagination that makes Carrizales mad: "In the *Sumario de la medicina* [Compendium of Medicine, published in 1498] Villalobos defines *amor hereos* [lovesickness] as a corrupt imagination that deceives the other potencies of the soul and the senses, by imposing on them idealized images of the desired person." Furthermore, Villalobos refers specifically to the "mad" desires of old men for young women: "A great madness is that of the old man who marries a young woman, because he is acting mad when he marries and he commits many mad acts after he is married" (Gran locura es la del viejo que se casa con la mujer moza, porque hace locura cuando se casa y hace otras muchas después de casado).[6]

While this argumentation shows that Carrizales would be considered pathological for Villalobos, it does not explain the curious fact that he seems insane even by the standards of our time, when the idea of an old man marrying a very young woman is not per se symptomatic of any mental disorder.[7] While Villalobos's characterization of the old man who "hace locura" is a form of Renaissance folly made

---

the earlier version that has come to be known as the "Porras" manuscript, in which the two consummate their adulterous passion (the ending in adultery is similar to that of the dramatic interlude *The Old Jealous Man*).

6. Mauricio de Iriarte, *El doctor Huarte de San Juan y su Examen de ingenios;* Otis Green, "El ingenioso hidalgo"; Gustavo Illades Aguiar, "Dos pacientes virtuales del médico Francisco de Villalobos: Anselmo y Carrizales," 104, 105n7 (quote from Villalobos, *Sumario de la medicina*).

7. Rather, in most countries such a situation involving the marriage of a thirteen- or fourteen-year-old is quite simply illegal.

famous by Erasmus in *Praise of Folly* (1509) and may well be an ill-advised enterprise, Carrizales's infirmity—as outlined in the above synopsis—predates his marriage. De Sousa's and Goldie's criteria for analyzing the emotions, on the other hand, provide the vocabulary to distinguish in which ways Carrizales is irrational, which helps us to appreciate why this literary character is so fascinating today. By definition as extreme reactions, Carrizales's affective experiences are clearly beyond normal limits, while at the same time they are both intelligible and structured. More importantly, it is the absolute lack, not just of a criterion of success to determine the rationality of his emotion, but of the *possibility* of such a criterion that makes Carrizales laughable when he is presented to the reader: "even while he was still unmarried . . . [at] the mere thought of the married state jealous thoughts began to disturb him, suspicions to torment him, and his imagination to alarm him" (*ES*, 152) (aun sin estar casado, pues con sólo la imaginación de serlo le comenzaban a ofender los celos, a fatigar las sospechas y a sobresaltar las imaginaciones, *NE*, 102). This does not fit Villalobos's notion of "imagination" (*imaginación*) well. The Renaissance doctor's use of the word *imaginación* does not imply that the woman is *imaginary*, but that an idealized image of the woman is fixed in the *imagination*, one of the three faculties of the mind.[8] In Carrizales's case, before he sees Leonora, there is clearly no real woman in mind, only an imaginary one, and yet that is when the reader learns that he is "the most jealous man in the world" (*ES*, 152).[9] Thus, his jealousy confounds de Sousa's apt distinction between an emotion (in which intentionality is directed at a target) and a mood (which lacks a clear target). As outlined in

8. The quotes from Villalobos's writings that Illades Aguiar uses to shore up his analysis demonstrate this on their own: "[T]he image of their beloved always figures and is always fixed in their thoughts, such that they are unable to occupy their imagination with anything else. . . . [R]ather they try with all of their might to increase their passion and confirm their illness with greater causes. . . . [T]hose in love are estranged from their imagination, and with it, their will" ([Q]ue la imágen de su amiga tienen siempre figurada y fija dentro de sus pensamientos, por donde no pueden ocupar jamás la imaginacion en otra cosa. . . . [A]ntes procuran con todas sus fuerzas de meterse mas adentro en la pasion, y confirmar su dolencia con mayores causas. . . . [L]os enamorados tienen ajena la imaginacion, y la voluntad con ella, Villalobos, *Curiosidades,* 488–89, quoted in Illades Aguiar, "Dos pacientes virtuales," 104).

9. It is not the case that the object of his emotion might be "fungible," that is, indistinguishably applied to one woman or another, which would point to an immature mind (de Sousa, *Rationality of Emotion,* 98–100).

my Introduction, de Sousa provides the example of "listless" for a mood and "sadness" for an emotion: one might be listless *because of* something but not *at* something ("I am not listless at low blood sugar"); in contradistinction, one is sad at a situation ("I am sad at the loss of something").[10] The example shows how a similar feeling might be caused in different ways, corresponding to an undirected mood versus a directed emotion. But this distinction does not hold for all emotions. Indeed, in the case of jealousy, there is no meaningful corresponding mood for the targetless feeling, making such an emotional response seem both pathological and illogical, not only by early modern standards but by contemporary ones as well.

With Carrizales's pathological character in mind, I turn to where Cervantes left off, the end of *The Jealous Old Man from Extremadura*, when the protagonist, instead of killing his wife, forgives her. Responding to this novelistic climax, the well-known mid-twentieth-century critic Agustín González Amezúa qualifies this act of forgiveness as Christian and anxiously suggests that there is nothing remarkable about it. Why not? According to González Amezúa, Carrizales was a good Christian, not "a Moorish dog nor a dirty Jew" (perro moro ni sucio judío).[11] Amezúa's offensive anti-Semitic outburst points to his own dis-ease. The act of Christian forgiveness is highly remarkable in the context of the story; in fact, it is another *extreme* peripeteia, not typical of Carrizales's previous actions, but rather contrary to them.[12] Considering this, if Carrizales's Christian ending is indeed remarkable, can his previous actions be better understood by conceiving them as un-Christian, or rather as non-Christian? In other words, where can we locate González Amezúa's "dirty Jew" in Cervantes's novella?[13]

10. De Sousa, *Rationality of Emotion,* 7.
11. Agustín González Amezúa, *Cervantes: Creador de la novela corta,* 2:266.
12. Just as his wealth is not typical of his previous poverty, or his licentiousness is not typical of his later abstemiousness. Although the extreme peripeteia become expected in this novella, that is not to say that the specific forms of the reversals are already incarnated in their opposites that come about later and are meant to shock the reader.
13. In addition to the Jewish and converso allusions that are analyzed in what follows, there are also evocations of Islamic culture in the novella. The early-twentieth-century critic Georges Cirot ("*El celoso extremeño* et *L'Histoire de Floire et Blanceflor*") first noticed textual parallels between Loaysa's breaking into Carrizales's house and the medieval story of *Floire and Blancheflor,* suggesting that Loaysa is a rescuer, Carrizales a prince, and his house a harem.

Throughout the novella, Carrizales is subtly Judaized through association with medieval and Renaissance stereotypically Jewish traits. As Sander Gilman has demonstrated, among the many faces of anti-Semitism in European culture is the frequent view that Jews are sexually aberrant, a stigmatization that he traces to the physical fact of circumcision. Jewish customs were so poorly understood by Christians that, according to Gilman, circumcision was often confused with castration, which might explain the common literary associations between Jewishness and impotence. In medieval Spain, such anti-Semitism took an explicit and often virulent form in poetic verses such as the *recuestas* of the *Cancionero de Baena* (ca. 1426–1430). Medieval poets such as Juan de Baena, Alfonso Álvarez de Villasandino, and Antón de Montoro (two of whom were conversos themselves) composed and performed poems in which the Jew or converso is the buffoon and object of derision.[14] The dishonor of these ridiculed people usually lies in their being labeled cuckolds, sodomites, or illegitimate children.[15] In the Spanish Baroque, the explicit association in the literary imagination of aberrant sexuality with Jewishness is still very alive in Francisco de Quevedo's satirical poetry.

These cultural associations form the backdrop for my reading of Carrizales as implicitly Judaized. His impotence is one form of aberrant sexuality, about which the narrator comments elliptically when alluding to the protagonist's failure to properly enjoy sexual relations with his young wife: "he began to enjoy the fruits of marriage, at least as well as he could" (*ES,* 155) (comenzó a gozar como pudo los frutos del matrimonio, *NE,* 105). If the use of the verb *to enjoy* (*gozar*) in conjunction with the metaphorical "fruits of marriage" were not enough to confirm the implied meaning, the reader is then told that

---

More recently, Cory A. Reed has studied Islamic elements in the novella and has argued that "Cervantes draws at least in part on the very Ottoman and Islamic models he emulates in his other fictional variations of the theme" (Reed, "Harems and Eunuchs: Ottoman-Islamic Motifs of Captivity in *El celoso extremeño,*" 200).

14. Sander Gilman, *The Jew's Body,* 191. I do not think there is much good evidence to consider Cervantes a likely converso, an idea proposed long ago by Américo Castro. However, even if he were, that would not be a reason to preclude anti-Semitism in his work, as the cases of Baena and Montoro (who were certainly conversos) demonstrate.

15. See Francisco Márquez Villanueva, "Jewish 'Fools' of the Fifteenth Century *Cancioneros,*" and Gregory S. Hutcheson, *Marginality and Empowerment in Baena's "Cancionero."*

Leonora had no opinion on such relations: "To Leonora, who had no experience of any others, these were neither appetizing nor unappetizing" (*ES*, 155) (los cuales a Leonora, como no tenía experiencia de otros, ni eran gustosos ni desabridos, *NE*, 105). Such sexual allusions are heightened by relating this passage to Cervantes's *Old Jealous Man*, the dramatic interlude (*entremés*) that is so thematically and linguistically similar (Carrizales is even referred to as "the old jealous man" [el viejo celoso, *NE*, 103] in the novella). In the interlude, the wife tells the other women who want to let the young man in that she does not know where her old jealous husband, Cañizares, keeps the key; in fact, she says, "I sleep with him, and I've never seen or felt that he has any key" (yo duermo con él, y jamás le he visto ni sentido que tenga llave alguna).[16] The quote not only calls into question his potency, but the lack of a phallic "key" suggests castration, which, as Gilman suggests, was a common popular misunderstanding of Jewish circumcision. Furthermore, Carrizales's later cuckoldry also pertains to this semantic category of aberrant sexuality.[17]

Other stereotypically un-Christian characteristics of Carrizales include the many references to his excessive wealth. Historian Robert Wistrich explains how, as medieval economies became ever more dependent on money, "Jews became associated in the popular mind with banking, money, exchange and the parasitical exploitation of a land-based Christian peasantry which formed the backbone of the European nations."[18] Thus the circumstantial fact that Carrizales is filthy rich—he himself claims that the dowry he provided for Leonora was "large enough for three women of similar status to marry and be considered rich" (*ES*, 181) (más de tres de su misma calidad se pudieran casar con opinión ricas, *NE*, 132)—and also that he came upon his money through shady mercantilism builds on the anti-Semitic stereotype, as does the immoral disposition he shows through avarice.[19] In yet another pecuniary reference, Carrizales is related metonymically to embezzlers (*alzados*) as the novella opens:

16. Cervantes, *El viejo celoso*, ed. Nicholas Spadaccini, 261.
17. In the published edition, Carrizales is not technically a cuckold; however, he dies, ironically, believing that he is. In contrast, both the Porras manuscript and *The Old Jealous Man* make clear that there is no ambiguity surrounding the horns that the old husband wears.
18. Robert S. Wistrich, *Antisemitism: The Longest Hatred*, 27.
19. Carrizales does not want to share his money except with members of his own family, which is why he wants to marry in the first place.

"he resorted to the same course of action as many other desperate people in that city, namely, that of seeking passage to the Indies. This was the refuge and shelter of the nation's destitute, sanctuary of the bankrupt,[20] safe-conduct of murderers, asylum and hiding place of those players called sharpers by experts in the art, common attraction for loose women,[21] the collective delusion of many, and the personal redemption of few" (*ES*, 150) (se acogió al remedio a que otros muchos perdidos en aquella ciudad se acogen, que es el pasarse a las Indias, refugio y amparo de los desesperados de España, iglesia de los alzados, salvoconducto de los homicidas, pala y cubierta de los jugadores a quien llaman *ciertos* los peritos en el arte, añagaza general de mujeres libres, engaño común de muchos y remedio particular de pocos, *NE*, 99). In the phrase *church of the embezzlers* (*iglesia de los alzados*), the idea of a non-Christian temple, of ill-gotten money, is explicitly mentioned. However metaphorical the word *church* (*iglesia*) may seem, it appears here as a corrupt alternative to a Christian church and a Christian life. Some of the other immoral types to whom Carrizales is related metonymically can also be linked to anti-Semitic stereotypes: medieval and early modern Jews were frequently thought of as murderers (*los homicidas*), not only for the theological concept of deicide, but, more popularly, in widespread stories of ritual murder especially of children.[22] Additionally, Jewish men were often construed as pimps, who were thus associated with prostitutes (*mujeres libres*).[23]

The stereotypical anti-Semitic references (based on race and ethnicity, that is, on "bad blood") are reinforced by allusions in the novella to the Hebrew scriptures. The Jewish references are found primarily in the association of Carrizales with the Pentateuch's jeal-

20. I differ with Lipson's translation, "sanctuary of the bankrupt"; I prefer "church of the embezzlers."

21. This might also be translated as "prostitutes."

22. Wistrich, *Antisemitism*, 30–32. The common idea that Jews engaged in ritual murder of Christian children is referred to, among other places, in the *Cantigas de Santa María,* by Alfonso X, the Wise: "[T]his sixth one is about how Santa María resuscitated the little boy whom the Jew killed because he was singing 'Gaude Virgo Maria' [Beautiful Virgin Mary]" ([E]sta VIa é como Santa Maria resuscitou ao menino que o judeu matara porque cantava 'Gaude Virgo Maria,' 1:40, 121–22).

23. In Cervantes's *Persiles,* which I will study in Chapter 5, negative moral associations between Judaism and jealousy are evoked with the Jewish character "la cruel Julia" (*Los trabajos de Persiles y Sigismunda,* ed. Juan Bautista Avalle-Arce, 456).

ous God. When Carrizales first falls for Leonora, having seen her in a window, he explains how he will shape her will by enclosing her in a protected space and teaching her his version of moral action: "I will lock her up and mould her according to my desires, and this way she will have precisely the temperament I will teach her to have" (*ES*, 152) (encerraréla y haréla a mis mañas, y con esto no tendrá otra condición que aquella que yo le enseñaré, *NE*, 102). This is analogous to Jehovah's placement of Adam in the Garden of Eden and to the stricture against eating from the Tree of the Knowledge of Good and Evil, according to Genesis:[24] "And Jehovah God had planted a garden in Eden to the East, and there he put the man he had formed" (Y auia plantado Iehova Dios un huerto en Heden àl Oriente, y puso alli àl hombre que formó, 2:8; "And Jehovah commanded the man, saying, Of every tree in the garden you will eat; but from the tree of the knowledge of good and evil, you will not eat; because on the day on which you eat from it, you will die" (Y mandó pues Iehova àl hombre diziendo, De todo arbol del huertó comerás: Mas del arbol de scíencia de bien y de mal, no comeras deel: por que el dia que de el comieres, morirás, 2:16–17).[25] The fact that Carrizales then provides his wife with companionship in the form of "two young girls of Leonora's age, who had been acquired so that Leonora might be able to pass the time with girls of her own tender years" (*ES*, 154) (dos doncellas de la misma edad de Leonora, que para que se entretuviese con las de sus mismos años asimismo había recebido, *NE*, 104) can be read as a parody of Jehovah's creation of Eve to provide companionship to Adam, so that he would not feel alone: "And Jehova God said, It is not good that the man should be alone; I will make him a helper who stands before him" (Y dixo Iehova Dios, No es bueno, que el hombre esté solo[;] hazerlehé ayuda que esté delante deel, 2:18).

Moreover, when Leonora, the slaves, and the servants first arrive

24. The sequence of events is similar, too: first Carrizales has the special house prepared; then he places Leonora in it; then he instructs her.

25. Unless otherwise indicated, Spanish quotes from the Hebrew scriptures and Christian Bible are from the first edition of Casiodoro de Reina's *Biblia*. Published in 1569, it was the first post-Tridentine Spanish translation from the original languages of the Bible. Preceding Reina's translation of the "viejo y nuevo testamento" are the Council of Trent's decrees concerning the limited prohibition of printing or possessing the Bible in translation. In my citations, I have made standard orthographic changes (e.g., from *u* to *v*) and expanded common abbreviations. The English translations of Reina's Bible are mine, and are meant only as close translations of Reina's text.

at the house, Carrizales speaks to them about their duties and responsibilities with language that suggests a covenant: "As soon as they stepped inside Carrizales preached a sermon to them all, entrusting them with the care of Leonora and charging them never, by any manner of means, to allow anyone beyond the second door, not even the black eunuch" (*ES*, 154) (y entrando en ella les hizo Carrizales un sermón a todas, encargándoles la guarda de Leonora y que por ninguna vía ni en ningún modo dejasen entrar a nadie de la segunda puerta adentro, aunque fuese al negro eunuco, *NE*, 104). The old man promises them a land of plenty, echoing by analogy God's offer to Abraham, Isaac, and Jacob of great economic prosperity and fecundity for loyal service: "He promised that he would treat and indulge them in such a way that they would not resent their confinement" (*ES*, 154) (Prometióles que las trataría y regalaría a todas de manera que no sintiesen su encerramiento, *NE*, 104–5), and the servants, in turn, agreed to obey him, like their prototypes in the Pentateuch: "The maids and slaves promised to do all that he required of them cheerfully, willingly, and enthusiastically" (*ES*, 154–55) (Prometiéronle las criadas y esclavas de hacer todo aquello que les mandaba, sin pesadumbre, con pronta voluntad y buen ánimo, *NE*, 105). Furthermore, just as it was necessary for the Jews to build the ark of the covenant to the exact specifications of Jehovah, Carrizales's redesigning of the house he purchases for his wedded bliss is essential to his plan of divine-like control: "He blocked up all the windows which faced on to the street, replaced them with skylights [dióles vista al cielo],[26] and then proceeded to do the same with all the other windows in the house" (*ES*, 153) (cerró todas las ventanas que miraban a la calle, y dióles vista al cielo, y lo mismo hizo de todas las otras de casa, *NE*, 103).

Within the confines of her imprisonment, Leonora is given everything she needs, becoming materially spoiled. She spends her time playing with dolls and consuming sweets in a potentially eternal state of childlike ignorance. The environment of abundance, plentitude, sweetness, and simplicity can be read as a grotesque allegory of the state of blissful ignorance in which the first couple lived in Eden before eating the fruit of the tree of the knowledge of good

26. Lipson's translation here is far from the words in Spanish; I prefer the more exact "leaving them with a view of the sky." The Spanish word *cielo* used here means both "sky" and "heaven."

and evil. The old man takes care of his people, jealously, providing them with everything except freedom, as Alban K. Forcione has argued; they lack the freedom to live in the outside world and the freedom to make choices on their own: "and in order to pass the time more pleasurably they developed a sweet tooth and few days went by without them concocting a thousand delicacies sweetened with honey and sugar. They had more than ample provisions of what they needed to indulge this habit, and their master was more than happy to supply them with these things since it seemed to him that in keeping them entertained and occupied in this way, they had no opportunity to start thinking about their confinement" (*ES*, 155) (y ellas, por pasarle mejor, dieron en ser golosas, y pocos días se pasaban sin hacer mil cosas a quien la miel y el azúcar hacen sabrosas. Sobrábales para esto en grande abundancia lo que habían menester, y no menos sobraba en su amo la voluntad de dárselo, pareciéndole que con ello las tenía entretenidas y ocupadas, sin tener lugar donde ponerse a pensar en su encerramiento, *NE*, 105). In this "land of sugar and honey," the windows of his house are all walled up; the only way to look, for those inside, is toward the sky (*el cielo*), or rather, toward heaven (*el cielo*): "he raised the walls enclosing the roof terraces in such a way that anyone entering the house had to look directly to heaven because there was nothing else to see" (*ES*, 154) (levantó las paredes de las azuteas de tal manera que el que entraba en la casa había de mirar al cielo por línea recta, sin que pudiesen ver otra cosa, *NE*, 104). They look toward heaven, but not by choice. Their celestial gaze is imposed on them by a jealous old man in a perverse rendering of the Garden of Eden before the Fall.

Discourse is controlled by Carrizales, who is, in Forcione's apt phrase, a "censor." The old man's presence keeps the stories of the maids from lascivious themes: "The entire house was redolent of chastity, seclusion, and restraint: not one of the old wives' tales which the maids used to recount to one another around the fireside during the long winter evenings ever betrayed the slightest hint of bawdiness, due to his presence in their company" (*ES*, 156) (Toda su casa olía a honestidad, recogimiento y recato: aun hasta en las consejas que en las largas noches de invierno, en la chimenea, sus criadas contaban, por estar él presente, en ninguna ningún género de lascivia se descubría, *NE*, 106). More significantly, Carrizales limits the visual representations in the home to images of women and still lifes (as does his counterpart in the interlude *The Old Jealous Man*): "The figures represented in the wall hangings which decorated his halls and drawing-rooms were all women, flowers, and woodland scenes" (*ES,* 156) (Las figuras de los paños que sus salas y cuadras adornaban, todas eran hembras, flores y boscajes, *NE,* 106). The tapestries on the walls reinforce the paradisiacal allegory, as they contain only scenes of nature, such as those of a garden, and hence mimic Eden ekphrastically. Carrizales becomes here the God of the Pentateuch, who sought to limit representations of other beings, demanding exclusive adoration, as in Deuteronomy 4:23–24: "Make sure not to forget your covenant with Jehovah your God, for he made a covenant with you, and not to make any sculpture, or image of any thing, as Jehovah your God has commanded. Because Jehovah your God is a fire that consumes, a Jealous God" (Guardaos no os olvideys del Concierto de Iehova vuestro Dios, que el concertó con vosotros, y os hagays esculptura, imagen de qualquier cosa, como Iehova tu Dios te ha mandado. Porque Iehova tu Dios es fuego que consume, Dios Zeloso). The Judaic nature of this law against representations is again pronounced in Leviticus 26:1, "Do not make for yourselves idols or sculptures, or raise pillars or place painted stones to worship in your land; because I, Jehovah, am your God" (No hareys para vosotros idolos, ni esculptura, ni os levantareys titulo, ni pondreys en vuestra tierra piedra pintada para ynclinaros à ella: porque yo Iehova soy vuestro Dios). Cervantes associates the prohibition of representations with a hyperbolically jealous subject, creating an analogy between the jealous God of the *Pentateuch* and the jealous Extremaduran.

Carrizales aimed to create a new cosmic order in which he was the center, the only man without any possibility of a rival. This amounts to a parody of nascent monotheism, in which one man is god and women are mortals. The jealous Extremaduran behaves as a self-fashioned god, attempting to gain complete control over his worshippers, displaying a jealousy that goes beyond the scope of what can be considered amorous and is more like Jehovah's ontological jealousy. Like Carrizales, who is called "the most jealous man in the world," Jehovah is eponymously jealous: "Jehovah, whose name is Jealous, a Jealous God is he" (Iehova, cuyo nombre es Zeloso, Dios Zeloso es, Exodus 34:14). Carrizales's jealousy is not merely that of one person toward another, but rather a jealousy in the order of being, the jealousy of a creator toward the beings he creates; a jealousy that seeks not only to be the center of someone's world, but to be the center of the universe.[27] But in contrast to the biblical Jehovah, who rested on the seventh day, Carrizales dies—so the reader is told at the end of the novella—"on the seventh day" (*ES,* 184) (al seteno día, *NE,* 135).

Carrizales's rival, Loaysa, completes the symbolic scene of Eden, as he tempts Leonora before the Fall. To seduce her, the young man uses serpent-like falsehoods and trickery.[28] Appropriately, Loaysa is metonymically linked to "the astute one who disturbs the human race"[29] (el sagaz perturbador del género humano, *NE,* 106). Clearly, the phrase aptly describes the serpent of Genesis: "the serpent was more astute than all the animals in the countryside" (la serpiente erá astuta mas que todos los animales del campo, Genesis 3:1). The animal disturbs (*perturbar*) the possibility of eternal peace for the human race (*género humano*). Furthermore, the phrase even invites an allegorical reading, for "the astute one who disturbs the human race" alludes not to Loaysa as an individual, but to his more general and abstract role as a "disturber" having an effect on all humanity, that is, not just on Carrizales's house.

Carrizales's primary un-Christian aspect, from a theological perspective, is his extreme jealousy. In the Hebrew scriptures, jealousy is often applauded or condoned. But in the New Testament (Christian Bible), it is criticized and linked disparagingly to the Jews. For instance, in Acts of the Apostles 5:17–18, jealousy is related to the "heresy" of the Jews: "Then, the Prince of the Priests rose, and all those who were with him, which is the heresy of the Sadduccees, were filled with jealousy. And they grabbed the Apostles and put them in the public prison" (Entonces levantandose el Principe de los Sacerdotes, y todos los que eran con el, que es la heregia de los Sadduceos, fueron llenos de zelo. Y echaron mano à los Apostoles, y puseronlos en la carcel publica). The association between Jews and

27. I recall in this light Sartre's idea that jealousy is a (male) desire of "laying hold of the world" (Sartre, *Being and Nothingness,* 562).

28. "And the woman said, the Serpent tricked me, and I ate" (Y dixo la muger, La serpiente me engaño, y comi, Genesis 3:13).

29. This is my translation. Lipson translates this phrase as "Scheming Meddler" (156). *Perturbador* is defined as "One who causes, or incites disturbance and worry" (El que causa, ò es motivo de la perturbacion è inquietud), and *perturbar* as "To change and upset the order and harmony that things had, or the peace and quiet in which they were found" (Inmutar y revolver el orden y concierto que tenian las cosas, ò la quietud y sosiego en que se hallaban), according to the *Diccionario de Autoridades* (1726).

jealousy is later repeated: "Then the Jews, having seen the company, were full of jealousy" (Entonces los Iudios, vista la conpaña, fueron llenos de zelo,[30] Acts 13:45). In Paul's First Epistle to the Corinthians, the reader is told that jealousy is antithetical to becoming a Christian: "because among you there is jealousy" (porque aviendo entre vosotros celos, 3:3). For jealousy is not part of Christian love (charity): "Charity is patient, is kind: Charity is not envious [or jealous]"[31] (La Charidad es suffrida, es benigna: la Charidad no tiene embidia, 13:4). Returning to González Amezúa's claim concerning Carrizales's consistent Christianity, it is highly dubious that Carrizales is a "faithful Christian" throughout the novella in his imitation of Christ. On the contrary, the characterization of Carrizales is greatly at odds with the Christian Bible.

When Carrizales sees Leonora in the arms of a young man, he is extremely jealous. Although the "spirit of jealousy" has certainly entered him, he does not follow the rules for wife-testing prescribed by the Book of Numbers, nor does he claim his prerogative under the Mosaic law against adultery (nor under the strict rules of the honor code).[32] Instead, remarkably, he forgives them both for what he believes they have done. As Fray Hernando de Zárate noted in 1593 on the Christian essence of forgiveness, "he who forgives offenses against him, in this he resembles God his father" (el que perdona las ofensas suyas, en eso se parece a su padre Dios).[33] In contrast to Christ in the New Testament, the Hebrew God is often described as unforgiving: "because he is a Holy God, a Jealous

30. Reina's gloss on the word *zelo* demonstrates that he does not mean "zeal" but rather a jealousy akin to envy: "stupid and envious of the good of the people" (tonto y embidioso del bien de las Gentes).

31. Reina glosses this section to clarify that by *envidia* he means "envy or jealousy" (envidia o celos); he also notes, "Or, it is not jealous, without knowledge of God" (O, no es zelosa sin sciencia de Dios).

32. Furthermore, according to Proverbs 6:34, jealous revenge is the natural reaction of the husband: "Because the irate jealousy of the man will not pardon on the day of vengeance" (Porque el zelo sañudo del varon no perdonará en el dia de la vengança). The Book of Numbers, chapter 5, outlines what the husband should do "[i]f the spirit of jealousy should fall upon him, and he were jealous of his wife" ([s]i viniere sobre el espiritu de celo, y tuviere celos de su muger, 5:14); these steps were intended to lead to the woman's death if she were guilty of adultery.

33. Zárate, quoted in González Amezúa, *Cervantes,* 2:266. González Amezúa adds here "and Christ in the Gospels forgave the adulterous woman, limiting himself to saying 'sin no more. . . .'" (y Cristo en el Evangelio perdonó a la mujer adúltera, limitándose a decir 'no peques más. . . .').

God; he will not have patience with your rebellions, and your sins" (porque el es Dios Sancto, y Dios Zeloso: no suffrirá vuestras rebelliones, y vuestros peccados, Joshua 24:19). Cervantes depicts in this novella an allegorical early modern Christian interpretation of the Bible: the punishing God of the so-called Old Testament gives way to the forgiving Christ of the newer Gospels. Carrizales's deathbed is that of Judaism, a disparaged and misunderstood morality that lives on in the blood of the conversos through the anti-Semitic concept of "bad blood" (*mala sangre*) that was promulgated in the 1449 statutes known as "blood laws," or, more literally, "blood cleanliness" (*limpieza de sangre*), as historian Henry Kamen explains. After the expulsion and forced conversions of 1492, those Jews who remained faced continued anti-Semitism, in the form of blood purity laws restricting their rights: "[T]he statutes of *limpieza de sangre* . . . kept out so many innocent people not only from posts of honour and trust but also from entering churches, colleges, convents and even unions and trade guilds." The historian Yosef Yerushalmi interprets this restriction on conversos as one of mistrust: "[T]he traditional mistrust of the Jew as outsider now gave way to an even more alarming fear of the *converso* as insider."[34] Like Carrizales himself, who is denigrated in part because of his old age, the alleged moral decrepitude of Judaism is encapsulated in the very term used traditionally to describe the Hebrew scriptures, that is, *Old Testament* (*Viejo testamento*).[35] According to early Christian writings, jealousy is immoral because it prevents the actualization of love. Pointing out how Cervantes pits jealousy against love, Forcione contends that "Cervantes clearly reveals that the liberty to know and choose is intimately connected with the liberty to love" (80). Indeed, jealousy appears as an obstacle to pure Christian love in the novella,[36] a love evoked antithetically, that is, in contrast to what the text portrays as dark, dead Judaism.[37]

In Carrizales there is indeed a transformation, or, in other words,

34. Henry Kamen, *The Spanish Inquisition: A Historical Revision,* 317; Yosef Hayim Yerushalmi, *Assimilation and Racial Antisemitism: The Iberian and the German Models,* 10.

35. Reina's 1569 Bible is explicitly a translation of the "viejo y nuevo testamento."

36. Marcel Bataillon, *Erasmo y España,* 783.

37. Forcione, *Cervantes and the Humanist Vision,* 80. Forcione's essay on *The Jealous Old Man from Extremadura* posits an opposition between Protestantism and Erasmian Catholicism, not between Judaism and Christianity, as I am main-

a conversion. When he is wandering like other depraved and lost ones in the New World, as well as when he is older and marries Leonora, Carrizales is anything but a forgiving Christian. Entombing a live girl, he stifles her development by withholding moral and physical freedom, jealously guarding her from the envious rays of the sun. His act at the end of the novella signals his metamorphosis from what he was before to what he becomes. What is the function of this transformation?

Carrizales's final emotional fit is a case of evidential jealousy: "He saw Leonora lying in Loaysa's arms, and both of them sleeping as soundly as if it were they who were under the influence of the ointment rather than the jealous old man" (*ES*, 179) (Vio a Leonora en brazos de Loaysa, durmiendo tan a sueño suelto como si en ellos obrara la virtud del ungüento y no en el celoso anciano, *NE*, 130). The visual confirmation of his jealous suspicion is an intense moment in the novella so horrible for him that he wishes he had no sense of sight. The act of seeing the beloved in another man's arms first provokes a terrible physical reaction: "Carrizales's heart stopped beating as he gazed at this bitter spectacle; his voice stuck in his throat, his arms hung helpless at his side, and he stood as if turned into a cold marble statue" (*ES*, 179) (Sin pulsos quedó Carrizales con la amarga vista de lo que miraba; la voz se le pegó a la garganta, los brazos se le cayeron de desmayo, y quedó hecho una estatua de mármol frío, *NE*, 130). The description of his jealous anagnorisis evokes the image of a dead man, cold and without pulse. For a brief moment his jealous anger revives his body and ushers in the traditional revenge-of-the-husband motif, as the "spirit of jealousy" enters him.

The narrator's description at this point is highly distanced and ironic, evoking in this way the typical, expected response of the comedia husband. Indeed, Carrizales's instinctual yet fleeting moment of seeking revenge parodies the jealous husbands of the honor plays by Lope de Vega and others (who often dignified vengeful jealousy

---

taining here. However, I call these interpretations complementary because Forcione himself mentions several other analogous oppositions "which were obsessive preoccupations in the religious culture of the age and could not fail to leave their mark on all approaches to such problems as ethical choice and the nature of the individual, whether religious or secular," among which is the one on which I am focusing: "law and love, ritualism and freedom, ceremonialism and authentic individual action, and *Judaism and gospel liberty*" (*Cervantes and the Humanist Vision*, 73n62, emphasis added).

as an appropriate response), in an act of literary criticism based on ethical grounds. More specifically, Carrizales's brief spark of vengefulness is suggestive in its allusion to the Veinticuatro's deeds in *The Commanders of Cordoba*.

In Chapter 1, I demonstrated how the Veinticuatro—like other honor-bound husbands, such as Peribáñez—was not guided solely by a rational sense of honor, but also by his jealousy, which is partially irrational. But the comedia privileges honor, condoning the Veinticuatro's behavior through the voice of the king. Focusing only on his protagonist's jealousy throughout the story, in the moment before the transformation, Cervantes has Carrizales think about his honor, as he encapsulates the climax of Lope's drama:

> Although anger worked its natural effect on him by reviving his dying spirits, his grief was so overwhelming that it would not allow him to draw breath. Yet he would have exacted the *revenge* which that great misdeed demanded of him if he had had weapons to hand. He therefore decided to go back to his room to fetch a *dagger,* and then to return to *remove the stains on his honour by shedding the blood* of his two enemies, even the blood of the entire household. Having made this *honourable* and necessary resolution, he returned to his room as silently and cautiously as he had come, whereupon his grief and anguish weighed so heavily on his spirits that, too feeble to do anything else, he fell in a faint across his bed. (*ES,* 179, emphasis added)

> ([Y] aunque la cólera hizo su natural oficio, avivándole los casi muertos espíritus, pudo tanto el dolor, que no le dejó tomar aliento. Y, con todo eso, tomara la *venganza* que aquella grande maldad requería si se hallara con armas para poder tomarla; y así, determinó volver a su aposento a tomar una *daga,* y volver a sacar *las manchas de su honra con sangre* de sus dos enemigos, y aun con toda aquella de toda la gente de su casa. Con esta determinación *honrosa* y necesaria volvió, con el mismo silencio y recato que había venido, a su estancia, donde le apretó el corazón tanto el dolor y la angustia que, sin ser poderoso a otra cosa, se dejó caer desmayado sobre el lecho. *NE,* 130, emphasis added)

In Carrizales's sudden decision to get the dagger, Américo Castro also detects a similarity to the plot of Lope's famous comedia. For Castro, the alternate ending of forgiveness is a way for Cervantes to distance his work from mass theater. I read the correlation as much stronger.[38] Like the Veinticuatro, Carrizales feels anger (*cólera*) and grief (*dolor*). When he imagines his vengeance, he thinks of shedding blood, and not just that of the adulterers, but "even the blood of the entire household." The terms *honor* (*honra*) and *honorable* (*honrosa*) both appear here as his concern for the very first time, though Carrizales has not worried about honor in the least until this very moment.[39] Indeed, he has led a largely dishonorable life, as we are told in the opening paragraphs (where he is compared to embezzlers, murderers, and prostitutes). His jealousy—unlike that of the jealous husbands of the comedias—has never been bound up with honor at all. That he thinks of honor now is an instance of his genre-bending, that is, his behaving like a theatrical character for the narrator's purpose of ironizing that response. The theatrical parody is reinforced by earlier allusions to Carrizales's dramatic nature: when he is nervously planning to ask for Leonora's hand, the narrator tells the audience, "Having recited this soliloquy not once but a hundred times, after a few days he spoke with Leonora's parents"[40] (Y así hecho este *soliloquio,* no una vez, sino *ciento,* al cabo de algunos días habló con los padres de Leonora, *NE,* 103, emphasis added). The term *soliloquy,* with its ironic grandiloquence, explicitly evokes the stage, as does the image of Carrizales rehearsing how he would ask for Leonora's hand a hundred times. Additionally, there is a theatrical element to the "singing" and "dancing" of the women around Loaysa, as these activities would have been part of most comedia productions of the day. In *The Commanders of Cordoba,* the luxurious and sensuous ambiance in the house in the scenes just preceding the honor-cleansing—witnessed in the women's preparation

38. Castro does not suggest, as I do, that Cervantes is specifically parodying Lope's play, but rather that his literary conception was different: "Thus the theme of the Commanders of Cordoba is made out—historical and poetic for Lope de Vega—but here this goes no further than being an illusory action." Castro describes what he sees as Cervantes's attempt to distance himself: "But the rejection of bloody vengeance in a case of adultery was also a way to distance himself from popular fashions, which were celebrated by Lope de Vega in his theater" (*Hacia Cervantes,* 342).

39. The word *honor* is only mentioned once previously in the novella, with respect to Leonora's thoughts, not Carrizales's.

40. This is my translation. Lipson translates this as "After repeating these words to himself, not once but a thousand times over the course of several days, he eventually spoke to Leonora's parents" (*ES,* 153); most importantly, I have chosen to translate the Spanish word *soliloquio* more closely, as "soliloquy."

for their adulterous lovemaking, as they spread perfumed sheets on the beds—is mimicked in the Dionysiac *singing* and *dancing* of the women under the influence of Loaysa. In their relationship to Pentateuchal themes, the singing and dancing might be evocative of the breaking of the covenant by the Israelites in the absence of Moses, and of his angry reaction upon his return from the desert, when he heard them with Aaron, *singing* and *dancing* around a young, new, and beautiful god: the golden calf. These actions were a direct violation of Jehovah's jealous command concerning nonrepresentation and idolatry. Not surprisingly, singing and dancing were often considered immoral in early modern Europe and were linked explicitly to this biblical scene of a broken covenant (for instance, in the woodcut illustration of Chapter 58 of Sebastian Brant's *Ship of Fools*).[41] In effect, the Veinticuatro's wife and niece, as well as Carrizales's eunuch and women, have broken their covenants with the Veinticuatro and Carrizales, respectively.[42]

The theatrical elements used to develop Carrizales's character and to evoke the ambiance of theater serve as a prefiguration for the most jealous husband's final sally onto the parodic stage. At the point in the novella in which he could try to seek revenge, the jealous

---

41. Attributed to Albrecht Dürer, the woodcut depicts a group of fools dancing around the golden calf. Brant's poem was composed in German and published in 1494 as *Narrenshiff*. It was soon translated into Latin as *Stultifera Navis* (1497) and reproduced in numerous editions all over Europe. An edition of a Latin text, *Stultiferae Naves* (The Ships of Women Fools), by Jacobus Ascenscius Badocus, which is loosely based on Brant's poem, was published in Burgos ca. 1500. Additionally, I would argue that López de Yanguas's poem, *Los triumphos de la locura* (The Triumphs of Madness [1521]), is indebted to both Badocus's and Brant's poems.

42. It is reasonable to search for such a reference to Lope's very famous play, based on an extremely popular ballad, in a work by Cervantes published about fifteen years after the first performance of the comedia, particularly given the well-known hostile sentiments Cervantes felt toward Lope's tremendous fame in Madrid at the time, in the full glory of what he disparagingly called the "comic monarchy." Cervantes also seems to parody *The Commanders of Cordoba* in his *entremés* titled *La cueva de Salamanca,* in which the *engañado* Pancracio (like the Veinticuatro) praises the faithfulness and chastity of his wife upon leaving on a trip and again upon his return (ahead of schedule). The traits he praises are in complete opposition to her true character, which is adulterous and scheming (she is hypocritical, like Doña Beatriz, and, as in Lope's play, she even has an accomplice—Cristina—who is having an affair with Leonarda's lover's friend, *el barbero*). However, Cervantes is more generous to the wife in that, not only does she succeed in continuing her affair, but also her lament concerning her lot in life is expressed sympathetically to the audience (247).

avenging husband (of the comedia) is no longer a fictional possibility. Like Don Quixote at the end of part 2, Carrizales goes to bed to die, his fictional illusion shattered. And the negative exemplary lesson to the reader should be this: the very honor that prided itself on blood pure of Jewish or Moorish taint (*limpieza de sangre*) is found to be ideologically sullied.[43] The anti-Semitic characterization of Carrizales—before his conversion—links the honor-bound, unforgiving husband with a Jewish origin, betraying the honor code's other main concern: that the family line not be tainted by Semitic blood. With Carrizales's change of heart, the symbolic Jew of jealous revenge is dead, to be reborn, upon his awakening, as the forgiving Christian: "'I do not blame you, ill-advised child'—and saying this he leaned forward and kissed Leonora's face as she lay unconscious—" (*ES*, 182) ([A] ti no te culpo, ¡o niña mal aconsejada!—y diciendo esto se inclinó y besó el rostro de la desmayada Leonora— *NE*, 133). Carrizales's conversion is complete; no longer following the letter of the law, he is moved by an internal disposition to forgiveness.

In this largely negative exemplum, Cervantes's criticism is meant to point out the absurdity of the jealous husband's actions. In the chapters above on Lope de Vega's drama, it is clear that male jealousy is usually treated quite seriously, related as it is to questions of honor. Like Carrizales's targetless jealous mood, these husbands must be jealous even before they have a wife, because they always have to protect their honor, which, to be most effective, requires jealousy (as we learn from Peribáñez). In addition, the Veinticuatro, the Duke of Ferrara, and Peribáñez all achieve grandeur from coming to grips with their emotion and acting on it. However, by relating jealousy to quasireligious and stereotypically anti-Semitic racial and ethnic attributes, Cervantes's novella strips it of all its propriety *before* the act of violence is considered, while the moral reprehensibility of the emotion is seen through the baseness of the man who experiences it.

Cervantes seems to have discerned that it is not solely a rational sense of honor that brings the Veinticuatro and other husbands to mass murder, but rather, an irrational form of pathological jealousy. Parodying Lope's ending, Cervantes's novella attempts to portray jealousy as neither honorable nor befitting a hero of the Christian

---

43. For Américo Castro's ideas on honor and blood purity in the Middle Ages, see *De la edad conflictiva*.

Reconquest such as Lope's Veinticuatro; rather, for Cervantes, jealousy is an obsessive feeling experienced by a cruel, old Semite. Ultimately, Cervantes's critique of the values of the honor play relies on negative stereotypes of Jews and conversos at a symbolic level. Cervantes draws upon the cultural vocabulary and stereotypes of his day to denigrate social practices deemed honorable by the society at large, which for him were abhorrent, by showing their internal contradiction: the rules of the honor code conflict; hence, it is an inherently irrational system.[44] The exemplarity of the story consists in demonstrating that the revered honor code is flawed and un-Christian. From the perspective of our time, Cervantes's allegory is morally troublesome: while attempting to enlighten readers of the ills of society—which would seem to indicate that he is an engaged author who is critical of his time—the allegory relies on the condemnation of the Other to make its point, what today might be considered bigoted and considerably less progressive than the Cervantes that most readers envision. In recent decades, some scholars have held that Miguel de Cervantes was a socially progressive writer with almost twenty-first-century sensibilities on gender, race, human freedom, and equality. He has been said to have denounced, through his literary writings, the institution of slavery, the subjection of women, and the discrimination of Christians against Jews, Moors, and Gypsies.[45] While these interpretations are popular, they are also being seriously questioned.[46] Certainly, the author of *Don Quixote* was not an outright promoter of misogyny or racism, and it is

---

44. The principle of noncontradiction is fundamental to rationality and logic.

45. For example, Joseph Ricapito discusses Cervantes as a "sympathizer" of the "marginalized" (Ricapito, *Formalistic Aspects of Cervantes' "Novelas ejemplares,"* 12–36), while Diana de Armas Wilson argues for Cervantes's protofeminism (*Allegories of Love: Cervantes' "Persiles and Sigismunda,"* 248–52).

46. Theresa Ann Sears, for instance, disputes de Armas Wilson's view, arguing that Cervantes's depictions of women most often fall into a very small number of traditional categories: "The tendency in recent criticism is to present a protofeminist Cervantes, an anti-Girardian who creates strong, free women and tender, sensitive men, both of whom are liberated from traditional roles, structures, and conflicts, into what de Armas Wilson has called '*learned* relations of complementarity and adjacency' (xv). . . . I have come to see this as a willfully unnuanced reading of the Cervantes corpus. A close look at the feminine characters and their decisions, as well as their fates, in the *Persiles* will help us to see why we must revise, yet again, our view of this most complex and often infuriating writer" (Sears, "Sacrificial Lambs and Domestic Goddesses, or, Did Cervantes Write Chick Lit? [Being a Meditation on Women and Free Will]," 54).

not my intention to demonize Cervantes as xenophobic or racist. Nor was Cervantes an apologist for the ills of his society, but, in a more complicated way, while he was alert to some of these, he was—like almost all of his contemporaries—simply not attentive to others.[47]

47. Even Bartolomé de las Casas, the sixteenth-century Dominican friar whose forceful defense of the rights of America's indigenous peoples earned him the title "Protector of the Indians," apparently saw nothing wrong with the enslavement of Africans. In Chapter 2, I quoted McKendrick's words on Golden Age male dramaturges' acceptance of patriarchal hierarchies, and it seems fitting to reiterate them here: "[O]ne cannot expect miracles, even of the great" (McKendrick, *Woman and Society,* 334). To deny that early modern Spanish ideology was virulently anti-Semitic is to cast a fog over the popular uprisings against Jews (such as the pogroms of 1391), the expulsion of 1492, and the racist blood laws against conversos that remained in effect throughout the seventeenth century.

Five
Cervantes's Virtuous Jealousy

> [I]t is important for a responsible, reflective, moral adult who experiences jealousy to know the aetiology of jealousy, and to know how many ways the emotion can lead one astray from the path of truth and appropriate and proportionate response, and how one's actions out of jealousy can be volatile, destructive of one's own purposes, and damaging to the other's sense of freedom.
>
> —Peter Goldie, *The Emotions: A Philosophical Exploration*

Although copious and multifarious, Cervantes's representations of jealousy are highly consistent in moral valence throughout his work, and tend to hold across generic boundaries (in prose, poetry, and drama). Indeed, the negativity of jealousy seems unequivocal in most of Cervantes's work, in whichever form it takes, be it novel, novella, ballad, comedia, interlude, or pastoral romance.[1] Examples of a monstrous jealousy are to be found everywhere in Cervantes's work. For instance, in the poem "The Ballad of Jealousy," jealousy lives in a cave filled with serpents, from which horrible moans are heard, and causes the death of poor Lauso, recalling the topos of dying from the effects of jealousy in the sentimental romance.[2] In the comedia *La casa de los celos* (The House of Jealousy), the emotion

---

1. His constant preoccupation with it, however, points toward its value as a literary theme. Denis de Rougemont asks rhetorically of adultery in *Love in the Western World,* "Without adultery, what would happen to imaginative writing?" (16). This statement would apply equally well to the role of jealousy in Cervantes.

2. It is well known that this was Cervantes's favorite among his *romances:* "I have written an infinite number of ballads, and the ballad of jealousy is the one I esteem among others that I find are quite bad" (Yo he compuesto romances infinitos / y el de los celos es aquel que estimo / entre otros que los tengo por malditos, *Viaje del Parnaso,* 4:40–42). Regarding the sentimental romance, Pa-

pervades all levels of the drama.[3] As others have noted, the vivid, symbolic stage directions in act 2 that describe the deathly jealousy "that inhabits this cave . . . with its blue tunic, on which are painted snakes and lizards, with a white, black and blue lock of hair" (que habitan esta cueva . . . con su tunicela azul, pintada en ella sierpes y largartos con una cabellera blanca, negra y azul) are similar to the descriptions in the ballad. In the comedia, jealousy is analyzed into allegoral parts that exit the cave: first, "despicable suspicion," followed by "curiosity," then "hopelessness" (*desesperación*), which finally causes death.[4] Stanislav Zimic's convincing interpretation of *The House of Jealousy* describes it as wholly malevolent. For Zimic, the play is unified by the theme of "egoism"—a notion quite similar to Américo Castro's and Ruth El Saffar's ideas on "solipsism" concerning *The Jealous Old Man from Extremadura*—from which all of the lovers suffer. Such egoism indicates that their love is not good, for it is only hypocritical self-love, that is, not true love.[5]

Similarly, in Cervantes's dramatic interlude *El juez de los divorcios* (The Divorce Judge), jealousy is an ill, considered one among many of women's negative attributes: "you are always grouchy, angry, *jealous,* worried, spendthrift, sleepy, lazy, quarrelsome, growling, and other effronteries of this kind which are enough to consume the lives of two hundred husbands" (andáis siempre rostrituerta, enojada, *celosa,* pensativa, manirrota, dormilona, perezosa, pendenciera, gruñidora, con otras insolencias deste jaez, que bastan a consumir las vidas de doscientos maridos). The hyperbolic statement connotes that jealousy disrupts peace and leads to death. In another scene in the same interlude, Minjaca pleads in front of the judge for a divorce from her husband "for four hundred [reasons]," among which the third is "because he is jealous of the sun that touches me" (porque tiene celos del sol que me toca), something of which the wives in both

---

tricia Grieve notes in *Desire and Death in the Spanish Sentimental Romance (1440–1550)*: "Once again [in *Cárcel de amor*], as in *Arnalte y Lucenda*, jealousy has sparked violence, a violence which turned against the jealous person" (49).

3. Maxime Chevalier points out that "the center of interest of th[is] *comedia* . . . resides in a series of variations on the theme of jealous passion" (Chevalier, *L'Arioste en Espagne [1530–1650]*, 442, quoted in Combet, *Cervantès ou les incertitudes du désir,* 329).

4. Cervantes, *La casa de los celos,* 181–82, 183. Note the use of typical jealousy symbols, such as the serpents and the color blue, which are common especially in the lyric tradition and will be discussed further in Chapters 6 and 7.

5. Stanislav Zimic, *El teatro de Cervantes,* 119–38.

The Old Jealous Man and *The Jealous Old Man from Extremadura* also complain.[6] Moreover, in a very different genre—the pastoral romance of *The Galatea*—the idealized world of peace and harmony is interrupted by violent incursions associated with jealousy. As Barbara Mujica has noted, these disturb the serenity of the pastoral, just as they did in *The House of Jealousy.*

Furthermore, in *Don Quixote,* jealous characters, situations, and subplots enliven numerous passages. For instance, to name but a few prominent examples, in Cardenio's tale, the intersecting love triangles almost lead to characters' deaths; in Ambrosio's recounting of Grisóstomo's story, the reader is told that jealousy is a form of delusion: "jealous imaginings and feared suspicions bothered Grisóstomo as if they were true" (le fatigaban a Grisóstomo los celos imaginados y las sospechas temidas como si fueran verdaderas); these obsessive, contrary-to-fact ideas lead to his death, which is most likely a suicide, as evinced by the theologically loaded term *hopelessness (desesperación).*[7] And in one last example from *Don Quixote,* in "The Tale of Foolish Curiosity," Lothario's jealousy of Camila's faithfulness leads to the tragic denouement after he sees a strange man leaving the house at night. Indeed, an un-ironically negative jealousy appears to permeate most of Cervantes's work.

Arising from this abundance of negative representations, an unusually strong consensus has arisen in Cervantine criticism that the emotion is an obstacle to true love, in the work of Cervantes. In this vein, Marcel Bataillon explains,

> From *The Galatea* to the *Persiles,* Cervantes caressed the idea of a love that was so elevated that it made itself inaccessible to jealousy. This reminds one of the purified but unreal humanity of pastoral romance. There is a beautiful page in Gil Polo's *Diana* against jealous suspicions: this sickness, this fever of love stricken hearts is scrutinized there with a severity which foretells Descartes's *Passions of the Soul.* Cervantes must have loved this page, which left in him a lasting trace. The insistence

6. Cervantes, *El juez de los divorcios,* 105–6 (emphasis added), 107. Recalling the Judaic characterization of Carrizales in *The Jealous Old Man from Extremadura,* Minjaca's husband is a surgeon (*cirujano*), thus he belongs to a stereotypically Jewish or converso profession.

7. Cervantes, *El ingenioso hidalgo don Quijote de la Mancha,* 1.14:184. The same term, *desesperación,* is used to describe one of the allegorical components of hellish jealousy in *The House of Jealousy* (183).

with which he returns time and again, in his novels and his stories, to this reproof of jealousy demonstrates that it was, in his judgment, not simply an affectation from the world of poetic shepherds but a fundamental truth.[8]

Arriving at a similar conclusion, Agustín González Amezúa argues from a negative perspective that Cervantes, the man, was certainly no lover because he could not appreciate the "truth" about jealousy, that is, that it is always a part of love: "Because jealousy is consubstantial and inseparable from true love . . ."[9] From Amezúa to Zimic, the critical appraisals signal considerable unanimity that there is a concept of "pure" or "true" love in Cervantes that, as Bataillon phrased it, is "inaccessible to jealousy." In large part, such considerations are accurate, as examples from a plethora of Cervantine texts clearly illustrate (as did the previous chapter's study of *The Jealous Old Man from Extremadura*). Nevertheless, critics have overlooked an important caveat, which is elaborated in Cervantes's last novel.

The Trials of Persiles and Sigismunda (1617)

In *The Trials of Persiles and Sigismunda,* the specter of jealousy is raised continuously and, for the most part, pejoratively. It is mentioned with such insistence that Juan Bautista Avalle-Arce remarks on it in his edition of the novel the first time the theme is evoked. His view concurs with that which I have identified as the critical consensus regarding pure love without jealousy: "This reference to jealousy is the first chord in what, throughout the entire novel, will develop into a majestic theme. Cervantes's concern with jealousy, evident in all of his work, indicates the ideal of pure love that he held on to, free of such despicable problems."[10] To be sure, the novel is largely about jealousy, and even its absence from certain sections calls attention to its importance. Recalling the metanarratorial comments

---

8. Bataillon, *Erasmo y España,* 783.

9. González Amezúa, *Cervantes,* 2:237. In this passage, González Amezúa is responding to Bataillon; he continues: "[Jealousy] is like the title of ownership that the person who loves exhibits . . . like a vigilant sentry who watches over this treasure of the soul." This view makes Cervantes contrast harshly with Lope de Vega, whose personal jealousy was briefly explored in Chapter 3, in relation to his writing.

10. Avalle-Arce, ed., *Persiles,* 22n21.

in *Don Quixote,* the narrator of the *Persiles* has allegedly censored a part of the manuscript that he is translating that had been dedicated wholly to a definition of jealousy because it was too long and repetitive: "It seems the author of this story knew more about being in love than being a historian, because he spends almost all this first opening chapter of the second book on a definition of jealousy prompted by the jealousy Auristela felt regarding what the ship's captain told her; but in this translation—for that's what it is—it has been removed because it's too tedious—besides being a topic often aired and discussed; instead we go straight to the truth of the matter" (Parece que el autor desta historia sabía más de enamorado que de historiador, porque casi este primer capítulo de la entrada del segundo libro le gasta todo en una definición de celos, ocasionados de los que mostró tener Auristela por lo que le contó el capitán del navío; pero en esta traducción, que lo es, se quita por prolija, y por cosa en muchas partes referida y ventilada, y se viene a la verdad del caso).[11]

The novel's narrator sets the stage for the harsh judgment of jealousy early on. In book 1, chapter 2, he describes, counterfactually, what Arnaldo (who believes erroneously that Periandro and Auristela are siblings, as they maintain) would have felt had he known that Periandro (who was actually Persiles) was not really the brother of Auristela with the phrase "the cruel lance of jealousy" (dura lanza de los celos), a metaphor that parodies Cupid's "arrow wound of love" (flechazo de amor) and is thus contrary to love. This affords the narrator an opportunity to ponder the enormous strength of jealousy: "[T]he thought that he was a man would have pierced his soul with the cruel [*dura*] lance of jealousy whose point dares penetrate the facets of the sharpest diamond. I mean to say that jealousy breaks through all security and prudence, the armor of love-stricken hearts" (*TP,* 24) ([E]l considerar que era varón le traspasara el alma con la dura lanza de los celos, cuya punta se atreve a entrar por las del más agudo diamante: quiero decir, que los celos rompen toda seguridad

---

11. Miguel de Cervantes, *The Trials of Persiles and Sigismunda, A Northern Story,* trans. Celia Richmond Weller and Clark A. Colahan, 101; Cervantes, *Los trabajos de Persiles y Sigismunda,* ed. Juan Bautista Avalle-Arce, 159. All English translations of the *Persiles* are those of Weller and Colahan, and all quotes in Spanish are to the edition of Avalle-Arce. Subsequent citations will be made parenthetically in the text by page number using the abbreviations *TP* (the *Persiles*) and *EP* (el *Persiles*).

y recato, aunque dél se armen los pechos enamorados, *EP,* 60). The power of male jealousy is hyperbolically destructive, as it can break even the hardest diamond (a strong, precious, and beautiful jewel). Later on, the violence of Arnaldo's jealous fury against Periandro is posited as a possibility to be feared. Although such statements in the novel are frequently counterfactual, the narrator is shown to be right in the case of Arnaldo. In book 4, chapter 4, Arnaldo speaks from experience of how the "disease" (*enfermedad*) of jealousy is worse than death itself: "Even though the causes leading to it are small, the effects it produces are great, depriving him, at the least, of his judgment, and at the most, of his life, for a jealous suitor finds it better to die in desperation than live with jealousy" (*TP,* 314) ([Y] aunque son pequeñas las causas que la engendran, los efetos que hace son grandes, que por lo menos quitan el seso, y por lo más menos, la vida; que mejor es al amante celoso el morir desesperado, que vivir con celos, *EP,* 426). For the male subject in Cervantes, the living hell of jealousy can be worse than death. Arnaldo's perspicuous analysis of jealousy, in which little causes engender great effects, points to Goldie's useful notion of proportionality of the emotions. This apparently paradoxical feature of jealousy demonstrates yet another reason why it is so mysterious. In fact, it is almost magical in the way it seems to work contrary to the rules of the natural world, in which small causes should produce like effects, and large effects should be produced by causes of consistent magnitude. Vives explained this disproportionality in the following way: "[T]he jealous person jumps at, seizes and exaggerates in his mind every little rumor in the air, adding the most unfair slander in every detail."[12]

Like the narrator, the title character, Persiles (who throughout most of the novel hides his real identity under the name *Periandro*), also condemns jealousy when lecturing the Valencian shepherdess he meets on the outskirts of Villareal: "Beautiful shepherdess, if it's jealousy, neither feel it nor provoke it, because if you feel jealousy you diminish your self-respect, and if you provoke it, your reputation. If the man who loves you is wise, knowing your worth he'll value you and love you well, and if he isn't, why would you want his love?" (*TP,* 259) (Hermosa zagala, si son celos, ni los pidas ni los des, porque si los pides, menoscabas tu estimación y si los das, tu crédito; y si es que

12. Vives, *Passions of the Soul,* 87.

el que te ama tiene entendimiento, conociendo tu valor, te estimará y te querrá bien, y si no le tiene, ¿para qué quieres que te quiera? *EP,* 360). That one should neither be jealous nor cause another to experience jealousy would seem to point to an unequivocally negative appraisal of jealousy by the story's hero. This passage demonstrates well the rational manner in which Periandro approaches the subject of conduct as it intersects with the emotions. His *dispositio* contains a logical demonstration, and he uses palpable *elocutio* by finishing with a rhetorical question obliterating the need for her to experience jealousy at all.

Another of the harshest condemnations of jealousy in the *Persiles* is again made by Periandro to the main female character, Sigismunda (who, likewise, is hiding her true identity, under the name *Auristela*). Like Lope de Vega's Beatriz and Casilda, Auristela fears that her beloved's eye will wander toward the beauty of another woman, in this case, "peerless Sinforosa" (la sin par Sinforosa). Her passion is so devastating that it causes her to become physically ill. In a letter to her, Periandro describes jealousy as a malevolent force that has driven her out of her wits:

> [I]t seems to me that either you don't know me or have forgotten yourself. Come to your senses, my lady, and don't let an empty and jealous suspicion make you forget the wisdom of your level-headed judgment and exceptional mind. Remember who you are and don't forget who I am; in yourself you'll recognize the greatest good any man could desire and in me all the steadfast love anyone could imagine. Then holding fast to this wise thought you'll never fear that other beauties might inflame me, nor imagine your incomparable beauty and virtue eclipsed by any other. . . . [L]ay aside fruitless jealousy and unfounded suspicions. (*TP,* 123–24)

> ([O] que no me conoces o que te has olvidado de ti misma; vuelve, señora, en ti, y no te haga una vana presunción celosa salir de los límites de la gravedad y peso de tu raro entendimiento. Considera quién eres, y no te se olvide de quién yo soy, y verás en ti el término del valor que puede desearse, y en mí el amor y la firmeza que puede imaginarse; . . . no temas que ajenas hermosuras me enciendan, ni imagines que a tu incomparable virtud y belleza otra alguna se anteponga. . . . [Q]uéndense aparte celos infructuosos y mal nacidas sospechas. *EP,* 188).

Imitating the content of his speech to the Valencian shepherdess, while adapting it to his personal circumstances, Periandro insists that he is virtuous, and she, worthy of love; thus, she has no reason to doubt his constancy. Again, his rational, eloquent mode of argumentation implies that jealousy is wholly irrational, and furthermore, that it is a form of insanity, or unreason. For her part, the reader is told, Sinforosa herself would be jealous, counterfactually, if she knew that Periandro and Auristela were not siblings (*EP,* 167). Jealousy, which is usually a hell for the subject, is now imaged as such for the male beloved of whom a female lover is jealous, as Periandro explains, "I'll request our departure from this land with all diligence and dispatch, for it seems to me that on leaving it I'll leave behind the Hell of my torment and come out into the Heaven of seeing you free from jealousy" (*TP,* 124) (La partida desta tierra solicitaré con toda diligencia y brevedad, porque me parece que, en salir della, saldré del infierno de mi tormento a la gloria de verte sin celos, *EP,* 188). Furthermore, in a series of images that recall Cañizares's obsessive jealousy in *The Old Jealous Man,* Periandro implores Auristela not to be jealous (although she is not actually present): "[W]hen two people love each other very much jealousy is stirred up just by the touch of the passing breeze, by the sunlight that falls on them, and even by the ground on which they walk. My lady . . . don't wound your dignity or your beauty and don't deprive me of the glory of my steadfast intentions" (*TP,* 121) ([Q]ue los celos se engendran, entre los que bien se quieren, del aire que pasa, del sol que toca, y aun de la tierra que pisa . . . [N]o hagas agravio a tu valor ni a tu belleza, ni me quites a mí la gloria de mis firmes pensamientos, *EP,* 185).

In another pertinent example in book 2, Policarpo's jealousy, which has been provoked by "malicious Cenotia," is explicitly imaged as illness and associated with the devil: "In short, the fury of the hellish disease of jealousy . . . took control of his soul" (*TP,* 148) (En fin, la rabia de la endemoniada enfermedad de los celos se le apoderó del alma, *EP,* 218). Jealousy is thus equated with demonic possession (*endemoniada*). Moreover, in book 4, Auristela becomes physically sick again, an illness brought about this time not by her own jealousy (which she has learned to overcome through reason) but by a spell cast upon her, on behalf of Hipólita, who is in love with Periandro. Hipólita enjoins the Jewish witch "cruel Julia" (la cruel Julia, *EP,* 456) to kill Auristela. The alliterative and vowel play emphasize her Judaic nature—*Julia, la judía, injuria*—creating an association between Jewishness and malignant jealousy that recalls Cervantes's characterization of Carrizales in *The Jealous Old Man from Extremadura*.[13] Typically, the most negative associations of jealousy in this novel are with female characters (Cenotia, Auristela, the Valencian shepherdess, Hipólita, Julia). It is seen as an evil, a sickness, and often linked to witchcraft. However, jealousy also has a positive role in the novel. In contrast to malignant jealousy, the good kind seems limited to that of male characters, and in particular, to Periandro's.

Both Periandro himself as well as the narrator discuss legitimate male jealousy: in book 2, the narrator declares, "There are three reasons for which a sensible man may legitimately weep: first, because he has sinned; second, because he has obtained pardon for it; and third, because he is jealous; all other tears are out of place on a dignified countenance" (*TP,* 116) (Por tres cosas es lícito que llore el varón prudente: la una, por haber pecado; la segunda, por alcanzar perdón dél; la tercera por estar celoso: las demás lágrimas no dicen bien en un rostro grave, *EP,* 178). Thus, when Periandro passes out and "cries as a jealous man," his behavior is "licit." His emotional reaction is based on a fear of losing Auristela, a fear that is correctly intuited by her and that is brought on by her telling him, not that she loves another man, but rather that she plans to abandon the pilgrimage and their plans of marriage to confine herself to a monastery (she has decided to give up on their quest).

More important to the reevaluation of jealousy as a positive emotion is Periandro's reflection on the topic of the Academy debate in Milan, "If there can be love without jealousy" (si puede haber amor sin celos). The announcement of the debate opens a space for Periandro to elaborate on the relationship between jealousy and love. Agreeing with a bold *sí* to the claim made in the debate's title, Periandro states that there *can* be love without jealousy. This view would be the "unrealistic" variety that Bataillon and others have privileged in their analyses. To his statement, Auristela adds that all love suffers from "fears" (*temores*): "And it seems to me love can never ever be free from such fears" (*TP,* 291) (a mí me parece que no puede

13. Furthermore, there is structural, thematic, and ideological similarity here to the poisoning of the title character in Cervantes's *El licenciado Vidriera* (The Glass Graduate) by the woman who is in love with him; in that novella, the woman hires another racial outsider, a Morisca, to administer the love potion that almost kills him and then drives him mad.

estar libre el amor [de temores] en ninguna manera, *EP,* 401).[14] Periandro then agrees with her and elaborates further. Strangely, he winds up professing not only that love can coexist with one type of jealousy—*temores*—but also, and more significantly, that the latter is a necessary companion to love: "'You've said a lot, my lady.... There's no one in love who, possessing what he loves, isn't afraid of losing it. There's no good fortune so solid it can't sway from side to side. There's no nail so strong it can stop the spin of the wheel of fortune. And if the desire that moves us to come quickly to the end of our journey didn't prevent it, perhaps today in the Academy I'd show there can be love without jealousy, but not without fears" (*TP,* 291) (Mucho has dicho, señora.... porque no hay ningún amante que esté en posesión de la cosa amada, que no tema el perderla; no hay ventura tan firme, que tal vez no dé vaivenes; no hay clavo tan fuerte que pueda detener la rueda de la fortuna; y si el deseo que nos lleva a acabar presto nuestro camino no lo estorbara, quizá mostrara yo hoy en la academia, que puede haber amor sin celos, pero no sin temores, *EP,* 401–2).

This statement adds more nuance to the view previously asserted by the novel's hero, in his rational and moral analysis of love that had to be untainted by jealousy (which he explained to both Auristela and the Valencian shepherdess). Furthermore, his last exclamation, as well as Auristela's—that love cannot exist without *temores*—contradicts his earlier agreement with the idea that there can be love without jealousy (he first agreed with the title of the debate). If *temores* are necessary in love, then logically there can be no love without jealousy.

How can Periandro—who has seemed so analytically rational—contradict himself so blatantly? Undoubtedly, he has borrowed Andreas Capellanus's notion that there are two kinds of jealousy, good and bad. In *The Art of Courtly Love* (ca. twelfth century), Capellanus distinguishes the noble "true jealousy"—which all lovers feel—from "shameful suspicion." "True jealousy" is always a part of love, in con-

---

14. Auristela attempts to contrast *celos* with *temores;* but, as I argue below, she is really distinguishing between two kinds of jealousy. In Spanish literature, the word *temor* is typically a form of jealousy. To wit, the following passage from act 2 of *Peribáñez and the Commander of Ocaña* puts it clearly: " . . . because sleeplessness is a door through which jealousy passes from love to fear" (que los desvelos son puertas / para que passen los zelos / desde el amor al temor, 2.349–51).

trast with "shameful suspicion," which can never be a part of love, for it doubts and debases the beloved's virtue. Capellanus goes on to say that all lovers must be jealous (that is, that jealousy is necessary in love), as he quotes "the rules of love," which allegedly came from the mouth of the god of love himself, the second of which reads: "He who is not jealous cannot love."[15] Periandro's comments on the debate agree with this commandment, that there can be no love without jealousy (that is, that the *temores* are a necessary condition). Periandro's distinction allows for a positive value of jealousy as protective of the beloved. Separating *celos* from *temores* (as Capellanus distinguishes "shameful suspicion" from "true jealousy") makes it clear that the kind of *temores* Periandro is describing is a form of suspicious jealousy, to the extent that the lover worries about and fears losing the beloved, as when Periandro cried and fainted because of the jealousy he felt. What is different from ordinary suspicious jealousy (*sospechas*) and similar to Capellanus's "true jealousy" is that the suspicious lover, in Periandro's view, has no right to doubt the beloved's faithfulness. When Auristela fears that Periandro will fall in love with Sinforosa, she wrongs him. In this masculinist world, female jealousy is considered superfluous; it has no function, because males do not rely on females for protection. On the contrary, there exists a protective kind of male jealousy. Periandro has the moral right to doubt the intentions of others, that is, of rivals who will inevitably be attracted to the beloved's outstanding beauty, but he has no right to doubt his beloved's intentions. In Golden Age literature and particularly in Cervantes's novels, male jealousy is inevitable, because so many of the women are exceptionally beautiful—more than one of them is described, contradictorily, as "peerless"—and thus each is desired by many rivals.

The notion of good, necessary (male) jealousy that Periandro elaborates on has three characteristics: first, it is suspicious, but rationally so; second, it is possessive (for its aim is to keep the beloved and the relationship); and finally, it is protective. I say "protective," because the beloved's true wish is to be with her lover (and this can not be doubted by the lover); hence, the male lover can assume he is protecting his female beloved from an unwanted suitor if one appears, for he does not doubt the fidelity and love of his beloved. This explains why, when Arnaldo makes an amorous advance, Periandro

15. Capellanus, *The Art of Courtly Love,* 103, 184.

assumes correctly that his role is to protect Auristela from the prince (from her perspective, he knows, the advance was unwanted).

Such a distinction into two types of one emotion was also advanced in the prologue to part 2 of *Don Quixote,* regarding envy: "I am also offended that he [the author of the apocryphal continuation of *Don Quixote*] has called me 'envious,' and that, as if I were an imbecile, has described for me what envy is; because, in truth, of the two types that exist, I only know the Holy type, the noble and well-meaning type" (He sentido también que me llame invidioso, y que como a ignorante, me describa qué cosa sea la invidia; que, en realidad de verdad, de dos que hay, yo no conozco sino a la santa, a la noble y bien intencionada).[16] This digression is most likely an allusion to Aristotle's distinction in the *Rhetoric* between emulation and envy: "Emulation is pain caused by seeing the presence, in persons whose nature is like our own, of good things that are highly valued and are possible for ourselves to acquire; but it is felt not because others have these goods, but because we have not got them ourselves. It is therefore a good feeling felt by good persons, whereas envy is a bad feeling felt by bad persons" (2.11). In *Don Quixote,* then, Cervantes uses the term *noble* for this kind of envy, for which I draw the parallel to Periandro's jealousy, because the latter is also characterized not simply as benign, but noble (the close relationship of jealousy and envy is where early modern philosophical discussions of these emotions often begin). Indeed, a modicum of jealousy is necessary, something that can also be inferred from *Don Quixote,* where, in "The Tale of Foolish Curiosity," Anselmo's problem—that is, his "impertinence"— is that he is not jealous enough to protect his wife and himself from harm, but rather he willfully brings on their tragedy. Similarly, in the *Persiles,* the barbarians lack jealousy, which is one of the prime reasons they are referred to with this derogatory label. Their lack of jealousy is described as an "embarrassment" (vergüenza), and their homeland is "the worst of all" (la peor de todas) due to their custom that a virgin bride must have sex with the brothers and other relatives of the groom on her wedding night; this is the fate from which Transila is running away when she meets the pilgrims (*EP,* 112).[17]

16. Cervantes, *Don Quijote,* pt. 2, prologue, 34.
17. This lack of jealousy among a people inhabiting "Northern lands" (tierras septentrionales) might be indebted to Vives's notion that Northern European men are much less concerned about their women's chastity (*pudor*) than other men (Vives, *Passions of the Soul,* 331).

The blameless aspects of jealousy that are explored by an experienced Periandro—a rational fear of losing the beloved, a suspicion of rivals, and the protection of the beloved from unwanted others—when taken together can be properly termed "noble fears" (which Capellanus calls "true jealousy") and are the only jealous qualities that Cervantes allows in his notion of "true love." Since Periandro is the hero of the novel, and is also perhaps Cervantes's most noble and Christian hero, not only his pronouncements but also his example would seem very important to an understanding of Cervantes's view of love and jealousy. Ultimately, the novel confirms Periandro's view as the Christian heroes arrive in Rome and are married, fulfilling their original plan.

Why did Cervantes eke out this positive role for male jealousy in his last work? One reason might be to represent a verisimilar psychology for Periandro. Bataillon and González Amezúa both described a lack of verisimilitude in Cervantes's view of love in accordance with the allegation that he subscribed to a notion of pure love in which jealousy must not rear its head. However, they both missed the fact that Periandro is jealous and that his jealousy is not only acceptable but indeed necessary in true love. I would argue that the love that Periandro feels is more verisimilar than pure unjealous love, which is the main reason that the novel accepts a limited positive role for jealousy.

In *The Trials of Persiles and Sigismunda,* jealousy is not unequivocally malignant, as it appears to be in the author's other literary texts, but rather its moral value is explicitly debated. Of course, with Cervantine irony, the debate is only announced, but never heard, because the heroes are not able to arrive at the required time at the "Academy of the Enthroned [or Elite]" (Academia de los Entronados). What the reader hears are Periandro's and Auristela's thoughts, not the academicians'. Nonetheless, the debate allows for a broadening of the view of jealousy. Suspicious jealousy is ultimately nuanced, allowing for a more verisimilar psychological representation of the male hero. In other texts, its exclusion from moral psychology led to the potential for an inverisimilar representation of the mind.

Most philosophers, including Vives, consider all forms of jealousy a vice. Contemporary philosopher Gabrielle Taylor argues that "[t]reating as a thing to be possessed what is in fact not a thing cannot secure the wanted good." Taylor's view is indebted to both Kant and Sartre, who, for similar reasons in their moral philosophies, require that humans not be treated as mere things. A few contemporary philosophers, however, including Goldie, have found a positive role for some kinds of jealousy, more in line with Cervantes's. As Goldie describes it,

> I agree that jealousy is a character trait which should not be left unchecked, because this emotion does tend to get out of control, but this is entirely consistent with not having a negative attitude towards all experiences of jealousy or towards the capability for having such experiences. There is no reason, therefore, why we should aim to have no jealous thoughts, or to be incapable of jealousy, rather than to be a person whose jealous thoughts are well grounded, appropriate, and proportionate. Furthermore, the person capable of jealous thoughts can be, all things considered, a better person than the person incapable of jealousy.

While not agreeing completely with the assessment of the grounds for positive jealousy in the *Persiles,* Goldie argues that jealousy "is not necessarily a vice." While in Taylor's view, Periandro would seem to treat his beloved as something to be possessed, there may be an important difference between possessing and protecting. Goldie, in fact, specifically argues that possessing is not a bad thing if what is aimed at is "protecting": "[B]eing protective of a relationship *may be* perfectly justified and appropriate." Moreover, Goldie's analysis of the emotions, and his emphasis on descriptive intelligibility rather than normative rationality and morality, lends credence to my view that jealousy is verisimilar: "Jealous thoughts and feelings so easily get out of control, leading us to do things which are far from being appropriate or proportionate. The reasons of the heart can be like this. But they are also perfectly intelligible and utterly human."[18]

Relying on Capellanus's distinction, Cervantes modifies his concept of true love in this novel, bringing his idealized Neoplatonic concept of love one step closer to earth, in a human instantiation, attempting to represent a true love that is at the same time psychologically verisimilar. In a paradox appropriate for jealousy itself, this novel is one of Cervantes's least verisimilar works, along with the *Coloquio de los perros* (Colloquy of the Dogs) and its conversing

18. Gabrielle Taylor, "Envy and Jealousy," 246–47, quoted in Goldie, *The Emotions,* 234; Goldie, *The Emotions,* 240, 238, 241.

canines. Indeed, the *Persiles* is full of fantastic representations, from monstrous cannibals and flying witches to Spanish-speaking wolves who feel pity. It is somewhat ironic, therefore, but nevertheless befitting the psychological verisimilitude approved of by the Council of Trent, that the hero's idealized human love becomes more true to life in this allegorical Christian novel. In fact, Periandro's full potential for heroism is possible only because of his position of knowledge and understanding. He not only feels jealousy, but knows what it is and when it is appropriate to experience it, and when it is not. Periandro is an expert on the emotions.

Six

Myth and the Fractured "I" in Góngora

> Only a subject can understand a meaning; conversely, every phenomenon of meaning implies a subject.
>
> —Jacques Lacan, *Écrits*

In early modern Spain, the invocation of Greco-Roman myths in literature was far from mere adornment. Yet myth is so common in the prose, theater, and poetry of the period that its semantic importance can easily be overlooked. It has been noted in previous chapters how Lope de Vega employed a variety of myths, including those of Juno, Jupiter, Argos, and Phaeton, to ground power relations within a drama. With respect to lyric, early modern poets from Garcilaso to Calderón frequently used myths for a variety of reasons and desired effects, oftentimes to draw a comparison to a psychological state, especially jealousy. Such is, for example, how Lope evokes pathos for the lyric voice in his Sonnet 56 of the *Rimas,* "That the forty-nine eternally," by comparing his affective torment to the physical torture of Tantalus and other mythological characters.

Góngora relied on myths to an even greater extent than Lope, basing some of his most important work on them. He wrote extensive poems on Pyramus and Thisbe and on Polyphemus and Galatea, as well as dozens of sonnets and other kinds of poetry in the tradition of Petrarch and Tasso, replete with allusions to mythological characters from Apollo to Zeus. Although writing in the Italianate tradition, and borrowing mythological and other images in the spirit of *imitatio,* Góngora never simply used his models slavishly—as Robert Jammes has pointed out—but rather, with his superlative creativity renewed whatever he put his pen to.[1] Famously heralded by the Poetic Group of 1927 for regenerating Spanish poetic language, the poet from Cordoba also brought new life to old myths, finding a way to say something novel about the human condition and, more specifically, about the splintered nature of human desire. One of the ways Góngora achieved this was by integrating divergent and conflicting iconographic representations of mythological characters into a single poem. Whereas the poetic and artistic representations that served as Góngora's sources usually presented one version of a myth, Góngora's poetic visualizations combined these versions into enigmatic entities that defy the notions of a privileged first-personal perspective and a unified subject.

This chapter focuses on the poem "Qué de invidiosos montes levantados" (What of the tall envious mountains)—a *canción* (song) that evokes multiple myths and draws on representations in art and literature of Vulcan, Venus, and Mars. The poem has been something of an enigma to critics for several decades. On the one hand, it is simply beautiful: Dámaso Alonso calls it "the most beautiful [song]"; Jammes identifies the poem as "one of the masterpieces of Góngora's work," while José María Micó praises it as "[o]ne of Góngora's best poems."[2] On the other hand, it is exceedingly strange, in the judgment of critics: Alonso remarks that "from this combination comes forth the strangeness of this song and not just a little of its ambivalent beauty," Micó refers to its "disturbing" and "complex" qualities and to its "many peculiarities," and Juan Ferraté exclaims in one essay, "What a strange poem!"[3]

My approach to this poem is the following: while relying on insights from psychoanalysis, I interpret important visual images in the poem by comparing Góngora's transformed iconography with that of intertexts from poetry and fine art.[4] In this way, my reading

1. Robert Jammes, *Etudes sur l'oeuvre poétique de don Luis de Góngora,* 545.

2. Dámaso Alonso, ed., *Góngora y el "Polifemo,"* 2:204; Jammes, *Etudes,* 425; José María Micó, "La superación del petrarquismo," 59.

3. Alonso, ed., *Góngora y el "Polifemo,"* 2:203; Micó, "Superación," 62, 71; Juan Ferraté, "Ficción y realidad en la poesía de Góngora," 312.

4. Góngora's interest in painting has been documented by Emilie L. Bergmann, who analyzes visual images in a few of Góngora's poems that are, according to her and Jammes, based on his contemplations of paintings, including one canvas of the Marquesa de Ayamonte as Cupid at the family villa in Lepe

of "What of the tall envious mountains" reconfigures what others have interpreted as strange incongruencies or disparate sections in the poem. The pronounced emphasis on visuality supports my art historical approach: the verb *to see* (*ver*) is used six times (lines 6, 9, 19, 25, 30, and 35). Also, the large middle section of the poem is a stilled scene of immobile, sleeping lovers, located in a traditional Renaissance bedroom interior, evoking the world of painting. I will show that the overt conflictedness of the poetic voice, and the explicit schism of the voice from his own "thought," supports the psychoanalytic aspect.

I begin by providing a general description and a literal reading of the poem. Then I briefly outline and critique the main interpretations. Finally, I elaborate my reading, show its explanatory efficacy, and conclude by suggesting a way to understand what Góngora has achieved here.

The poem is composed of six nine-line stanzas and a send-off of three lines (all of which are hepta- or hendecasyllabic). It is a *canción* and borrows one of the strophic forms that Petrarch cultivated (the canzone) and that has origins in the medieval tradition of *fin amor,* or courtly love.

> What of the tall envious mountains,   1
> made treacherous by capped snow,
> that prevent me from seeing your sweet, beautiful eyes.
> What of the rivers, that are frozen over with ice,
> that are brimming over with water,   5
> that defy me from seeing them again.
> And what, tricking these impediments
> my noble thought,
> in order to see you, dons feathers, walks on air.

(Bergmann, *Art Inscribed: Essays on Ekphrasis in Spanish Golden Age Poetry,* 209–25). Unlike most of his contemporaries, Góngora apparently never had the opportunity to leave Spain on any voyage (Angel Pariente, *Góngora*), and thus would never have seen the Florentine and Roman masterpieces that so influenced Cervantes's thought and writing, as discussed by de Armas in *Cervantes, Raphael and the Classics.* However, that is not to say that he did not come into contact with paintings on mythological subjects. Certainly as one of the most renowned poets of his day he had access to the court and to the homes of the aristocracy. His travels in Spain, and his stays for extended periods of time in and around Madrid as a guest of illustrious patrons are documented. My contention here is that if he did not see the particular paintings I write of, he could have seen copies or imitations based on them.

It does not excuse either the obscurity   10
of the dark night or the ice,
and it can resolve, with trickery, the greatest difficulty.
There are no guards or locks secure enough today
to deny it your person,   14
that it cannot skillfully undermine.
Nor will any deed embarked upon by
your husband—when he does battle—
escape its careful watch, or not be envied by me.

There you fly, pleasure of my sorrows,   19
with equal impunity
you penetrate the abyss, you scale the sky;
and while I await you in the chains
of this rabid absence,   23
your wings humble the wind itself.
Now I see that you land
where the embroidered cloth
covers a bed and conceals a thousand caresses.

Too late did you beat your envious feathers,   28
otherwise in her pleasurable exhaustion
you would have seen (her voice dead, her hair loose)
the white daughter of the white foam
in the arms of—I'm not sure what to call him—   32
a fierce Mars or a beautiful Adonis;
but now tied around his neck,
you can see her sleeping
and him transported—almost—to the next life.

Her arm naked, her breast uncovered,   37
contemplate the rising vapors from the frozen fire
born of the temperate snow,
and the husband, striking an almost dead figure,
who drinks the silence of her slumber   41
with solicitous sweat.
Sleep, for the winged god,
the master of your souls,
watches over your slumber with his finger to his lips.

Sleep, oh gracious couple of noble lovers,   46
in the happy knots
of the bonds of Love in which Hymen has tied you;
while I, exiled,
seek pity with my tears from these oaks   50

and naked cliffs.
Upon waking, culminate
your happiness by remembering;
would that your bed be a soft battlefield.

Song, tell my thought   55
to close the bed curtain
and return to the unhappy one who walks.

(¡Qué de invidiosos montes levantados,   1
    de nieves impedidos,
me contienden tus dulces ojos bellos!
¡Qué de ríos, del hielo tan atados,
    del agua tan crecidos,   5
me defienden el ya volver a vellos!
    ¡Y qué, burlando de ellos
    el noble pensamiento,
por verte viste plumas, pisa el viento!

Ni a las tinieblas de la noche oscura   10
    ni a los hielos perdona,
y a la mayor dificultad engaña;
no hay guardas hoy de llave tan segura,
    que nieguen tu persona,   14
que no desmienta con discreta maña;
    ni emprenderá hazaña
    tu esposo, cuando lidie,
que no registre él, y yo no invidie.

Allá vueles, lisonja de mis penas,   19
    que con igual licencia
penetras el abismo, el cielo escalas;
y mientras yo te aguardo en las cadenas
    de esta rabiosa ausencia,   23
el viento agravien tus ligeras alas.
    Ya veo que te calas
    donde bordada tela
un lecho abriga y mil dulzoras cela.

Tarde batiste la invidiosa pluma,   28
    que en sabrosa fatiga
vieras (muerta la voz, suelto el cabello)
la blanca hija de la blanca espuma,
    no sé si en brazos diga   32
de un fiero Marte o de un Adonis bello;
    ya anudada a su cuello,

podrás verla dormida,
y a él casi trasladado a nueva vida.

Desnuda el brazo, el pecho descubierta,   37
   entre templada nieve
evaporar contempla un fuego helado,
y al esposo, en figura casi muerta,
   que el silencio le bebe   41
del sueño con sudor solicitado.
   Dormid, que el dios alado,
   de vuestras almas dueño,
con el dedo en la boca os guarda el sueño.

Dormid, copia gentil de amantes nobles,   46
   en los dichosos nudos
que a los lazos de Amor os dio Himeneo;
mientras yo, desterrado, de estos robles
   y peñascos desnudos   50
la piedad con mis lágrimas granjeo.
   Coronad el deseo
   de gloria, en recordando;
sea el lecho de batalla campo blando.

Canción, di al pensamiento   55
   que corra la cortina
y vuelva al desdichado que camina.)[5]

The poet, unable to see his beloved, complains in apostrophe of
the Petrarchan-style "being in her absence" (*ausencia*) provoked by
what he calls the "envious" mountains and the terrible conditions,
including snow and ice, elements of nature that he imbues with envy
of his love ("IML," 1–4). Because of this situation he sends his "noble
thought" (noble pensamiento, "IML," 8) to investigate his suspicions
of her. He seems jealous. Despite the terrible conditions that deny
him the pleasure of seeing his beloved (who is referred to in line 3
through the mention of her "sweet, beautiful eyes" [dulces ojos bel-
los]), the "noble thought" will put on feathers ("IML," 9) and fly to
see her.

---

5. Luis de Góngora, "Qué de invidiosos montes levantados," in *Canciones y
otros poemas en arte mayor: Edición crítica,* 87–91. Subsequent citations of this
poem will be made parenthetically in the text by line number using the abbreviation "IML."

In the second stanza, the lyric voice continues explaining that this detached noble thought can see all, that nothing can stop it (not nature nor people ["IML," 10–15]). The voice insists that all will be revealed, even the battles of love—after the Ovidian metaphor—between the lady and, yes, her husband ("your husband—when he does battle" [tu esposo, cuando lidie, "IML," 17]). And now the lyric voice informs the reader that he will *envy* the husband and wife ("IML," 18).

The poet continues with the flight of his "thought" and how it can "penetrate" any place; no guard or lock can keep it out ("IML," 13). In the third stanza the poet turns to his self-portrait: he describes himself, in contrast to the free-flying thought, as "chained" in a "rabid absence" from his lady (en las cadenas / de esta rabiosa ausencia, "IML," 22–23). At the end of this stanza, the flying thought arrives at the bed of the couple:

> Now I see that you land
> where the embroidered cloth
> covers a bed and conceals a thousand caresses.
>
> (Ya veo que te calas
> donde bordada tela
> un lecho abriga y mil dulzoras cela. "IML," 25–27)

Then, in the fourth stanza, something happens that some critics have called "strange," and others "ironic": the flying "thought" imagined by the poet arrives too late for the lovemaking ("Too late did you beat your envious feathers" [Tarde batiste la invidiosa pluma, "IML," 28]). Thus there is no account in the poem of the acts of love, but only a description of the two (postcoital) lovers in a very tired state. Both are compared here to mythological characters, the man to Mars and Adonis ("of . . . a fierce Mars or a beautiful Adonis" [de un fiero Marte o de un Adonis bello, "IML," 33]) and the woman, through a clear metonymy, to the goddess of love and beauty herself, Venus ("the white daughter of the white foam" [la blanca hija de la blanca espuma, "IML," 31]). This visual image, emphasizing her sheer whiteness, evokes iconographic representations of Venus as originating from the whiteness of the sea, as in Sandro Botticelli's famous *Birth of Venus* (from the white seashell, in the case of this painting).

The fifth stanza describes her nakedness and the man's sweaty and sleepy state; the poet calls the man "an almost dead figure" (figura casi muerta, "IML," 40). Then, the poet addresses the couple and commands them to sleep, assuring them that Cupid will help them continue in slumber, with the ekphrastic image of the flying boy-god holding his finger up to his lips ("Sleep, for the winged god . . ." [Dormid, que el dios alado . . . , "IML," 43]).

The sixth stanza continues with the sleep command *Dormid,* and here the poem becomes an exaltation of the couple, in which they are referred to as noble lovers and their bonds of love are seen to be proffered, in line 48, by the (very obscure) god of marriage, Hymen. Again, however, in this stanza, the poet points out his lot in contrast to theirs: in line 49 and following, he describes himself as a lonely, crying exile (*desterrado*) seeking pity from naked cliffs and oak trees (de estos robles / y peñascos desnudos / la piedad con mis lágrimas granjeo). Then, switching back to the couple, he wishes them, ostensibly, good lovemaking in the future: "that your bed be a soft battlefield" (sea el lecho de batalla campo blando, "IML," 54), once again evoking the Ovidian *love as battle* topos.

Following this last full stanza is the send-off, in which the song itself is addressed by the poet. In this case, the poet asks the song to tell the flying thought to close the bed curtain on the lovers and then to return to him. The poem ends with another self-description of the lyric voice as "the unhappy one who walks" (el desdichado que camina, "IML," 57).

In their readings of the poem, most critics have fixed their attention either on the loving couple in bed or on the lonely outsider. For instance, Dámaso Alonso's interpretation is that the song is an epithalamion, a poem that serves to celebrate the wedding of a real, live couple. This idea is based primarily on linguistic similarities between sections of this poem and two by Tasso that were explicitly epithalamia: (1) "celebra le nozze del signor Alfonso d'Este, il giovine, e della signora donna Marfisa d'Este" (to celebrate the marriage of signor Alfonso d'Este, the younger, to signora Marfisa d'Este) and (2) the sonnet "Coppia gentil, cui scelse a prova Amore" (Noble couple, whose unflagging choice Love), which was explicitly written for "le nozze del signor Gio. Battista Azzolino e della donna Isabella Assalti" (to celebrate the marriage between signor Giovanii Battista Azzolino and Lady Isabella Assalti). Alonso is right that Góngora's poem participates in linguistic borrowing—in the tradition of *imitatio*—from these and other poems. Indeed, as he points out, the poem even contains phrases that are clearly taken right from the Italian, for example, Góngora's "Sleep, oh gracious couple" (Dormid, copia gentil, "IML," 46), *copia* coming from the Italian word for "couple," not the Spanish, which is *pareja*.[6]

However, there are two main problems with Alonso's interpretation: that the poem has no epithalamic title is the first. In the poems by Tasso, as well as in epithalamic paintings of the sixteenth century, the names of at least one member of the celebrated couple are indeed made explicit. It is clear that these titles do little more than indicate that the poems are in fact epithalamia, mentioning, as they do, the names of the specific, illustrious people whose weddings are being feted. Second, and more importantly, Alonso's epithalamic interpretation cannot make good sense of the self-portrait of the lyric voice as the "exiled" one in "chains," "the unhappy one who walks," since such a voice emphasizing its own loneliness is anomalous to the genre of the epithalamion.

In contrast to this approach, other critics, such as Giulia Poggi, have concentrated on the poem as a lover's lament and illuminated its roots in the classical tradition of Propertius. Clearly, along these lines, it also has antecedents in the work of Petrarch, which the early Góngora commentator José García de Salcedo Coronel pointed out.[7] This type of focus, however, overlooks, among other things, the importance of the good wishes that the poet bestows on the celebrated couple, good wishes that are, of course, anomalous in the love lament.

José María Micó has improved on these partial interpretations by paying close attention to both the part on the unfortunate lover and the part on the fortunate lovers. He rightly calls the protagonist "complex" and the poem, with its two parts, full of "peculiarities." After a careful, detailed, and enlightening analysis of the sources of verses from Italian and other authors, Micó's conclusions are that Góngora's poem surpasses its Petrarchan sources, and that the poem is not an epithalamion, contra Alonso.[8]

In my reading, I take Micó's interpretation one step further and demonstrate how this purportedly "strange" and "peculiar" poem is in fact unified. The key to a unified reading is in finding the

---

6. Alonso, ed., *Góngora y el "Polifemo,"* 2:201–3.

7. Petrarch's poem 37 of his *canzoniere* contains images of mountains and rivers, and the line "How many mountains and waters" (Quante montagne ed acque [in Alonso, ed., *Góngora y el "Polifemo,"* 2:202]).

8. Micó, 100–102. Hence the title of Micó's essay, "La superación del petrarquismo." Regarding other poems, Ulrich Schulz-Buschhaus has described a similar phenomenon as Góngora's early style; see Schulz-Buschhaus, "Der frühe Góngora und die italienische Lyrik," 231.

right myth on which the poem is based, through association of the poem's visual images with early modern iconography. Ironically, as this study will show, the unified reading of the poem points to the disunity—the fractured "I"—of the lyrical subject.

In what follows, I make two overall claims: First, the myth that binds the two "parts" together, that forges them into place, is the myth of Vulcan, god of the forge. Second, the poem appears disjoint because it is about inner, subconscious conflict in the lyric voice arising from the subject's jealousy. Along the way, I will connect these two claims by relating the poem to the visual arts.

The conflicted mind of the lyrical subject is represented through allusions to two disparate traditions of the myth of Venus and Mars. These two versions are forged into one, a melding together of opposites that maintains the enormous tension of the opposing versions. This inherent tension has led to the reception of this poem as strange and bizarre. In effect, what Góngora did was to depict multiple, incompatible iconographic representations on one canvas. It is through an exploration of the poem's dialogue with early modern European art that the alleged enigma is resolved. While previous treatments of the Venus and Mars myth in art and poetry were on one or another "tradition," Góngora perceived a link between the two divergent and irreconcilable versions of the myth and fused them together, creating what I call a "polysemous myth."

The most famous version of the Mars and Venus story is the one depicted by the sixteenth-century Venetian painter Jacopo Tintoretto in his *Vulcan Teaching Venus and Mars* (see fig. 1). The source for this painting is book 8 of Homer's *Odyssey,* and it is also told in book 4 of Ovid's *Metamorphoses.* This is the story of how Mars and Venus deceive Vulcan, Venus's husband, and commit adultery. Vulcan learns of the adultery through Helios (the sun), who sees all, and he becomes very jealous. But as Vulcan does not see himself as a fit contender in a match against the god of war, instead of a fight, he sets a trap of chains for the adulterous lovers in bed.

The opposing and incompatible version of the myth, made famous in paintings of Mars and Venus by Piero di Cosimo, Botticelli, and Veronese, originates from a more obscure literary tradition that probably has origins in the writings of Pausanias:[9] Mars and Venus are a married couple who symbolize the uniting of two cosmic

9. Erwin Panofsky, *Studies in Iconology: Humanistic Themes in the Art of the Renaissance,* 164.

Figure 1. Jacopo Tintoretto, *Vulcan Teaching Venus and Mars*. Erich Lessing/Art Resource, New York. Kunsthistorisches Museum, Vienna, Austria.

forces—war and love—and who give birth to Harmonia (Harmony). This version of the myth is invoked implicitly in epithalamic poems such as the ones by Tasso mentioned by Alonso, and explicitly in epithalamic paintings.

In "What of the tall envious mountains" the conflicting traditions are expressed simultaneously, creating a palpable tension: Venus and Mars are present both as the married couple typical of the epithalamion and as the adulterous lovers engaged in the cuckoldry of Vulcan.[10] In the poem, the presence of the myth's epithalamic version is clear and is implicitly accepted by all critics of the poem.

10. Despite the common view that art in sixteenth-century Spain consisted only of religious subjects (for instance, see Mary Cable, *El Escorial*), Philip II had a penchant for mythological paintings (particularly for female nudes). He famously commissioned Titian in about 1560 to paint a series of "poesie," or paintings on mythological stories, contrasting sad and happy pairs of lovers that remain "among the most beautiful and sensual paintings in the history of art" (Rosemarie Mulcahy, *The Decoration of the Royal Basilica of El Escorial,* 10–11). The incredible collection of cinquecento Venetian works at the Prado was begun by Philip II, and many of these paintings were in Spain at one of the royal collections before or at the time Góngora's poem was written. According to a partial inventory done in the sixteenth century, the following paintings were found among the royal Guadajoya collection (some identified by painter, others

The physical attributes of both the lady and the husband are hyperbolized through comparisons with these beautiful gods. The man is explicitly compared to Mars ("a fierce Mars," "IML," 33), while the allusion to Venus is metonymical ("the white daughter of the white foam," "IML," 31), referring to her depiction in painting as light-skinned, nude, or white-clad, and to her origins in the sea foam as described by Hesiod.[11] In addition, her identity is clarified by reference to her best-known lovers, Mars and Adonis. In Góngora's poem, the beautiful lovers, as Venus and Mars, are found in bed, after having made love, with Cupid at their side (Cupid or Amor is mentioned as "the winged god" [el dios alado, "IML," 43]), just as the three are found in Piero di Cosimo's *Mars and Venus*. In this painting, the iconography is very similar to the scene drawn by Góngora of the postcoital sleeping lovers: a bare-breasted Venus, with her white toga draped over part of her body, lies with a sleeping and sweaty armored Mars, while Cupid looks over the scene. In Góngora's poem, the lady's arm is nude and her breasts are bare, while the husband is described as physically exhausted. Góngora's differs, however, in that his Venus is asleep. This image of a sleeping Venus may be a tribute to Giorgione's painting *Venus Asleep* (ca. 1510), which, according to Helen Roberts, is the first rendition of this theme in art or literature and which "seems to have served as a source of inspiration for many later renderings of nude female sleepers."[12] Giorgione, a teacher of Titian's, was of the Venetian school—a school for which the Spanish Hapsburgs had a marked preference. He depicts Venus's full nude body reclining and asleep with her bare right arm posed in a bent position, and her right hand behind her head ("her arm naked" [Desnuda el brazo]), which makes her breast stand out more prominently ("her breast uncovered" [el pecho descubierta]) ("IML," 37). As in Góngora's poem, her hair is loose and runs over her shoulder (suelto el cabello). Giorgione's painting is the known source for Titian's famous *Venus de Urbino* (ca. 1528). In the two paint-

not): Correggio's *Leda and the Swan*, as well as a *Mars* and a *Mars and Venus*. A subsequent inventory of the Real Alcázar of Madrid, performed in 1636, revealed the presence, among many other paintings, of Titian's *Venus and Cupid*, *Venus and Adonis*, and *Sleeping Venus*, and Veronese's *Venus and Adonis* (Fernando Checa, *El Real Alcázar de Madrid*, 407).

11. Hesiod, *Theogony*, ll. 190–200. According to the ancient Greek poet, this foam gathered around Uranus's severed testicles; *aphros*, the root of *Aphrodite* (the Greek name of Venus), means "sea foam."

12. Helen Roberts, *Encyclopedia of Comparative Iconography*, 846.

ings Venus strikes a similar pose, lying nude on a white sheet that covers an embroidered cloth or bedcover; the most obvious differences between the two are that Titian portrays Venus awake rather than asleep, and situates her in a lavish bedroom rather than in the Venetian countryside. Góngora seems to borrow iconography from both paintings: his Venus is asleep, as in Giorgione's painting, but in a lavish interior. That both Mars and Venus are sleeping (or almost asleep) in Góngora's interior bedroom scene might imply that the lovers have nothing on their conscience, no cares or worries, along the lines of the epithalamic version. In lines 41–42, Góngora uses alliteration with the s sound to emphasize the visual image of the "sweat" (*sudor*) on the man's body and the "sleep" (*sueño*) he needs, and hence, the corporeality of the lovemaking, as he describes the husband "who drinks the silence of her slumber with solicitous sweat" (que el silencio le bebe / del sueño con sudor solicitado).

Another important element revealing the presence of the epithalamic tradition is that the poet bestows good wishes on the lovers, as he calls them "gracious couple" (copia gentil, "IML," 46). The painter or poet of an epithalamic scene implicitly wishes the subjects well, as the intention of the work is to celebrate their good fortune. Writing on the relationship between these two traditions involving Venus, the renowned art historian Erwin Panofsky explains that in epithalamic painting, Vulcan is implicitly invoked as well, since Mars's armor—which is iconographically necessary to identifying this lover as the god of war, just as are the lamb and staff to a depiction of the young John the Baptist—always signals the absence of the god who made the armor, that is, cuckolded Vulcan.[13]

In Góngora's poem, the conflicting Homeric version of this myth is operative more explicitly, too. The tradition of the adulterous lovers is drawn out, first of all, by the presence of the jealous voice at the very beginning of the poem. This jealous voice is that of the poet as Vulcan. As I mentioned above, the lyric voice implies to the reader in the opening lines that he has a right to feel jealousy; it is not until line 17 that the reader learns that the lady is married.

Second, the mention of Adonis in line 33 ("a fierce Mars or a beau-

13. Panofsky, *Studies in Iconology,* 162. Marcia L. Welles draws out the corollary to this point well in her examination of Velázquez's painting *The Forge of Vulcan,* in which Mars's cuckoldry of Vulcan is implied by the presence, in the forge, of the armor Vulcan has created for the god of war (Welles, *Arachne's Tapestry: The Transformation of Myth in Seventeenth-Century Spain,* 140).

tiful Adonis"), while serving, of course, to hyperbolize the husband's physical beauty, brings up the theme of jealousy and adultery again, and casts doubt on the purity of this love. That the poet mentions two potential values and not one, despite the conjunction *or*, functions to evoke the theme of infidelity. Two potential lovers are mentioned: Mars *and* Adonis. The affair between Venus and Adonis is illicit in Ovid's *Metamorphoses*, leading to Mars's fury and, ultimately, to Adonis's death by the wild boar, and evokes images like that of Paolo Veronese's painting *Venus and Adonis* (ca. 1550, see fig. 2), in which the lovers display lascivious expressions on their faces, portrayed by sly smirks. The overt sexuality of the painting—the focal point depicts Adonis's hand on Venus's breast—coupled with their facial expressions reveal the obvious awareness of their wrongdoing, in contrast to the bliss represented on the characters' countenances in Di Cosimo's epithalamic *Venus and Mars*.

Third, the iconography of this bedroom scene, with a raised bed curtain (*cortina*) through which the poet's "thought" and the poem's reader may peer in on lovers in a bed, evokes an adulterous love and specifically the adulterous love of Mars and Venus. The description seems partially to imitate one of the many sixteenth-century European woodcut illustrations of that section of the *Metamorphoses* on the adulterous love of Venus and Mars, such as, for example, the one in Micyllus's edition, *Vulcan Netting Venus and Mars*, probably by the artist Christopher Murer (1582; see fig. 3). In the illustration of this passage from book 4, Cupid holds up the bed curtain so that all of the gods (in the upper left-hand corner) may look in on these lovers in the throes of passion, just as Vulcan begins to net them.

Góngora alters the iconography significantly, yet leaves behind telling traces: In Góngora's poem, the winged curtain-raiser is not love (Amor or Cupid), but rather, its antithesis, jealousy (the poet). The peeping gods are not mentioned in his poem; rather, the ones depicted in the woodcut are replaced by the readers of the poem, who have been brought to this secret place by the poet, who has netted the lovers for our viewing pleasure. Góngora's action here in netting them (and they are tied in "knots" [*nudos*], says the poem) is much like the action of Vulcan in Tintoretto's *Vulcan Teaching Venus and Mars*. In his painting, Tintoretto chose to portray the moment in which Venus and Mars are caught, in flagrante, in the chains placed there by Vulcan, who watches over the scene with an angry countenance. Mars is hiding, while Venus is stupefied and motionless. And

Figure 2. Paolo Veronese, *Venus and Adonis*. Kavalier/Art Resource, New York. Alte Pinakothek, Munich, Germany.

the gods, mentioned by Ovid and present in most woodcut illustrations, are absent, just as they are in Góngora's poem.

The poet's depiction is importantly an interior scene, like Tintoretto's and Murer's (and unlike di Cosimo's). This locates the intrusion of both Vulcan and the reader/viewer in a more private realm: because they are inside, behind a bed curtain, our intrusion is more overt. Unlike Galatea and Acis, who, in Góngora's *Fábula de Polifemo y Galatea,* make love on the seashore, these lovers have the

Figure 3. [Christopher Murer?], *Vulcan Netting Venus and Mars,* from Ovid's *Metamorphoses,* 4:162. *Metamorphoseon Libri XV,* by Ovidii Nasonis, ed. Jakob Micyllus (Leipzig: Steinmann, 1582). Courtesy of the Bancroft Library, University of California, Berkeley.

expectation of privacy, which is violated by the "penetration" of the flying thought ("IML," 21).

The iconographic emphasis in the poem on the adulterous love between Venus and Mars evokes the unnamed mythological figure who completes the triangle and, yet, has gone unnoticed by critics: Vulcan, god of the forge. The self-portrait of the lyric voice in the first three stanzas, and especially in the sixth stanza, demonstrates further the presence of Vulcan. In line 49 and following (stanza 6), the poet laments,

> while I, exiled,
> seek pity with my tears from these oaks
> and naked cliffs.

> (mientras yo, desterrado, de estos robles
> y peñascos desnudos,
> la piedad con mis lágrimas granjeo. "IML," 49–51)

These important images of nature at the very end of the *canción* recall the "mountains" and "rivers" (*montes* and *ríos*) of the first stanza, and once more situate the poet in his desolate space: alone, "in . . . chains," "exiled," "with my tears," phrases that demonstrate his immobility and stagnation. The semantics and morphology of the vocabulary contrast his state with that of the fortunate lovers. While bare-breasted Venus is explicitly "nude," and the couple sleeps in "happy knots" (dichosos nudos, homonymic with *nudos,* meaning "nude"), the poet is left with only "naked cliffs" (peñascos nudos, "IML," 50). The poet recognizes his physical inferiority with respect to the idealized lover, his essential difference from a "fierce Mars or a beautiful Adonis"; he is connected in this way to Vulcan, whose physical ugliness and lameness were what led to Venus's straying in the myth. The doleful lament of the inferior who watches the flawless Mars with the perfect Venus evokes the figure of Vulcan.[14] Additionally, the flying thought that sees what the poet cannot and reports back to him is analogous to Helios's reporting to Vulcan of the affair in Ovid's version of the myth.[15] The idea of catching the couple in flagrante in his net is problematized with the reference to the "happy knots" placed on the couple by Hymen.

The voice of the melancholy, jealous lover in the poem who does not see himself as a match for Mars is that of Homer's Vulcan. Góngora transforms and renews the myth by having Vulcan place the chains not on the lovers, but on himself: "in the chains [*cadenas*] of this rabid absence" ("IML," 22–23).

Further allusions to the poet as Vulcan point to the origins of the god of the forge. Because of Vulcan's physical ugliness, he was the only Olympian god banished from the Palace of the Gods. "Banished" or "exiled," of course, is one of the primary meanings of the word *desterrado,* a predicate adjective stressed greatly in the poem immediately after the pause indicated by the comma (mientras yo, desterrado ["IML," 49]). This hendecasyllable displays primary stress on the sixth syllable (the *a* in *desterrado*)—and, of course, on the obligatory tenth—and supernumerary stress on the third (*yo*), further emphasizing the condition of the "I." Piero di Cosimo's painting, *The Finding of Vulcan,* follows the tradition elaborated by Servius, that

14. These two contrasts are perfect examples of what Baltasar Gracián called "improporción," which for him was the greatest manifestation of Góngora's genius (Gracián, *Agudeza y arte de ingenio,* 2 vols., ed. Evaristo Correa Calderón [Madrid: Castalia, 1969], 2.64).

15. A few years later, this scene—Helios informing Vulcan of the affair, with the aid of Mercury—would be famously portrayed in Velázquez's *Forge of Vulcan.*

Vulcan's mother, Juno, threw him to the earth, disgusted by his physical deformity, by his monstrosity, because he had a club foot.[16] After falling to the earth, the slightly deformed Vulcan was shown compassion by nymphs, inhabitants of the island of Lemnos. This compassion is perhaps what the poet is seeking in line 51, when he refers to his search for "pity." Thus the poem's reader, if he or she is moved to pity, becomes one of the Lemnian nymphs, despite Góngora's erasure of the nymphs from the canvas.

The identification of the lyric voice with the god of the forge works to represent a psyche in inner turmoil, in a very modern way. At the beginning of the poem, he describes the mountains as "envious" of his love for the lady, and in his complaint of such envy, he appears possessively jealous, in the sense of guarding his love relationship (for envy is wanting the good that others have, while possessive jealousy is wanting to keep for oneself the good one believes one already enjoys). This first adjective in the poem—*invidioso* in line 1—makes the reader think that the poet is in fact the lover of the lady with whom he wishes to be. It is to the reader's great surprise, then, at the end of the second stanza, that the poet reveals that the lady is married (and later, that she is happily married) and the poet admits that he is the one envying the two of them. The couple, in turn, at the end of the third stanza, is attributed the feeling of jealousy, through their metonymical association with the "guarding, concealing bedcover."[17]

Such conflicting psychological revelations—the world is envious, I am envious, I am jealous, they are jealous—begs a response from that branch of knowledge that studies conflictedness: Freudian psychoanalysis. In his essay "Some Neurotic Mechanisms in Jealousy, Paranoia and Homosexuality," Sigmund Freud theorizes that people ascribe to others emotions that they themselves feel unconsciously. For instance, the idea that others cannot be trusted is an insight that one may glean from knowledge (usually unconscious) that one is, oneself, untrustworthy. This psychological mechanism is operant in the poem. In the first line, the poet attributes the negative sentiment of "invidia" to Nature, fearing that it seeks to keep the beloved from

---

16. Servius, *Commentary on Vergil*, quoted in Panofsky, *Studies in Iconology*, 36.

17. "Ya veo que te calas / donde bordada tela / un lecho abriga y mil dulzoras cela" ("IML," 26–28). The word *celar* used here to describe the personified action of the bedcover means "to conceal," but also may evoke a popular etymology relating the word to *celos* (jealousy), described in Covarrubias's *Tesoro* (1611).

him; the attribution of this sentiment to something outside of himself more correctly points to knowledge of his own envy. This "neurotic mechanism," to borrow Freud's phrase, is the first indication in the poem that something is in turmoil in the voice's unconscious. Love is a battle, indeed, but the battle is that within a fractured subjectivity, in the voice's own mind.[18]

With respect to inner turmoil, first of all, then, the lyric voice does not seem consciously to know who is rightfully jealous or envious of whom. Second, the first line in the fourth stanza, referring to his flying thought, is very revealing. In passing from the third to the fourth stanza, there is a significant ellipsis: "Too late did you beat your envious feathers" (Tarde batiste la invidiosa pluma, "IML," 28). This idea simply does not make any sense, if held to logical scrutiny. The poet has created an imaginary construct, his own flying thought, to have it fly to see his lady and her husband engaged in amorous exploits. Why would such a construct, created by the imagination, be limited by the concept of time? Furthering this contradiction, in the second stanza, the poet insists that his flying thought can do all, but obviously it cannot. In effect, the "plumas" or "feathers" that the thought dons in order to fly do more than just enable it to do that: indeed, they help cover up his thought, to give it the appearance of something that can soar toward the heavens, while in truth it is grounded on the earth like the "chained" one who "walks" on its surface (that is, the "pensamiento" is not noble, not heavenly, but base and earthly, just as Vulcan is earthly, as an exile from the heavens).

What this ellipsis, in fact, reveals is yet another level of the psychological conflict: the subject has, on the one hand, a conscious desire to witness the sex act (what some theorists of jealousy, including Stendhal, Freud, and Girard, have called "a fascination with the rival"), while, at the same time, there is a subconscious repression, or blocking out, of the sex act from the imagination. The bizarre idea that "thought has arrived too late" is an example of a clever defense mechanism designed by the lyric voice's unconscious mind to protect itself from the extremely harsh vision. Clearly, there has been what Freud calls "censorship" of disturbing material, more typical, for the Viennese doctor, of daydreams than of dreams.[19] At the moment in which he is about to visualize his most hated yet most

18. Freud, "Some Neurotic Mechanisms," 226.
19. Freud, *The Interpretation of Dreams,* 526–45.

desired scene, the lyric voice creates an excuse for not witnessing it in his daydream.

Yet another indication of inner turmoil is the conflict between the lyric voice's envious, dejected feelings and his good wishes, which is the "strange" combination, for critics. He really desires to wish them well (in the third and sixth stanzas). At a conscious level, his envy and jealousy are unseemly, so he tries to suppress them.[20] He really wants her, but his want is base. However, moral compunction alone cannot quash this immense desire. In a simile describing the husband, he reveals further fantasies of possessing the woman, through ill will befalling her spouse. First, he describes the husband as "an almost dead figure" (figura casi muerta, "IML," 40), revealing his unconscious desire to kill him or see him die; later, the poet's wish "that your bed be a soft battlefield" ("IML," 54) might be a veiled desire for the husband to become impotent. In this sense he wishes upon his rival—the Mars figure—a metaphorical and sexual version of the lameness that he himself suffers. This desire to be noble while harboring suppressed hostility is the root, then, of the neurotic conflict, which expresses itself visually through the juxtaposition of contradictory visual images that were iconographic in classical and Renaissance art and literature.

In "What of the tall envious mountains," Góngora has done three very innovative things with literary and artistic traditions. First, as I have detailed, he has merged two disparate versions of the Mars-Venus myth, superimposing incompatible scenes as depicted by artists such as Tintoretto, Veronese, Piero di Cosimo, and Murer. This forging of opposites is founded on the similarities between the two, and leads to the creation of a polysemous myth.

Secondly, the web of complications arising from the juxtaposition of well-known iconographic representations of Vulcan, Venus, and Mars points also to a Góngora who dexterously attempts to demonstrate in this poem the superiority of poetry to painting. This agonistic intention of his poetry has been adduced by Emilie Bergman in her book on ekphrasis.[21] In this vein, Góngora seems to be implying

20. Such envy of another's good fortune has always been considered morally repugnant, at least since Aristotle's *Nichomachean Ethics;* as for why a man would want to conceal his jealousy, this has been adduced by Capellanus in *The Art of Courtly Love* and later by Roland Barthes in *A Lover's Discourse*: it maligns the woman's character.

21. Bergmann, *Art Inscribed,* 108–9.

to the reader that it would be impossible to weave such a net of intricate meanings into one tapestry or paint them onto one canvas, but that he can do so in one very beautiful poem. Thirdly, Góngora has inverted the values of the medieval courtly love or *fin amor* tradition of Old Occitan poetry of the twelfth and thirteenth centuries, a tradition in which the male poet laments separation from his married lady. In *fin amor* poetry, such as that of Bernart de Ventadorn, the husband was almost always described as "ugly," "jealous," "old," and "dull," and the love between husband and wife was seen, paradoxically, as illegitimate because the institution of marriage was based not on love but on a system akin to proprietary laws. The true or "noble love," in contrast, was—in the ideology of *fin amor*—the rarely consummated, adulterous love between poet and lady.[22] With the presence of the Vulcan figure, what seems like the legitimate love between husband and wife in Góngora's poem must also be considered illegitimate, since they are, at the same time, adulterers. Whereas desire is unproblematic in courtly love poetry—the poet's love is noble, the husband's is always ignoble—Góngora's more complex treatment, based on incongruous iconographic juxtapositions, corresponds to the Vulcan-subject's conflicted desire, seen in defense mechanisms, expressed illogicality, and a censored daydream. In this way, Góngora uses jealousy to reveal the underpinnings of the unconscious as he forges a modern notion of the psyche.

---

22. Moshe Lazar, "Fin'amor," 74. In the sixteenth century, Garcilaso de la Vega is still steeped in this tradition when, in his Second Eclogue, he refers to his beloved Isabel Freire's husband as a Cyclops (Elías L. Rivers, *Garcilaso de la Vega, Poems: A Critical Guide,* 66).

Seven

Góngora on the Beautiful and the Sublime

> **When my sword passed from its sheath right through his chest, it seemed to everyone that my sword and his voice together imitated thunder and lightning.**
>
> Calderón, *A secreto agravio, secreta venganza*
> (Secret Vengeance for Secret Insult)

As the chapters of this book attest, the myriad shapes and kinds of jealousy were of great concern for early modern Spanish writers. Such interest grew from the Renaissance to the Baroque. It could be said that Baroque writers found in jealousy a polyvalent designation by which to express their art, one whose dynamism was favorable to what René Wellek calls "the baroque literary style," that is, the figures and tropes most favored by Baroque writers and poets. Indeed, in the work of the Spanish Baroque poet par excellence, Luis de Góngora, jealousy expresses the poetics of a new age, pitting Renaissance aesthetic notions of beauty against the destructive power of the sublime.

On the Beautiful

In "Las flores del romero" (The Rosemary Flowers), a *romancillo* from 1608, Góngora is primarily concerned with the feelings of the jealous lover, in this case, "una niña," a young woman or girl (her age is indeterminate). In the poem's three stanzas, the poet addresses the *niña* in apostrophe.[1] The first stanza is brief, and the second half of it will become the refrain:

1. A *romancillo* is a short ballad containing lines of fewer than eight syllables retaining the assonantal pattern of *romance*. There are several examples

157

Rosemary flowers, dear little Isabel, today are blue flowers, but tomorrow will be honey.

(Las flores del romero,
niña Isabel,
hoy son flores azules,
mañana serán miel.)[2]

The emotion of jealousy is introduced at the very beginning, through the use of the adjective *azules,* the color that corresponds to this passion, according to the literary conventions of the Golden Age. The second stanza begins:

Girl, you are jealous, jealous of that one who is lucky, because you seek him, but he is blind, for he does not see you, he is ungrateful, because he angers you, and he is overly self-confident, because he does not apologize today for what he did yesterday.

(Celosa estás la niña,
celosa estás de aquél
dichoso, pues le buscas,
ciego, pues no te ve,
ingrato, pues te enoja,
y confiado, pues
no se disculpa hoy
de lo que hizo ayer. "FR," 5–12)

It seems that the "lucky" one (aquel dichoso) has not treated the girl well, though the nature of his offense is not made explicit. In some way, he has given her reason to suffer jealousy: "he does not apologize today for what he did yesterday." The use of the preterit for the wrong he committed, *hizo* ("FR," 12), in a report by the extra-diegetic lyric voice, makes it likely that he did in fact do something to cause her jealousy. Thus, her emotional experience is typical of female dramatic jealousy, which is generally not suspicious, but evidential or fait accompli. Similarly, given that the beloved has acted in some

---

in Góngora's oeuvre of romancillos and romances with the flavor of traditional poetry, in which a *niña* suffers for love; see also "La más bella niña" (The most beautiful girl [1580]) and "Lloraba la niña" (The girl was crying [1595]). However, jealousy is an important element only in this poem, not in these others.

2. Góngora, "Las Flores del romero," in Dámaso Alonso, ed., *Góngora y el "Polifemo,"* 2:50–51. Subsequent citations from this edition will be made parenthetically in the text by line number using the abbreviation "FR."

way, Isabel's jealousy meets de Sousa's criterion for rationality, in that the target is "jealousy provoking." That is, the "lucky" one has done something wrong of which the girl has secure knowledge, either directly or indirectly.

As analyzed in Chapter 2, it was typical of the literature of this period to treat women's jealousy only when it had a known basis in fact, unlike, say, the suspicious and possessive, often irrational, kind of male jealousy that Cervantes describes in *The Old Jealous Man*. In contrast to the monstrous, hyperbolic jealousy of Lope's Sonnet 56 of the *Rimas,* "That the forty-nine eternally," this woman's jealousy would have to be described as *hypobolic* and, as I will later explain, beautiful.[3] To be sure, there were mythological models of extreme female jealousy, the greatest example of which was Euripides' *Medea* (a tale retold by Ovid in the *Metamorphoses*). It is culturally telling that neither Góngora nor his contemporaries chose to elaborate this myth, save for scattered references. Rosemary Lloyd's reflection about the threat to men of women who actively experience powerful emotions once more comes to mind.[4] To this end, it seems, Lope de Vega ridicules female jealousy in *Jealous Arminda* and *The Dog in the Manger*. In this romancillo, Góngora has no desire to ridicule, but he certainly does not represent female jealousy in the same way that he represents the male variety. The emotional experience that lends itself to hyperbole when felt by male characters is now gentle, quaint, and beautiful. Góngora thus captures Goldie's notion of *feeling towards* an object as he incorporates gender—what Nancy Armstrong has called "the root of human identity"—into the personal perspective.[5]

Perhaps the beloved paid another girl too much attention by looking at her. This would explain why the poet calls him "blind" and exclaims that "he does not see you," meaning more broadly that he does not have eyes for her. Now she suffers because she would like to speak with him but he is not to be found. For the poet, the girl's suffering is a good sign that the two in fact do love each other, com-

3. The beautiful has been connected with the female and the sublime with the male in eighteenth-century treatises on the sublime and the beautiful (see Leslie E. Moore, *Beautiful Sublime: The Making of "Paradise Lost" 1701–1734,* 62–74).

4. Lloyd, *Closer and Closer Apart,* 9.

5. Nancy Armstrong, "Some Call It Fiction: On the Politics of Domesticity," 580.

paring them to "those who have loved each other much" (aquellos / que se han querido bien, "FR," 15–16), and hence agrees with Ovid's and Capellanus's idea that jealousy discloses the intensity of love. This is very different from "A los celos" (To Jealousy), also known as "O niebla del estado más sereno" (Oh fog of the most serene state), Góngora's 1582 sonnet in which male jealousy is anathema to love, and from Cervantes's notion that jealousy has no part in love, except in the *nobles temores*. Such conceptual claims as Lope's "there is no love without jealousy" and Cervantes's "there is no jealousy in love" are not part of Góngora's vocabulary in the romancillo. The treatment of jealousy depends here on the feelings as qualia that constitute an important element of emotions, not on ideas or beliefs, or on the statement of universal laws.

As the poet continues, he asks the girl to have hope, for he believes in their love:

> Let hope dry up all that you cry for him; because the jealousy between those who have loved each other much, today is blue flowers, but tomorrow will be honey.

> (Enjuguen esperanzas
> lo que lloras por él;
> que celos entre aquellos
> que se han querido bien,
> *hoy son flores azules,*
> *mañana serán miel.* "FR," 13–18)

The image of hope born of tears (Enjuguen esperanzas) demonstrates the poet's optimism in the benign quality of this fleeting jealousy. This idea is repeated with great simplicity in the metaphorical refrain about blue flowers and honey: You need not worry; although today you feel jealousy, tomorrow life will be sweet again.

In the final stanza, the poet wishes to give the *niña* even more reason for hope:

> Dawn of yourself, as you wake to enjoy your pleasure, your tears eclipse your pleasure; calm your eyes, and give no more pearls, because that which befits the dawn is ill suited to the sun. Undo, as if it were a fog, all that you cannot see, because suspicions between lovers, and the disputes that ensue, today are blue flowers, but tomorrow will be honey.

> (Aurora de ti misma,
> que cuando a amanecer
> a tu placer empiezas,
> te eclipsan tu placer,
> serénense tus ojos,
> y más perlas no des,
> porque al Sol le está mal
> lo que a la Aurora bien.
> Desata, como nieblas,
> todo lo que no ves;
> que sospechas de amantes
> y querellas después,
> *hoy son flores azules,*
> *mañana serán miel.* "FR," 19–32)

Jealousy has arisen in the young woman because of the actions of her beloved, which make it impossible for her to have fun or enjoy herself, expressed in a metaphor that focuses on the sense of sight: jealous tears "eclipse your pleasure," that is, they blind her. The poet continues with his emphasis on sight, telling the girl, "calm your eyes" (serénense tus ojos), meaning the eyes should cry no more, at the same time that he suggests that the tears are the eclipsers in the previous metaphor. The tears are also "pearls" of "dawn." In a celestial conceit, the tears belong to the realm of dawn because they are like pearls of dew (*perlas del rocío*), a common metaphor in high poetry. As Dámaso Alonso explains, "the dew" is an element that does not correspond to "the sun," and thus, the poet asks the woman not to cry any longer.[6] The sun that is to come up tomorrow has the power to "[u]ndo . . . all that you do not see." That is, the jealous suspicions that have no basis other than the imagination will disappear, in a comparison to the action of the sun in Nature: at dawn there is often fog that lifts only when the sun rises. The fog (*nieblas*) appears in a visual simile once more, in that it obscures sight, though it is easily lifted. There is unity in this stanza beyond this extended metaphor, since the imagery began with the celestial verb *to eclipse* (*eclipsar*), thus making a full circle—or orbit—back to the dew that eclipsed her pleasure. The refrain itself fits well into this scheme, since the "honey" (which will replace the "suspicions"

---

6. Alonso, ed., *Góngora y el "Polifemo,"* 2:52.

and "disputes") is golden, and thus has the same color as the sun, creating a perfect harmonious correspondence.

It is worth noting that this poem shares lexical affinities with the first line of Góngora's 1582 sonnet that begins "Oh fog of the most serene state" (O niebla del estado más sereno). In the romancillo, the poet implores the young woman to "calm" her eyes (serénense); in the sonnet, the man is "serene" (sereno) before he becomes jealous. In both poems, jealousy is metaphorized as a "fog" that blinds. Notwithstanding such similarities, the emotion is not treated hyperbolically in the romancillo. In fact, in it the sun can easily "undo" the fleeting "fog" (it is treated as a quotidian process of Nature). This metaphor focusing on the ephemerality of (female) jealousy in the romancillo contrasts with the eternality of (male) jealousy in the sonnet.

The sonnet has an "I" sufferer who is almost not felt (there is only one use of a first-person pronoun), but it is an imitation of sonnets by Sannazaro and Garcilaso de la Vega, in which the male "yo" was more strongly perceived. Evidently, Góngora conceived of hyperbolic jealousy as that of a man, while the weaker, transient, ephemeral variety is a better description of that of a woman. The poets of love— in the line of courtly love, dolce stil novo, Petrarchism—were largely men who celebrated a beloved lady, or sang of their suffering, which was provoked, they often claimed, by her. But the protagonist of the romancillo is female, and the poet has difficulty identifying with her plight (it is the only poem by Góngora in which a woman suffers from jealousy). He feels compassion for her, but clearly for the poet jealousy is not such a grave matter for a woman, and it is even less so, perhaps, for a niña. Additionally, he makes recourse to the same double standard as Lope de Vega. That mere "suspicions" are blamed— implicit in his saying that life will be sweet when the suspicions disappear—in a poem that refers to fait accompli jealousy recalls Lope's Jealous Arminda: suspicion is blamed for loss of happiness, even when the jealousy is fully rational and based on intersubjectively available information.

This weak female jealousy that love will overpower is ultimately immersed in the Neoplatonic aesthetics of Beauty, wherein an orderly love will emerge from a previously disordered state. The origin of Beauty is described by Marsilio Ficino in his Commentary on Plato's "Symposium" (ca. 1475): "The attractiveness of this Orderliness is Beauty. To beauty, Love, as soon as it was born, drew the Mind, and led the Mind formerly un-beautiful to the same Mind made beautiful. . . . Who, therefore, will doubt that Love immediately followed Chaos, and preceded the world and all the gods who were assigned to the various parts of the world?" Love, for Ficino, is equated with beauty: "When we say Love, we mean by that term the desire for beauty, for this is the definition of Love among all philosophers." Love creates order where there was none, instilling "harmony," which is what the poem's sweet honey of tomorrow (mañana serán miel) represents, as does the realignment of the natural world (the sun, the dew, etc.). As Ficino explains, "Beauty is, in fact, a certain charm which is found chiefly and predominantly in the harmony of several elements." Furthermore, Ficino emphasizes the common attributes of love and beauty, among which are "youth" and "handsomeness," which perhaps explains the youth of the *niña*. And as the poet tries to calm the fears of the young woman and reestablish celestial harmony, he may be alluding to Ficino: "Love is clearly said to soothe with his song the minds of men and gods."[7] In his songlike romancillo, Góngora's lyric voice becomes the god of love, creating harmonious beauty.

The modern aesthetics of Kant includes a notion of beauty that shares elements with this weak female jealousy overcome by love. In his *Critique of Judgement* (1791), Kant contends, "For the beautiful is directly attended with a feeling of the furtherance of life, and is thus compatible with charms and a playful imagination."[8] For Kant, Beauty is posited in radical contrast to the aesthetics of the sublime, which is imaged by Góngora as male. Such sublime male jealousy is found in several poems, among which are the sonnet "Oh fog of the most serene state" and the *Fábula de Polifemo y Galatea* (Fable of Polyphemus and Galatea).

On the Sublime

The last century has left us with three main views of Góngora's *Fable of Polyphemus and Galatea*. In the first—which characterizes both Dámaso Alonso's and Alexander A. Parker's interpreta-

---

7. Marsilio Ficino, *Commentary on Plato's "Symposium,"* 1.3.128; 1.4.130; 5.7.175; 5.9.178.

8. Immanuel Kant, *Critique of Judgement,* trans. James Creed Meredith, 91 (Ak. 5:245). Page and section numbers refer to the Meredith translation of *Critique of Judgement* and also to the standard edition of Kant's work in German, known as the *Akademie* (see *Kant's Werke: Akademie-Textausgabe*).

tions—the poem is said to concern opposing dualisms (monstrosity/beauty, darkness/light, love/jealousy) united and balanced in an organic whole.[9] According to the second view, the positive values in this dualism are celebrated; for R. O. Jones, these are beauty and life, while for Robert Jammes, they are love and other pastoral ideals.[10] The third holds that the negative values of the dualism triumph; for instance, Melinda Eve Lehrer interprets much of Góngora's poetry, including the *Polifemo,* as "beautiful pastorale[s] . . . built up and then shattered." Along similar lines, R. John McCaw treats the poem's subversion of pastoral: "The contradiction between Polyphemus' words and deeds, then, signif[ies] the triumph of instinct over intellect, and, generally, the deflation of the integrity of pastoral ideals."[11] In what follows, I will support the third view by providing a new reading of the poem: the *Polifemo* is not a celebration of love, but rather a representation of love's destruction by jealousy. Góngora found in jealousy a representation of sublime experience, anticipating one of the dominant topics of eighteenth- and nineteenth-century aesthetics, and this sublime power of jealousy, the destroyer of love, is the focus of the poem.

The human emotion of jealousy is often described in literature in the most hyperbolic terms, reflecting perhaps the actual strength of the affective experience. Calderón and Lope de Vega, among others, provide good examples of this; hence the title of the former's play, *Jealousy, the Greatest Monster,* and Lope de Vega's horrific realization in his sonnet "That the forty-nine eternally" that "to see another lover in the arms of one's lady" (otro amante en brazos de su dama)[12] is life's worst torment, worse than the tortures suffered by the Danaids, Tantalus, Ixion, Sisyphus, and Prometheus. However, Góngora's use of hyperbole raises the theme to its Olympian zenith, indeed, beyond the bounds of conceptuality. Whereas the

9. Alonso, ed., *Góngora y el "Polifemo,"* 1:186–207; Alexander A. Parker, ed., *Fábula de Polifemo y Galatea,* 111–16. Parker argues, for example, "But when praising beauty, Góngora does not forget ugliness; when praising life, he does not forget death. . . . Consequently, Góngora's art has indubitable equilibrium and harmony" (*Fábula,* 116).

10. R. O. Jones, ed., *Poems of Góngora,* 36–37; Jammes, *Etudes,* 533–54.

11. Melinda Eve Lehrer, *Classical Myth and the "Polifemo" of Góngora,* 57; R. John McCaw, "Turning a Blind Eye: Sexual Competition, Self-Contradiction, and the Impotence of Pastoral in Góngora's *Fábula de Polifemo y Galatea,"* 32.

12. Lope de Vega, Sonnet 56, in José Manuel Blecua, ed., *Obras poéticas de Lope de Vega,* 56n, l. 13.

poetics of the day described a harmonious beauty in which the poet was encouraged to amaze the reader with *admiratio* or *maraviglia,* Góngora surpasses these tropes. I will show here how jealousy gave Góngora the opportunity to speak about something beyond the phenomena and experience of the world and beyond the poetics of his day: the sublime.

I am not using the term *sublime* as it was sometimes used in Renaissance and Baroque Europe as a synonym for "great" or "elevated,"[13] nor in Longinus's specialized sense as referring to *phusis* being revealed by the poet's effortless concealment of his *technè,* and having the effect of uplifting the reader's soul.[14] Along these lines, sixteenth-century theoreticians prescribed *admiratio* in poetry, as canonized in Francesco Patrizi's *Della poetica* (On Poetics, 1586), where he writes on *mirabile:* "[T]he poet should always strive, as his work and end, to cause admiration [fare mirabile] on whatever subject he happens to put to hand, in whichever reader who happens upon his work, for not all readers are alike."[15] Although these uses well describe the kinds of metaphors created by Góngora's precursors and contemporaries, they do not adequately portray the magnitude of his images.

I propose that Góngora's images are "sublime" in the *modern* aesthetic sense, as developed by Edmund Burke, Joseph Addison, and Johann Georg Sulzer in the eighteenth century and systematized by Kant in *Critique of Judgement* in 1791.[16] For Kant, the sublime

13. For instance, in the sense of "great," one aspect of the early debate over Góngora's style concerned "the use of humble words interspersed with sublime ones" ([e]l uso de palabras humildes entretexidas con las sublimes [Pedro Díaz de Rivas, *Discursos apologéticos por el estylo del Poliphemo y Soledades,* 36]).

14. In contrast to my usage, the contemporary critic Piero Boitani employs the term *sublime* in Longinus's sense (*The Tragic and the Sublime in Medieval Literature,* 9). Also, Roberto González Echevarría uses two of Longinus's elements to demonstrate how José Lezama Lima interpreted Góngora as sublime, as shown through a study of Lezama Lima's essay on Góngora and his allusion to a passage in Góngora's *Soledades* in his novel *Paradiso* (González Echevarría, "Lezama, Góngora y la poética del mal gusto," 433).

15. Francesco Patrizi, *Della poetica,* quoted in Bernard Weinberg, *A History of Literary Criticism in the Italian Renaissance,* 2:784–85. With respect to Góngora's *Soledades,* Marsha S. Collins contends that notions from Longinus's sublime and various Renaissance treatises inform the kind of *admiratio* that Góngora employed in it (Collins, *The "Soledades," Góngora's Masque of the Imagination,* 115–17).

16. Paul Guyer, *Kant and the Experience of Freedom,* 258–59.

is an experience wherein the subject's reason and imagination are overwhelmed by a scene of such great magnitude or power that it defies the subject's conceptual ability. He distinguishes two types: the *mathematical* and the *dynamic*. The subjective experience of the mathematical sublime occurs when the enormity of the object defies conceptualization. It cannot be conceived of in its entirety, nor can it be fully perceived by the observer (such as an Egyptian pyramid for a close-standing observer). The dynamic sublime is experienced when something defies being fully conceptualized because of its tremendous force in motion (such as a raging storm).[17]

It is well known that this Kantian framework had a tremendous impact on European Romantic poetry. Yet one sees the stirrings of the modern conception of the sublime already in the early modern period in Góngora. The phenomenology of the sublime, as described by Kant, is anticipated in broad strokes in Góngora's poetry, notwithstanding the fact that the most influential poetics of his time—Patrizi's *On Poetics,* Tasso's *Discorsi dell'Arte Poetica e del Poema Eroico* (Discourse on Poetics and the Heroic Poem), and López Pinciano's *Philosophia antigua poética* (Ancient Poetic Philosophy)— make no reference to it. Indeed, Góngora expresses the dual varieties of the sublime in two poems: he develops a representation of the mathematical sublime in the 1582 sonnet "Oh fog of the most serene state"; and in the *Polifemo,* he instantiates jealousy in the humanly endowed monster Polyphemus, in what amounts to not only an evocation of the dynamic sublime, but also a descriptive poetics for the *geist* of a new age, the Baroque sublime.

Long before he created the *Polifemo,* Góngora first represented the sublime power of jealousy in the 1582 sonnet. Thus, I will first examine this poem to elucidate Góngora's treatment of jealousy as a locus of the mathematical sublime. I will then demonstrate how the *Polifemo* embodies a representation of the dynamic sublime, and as such, is really about the destruction of love by jealousy. Through comparison to classical and Renaissance precursor texts I will illustrate how Góngora moved beyond *admiratio* to the modern sublime.

---

17. Kant's system also includes an aspect—not evoked by Góngora—that was, for him, one of the most important, that is, the moral component of aesthetic experience. For Kant, the sublime instructs the subject of the categorical imperative and the subject's own autonomy even in the face of a potentially hostile world.

Mathematically Sublime Jealousy:
"Oh fog of the most serene state" (1582)

In one of his earliest sonnets, Góngora treats the theme of jealousy with great artifice. The poem was first published by Pedro Espinosa in his *Flores de poetas ilustres de España* (Flowers of Illustrious Spanish Poets, 1605), and both the so-called anonymous commentator and Salcedo Coronel noted that "Oh fog of the most serene state" was based on Jacopo Sannazaro's Sonnet 23.[18] The similarities to Sannazaro's sonnet are undeniable, and there is ample evidence to suggest that Góngora's sonnet is an imitation not only of this Italian poem, but also of a later version of the same in Spanish, namely, Garcilaso de la Vega's Sonnet 39, "Oh jealousy, terrible reins of love" (Oh çelos, de amor terrible freno). The latter is a beautiful translation of Sannazaro's sonnet, and contains lexical peculiarities that then reappear in Góngora's more original *imitatio*. J. P. W. Crawford identifies several similar Spanish versions of this Sannazaro sonnet, while Ulrich Schulz-Buschhaus compares a few Italian versions— also imitations of Sannazaro's sonnet—that, unlike Góngora's, do not surpass their model in any substantial way.[19] Here is the model sonnet on which these imitations are based:

1–4. Oh jealousy, horrible rein to lovers, that at once you turn and hold me so strong. Oh sister of impious bitter Death, with your gaze you upset the serene sky;

5–8. Oh serpent hiding in a sweet hollow of rejoicing flowers, that has killed my hope; after prosperous outcomes, bad luck; in tender foods, sour poison;

9–11. From which infernal valley of the world did you exit, Oh cruel monster, Oh plague of mortals who makes my days so dark and sad?

12–14. Go back, do not double my ills. Oh unhappy fear, why did you come? Wasn't Love enough with his arrows?

18. Biruté Ciplijauskaité, ed., *Sonetos completos,* by Luis de Góngora, 244. J. P. W. Crawford notes that this poem might not be a direct imitation of Sannazaro's, but rather of one of the many Spanish imitations: "Sannazaro's poem was probably translated more frequently in Spain than any other Italian sonnet, and, since Góngora's sonnet shows no close verbal similarities, it probably does not depend upon direct imitation" (Crawford, "Italian Sources," 126).

19. Crawford, "Notes on the Poetry of Hernando de Acuña; Notes on the Sonnets in the Spanish *Cancionero General de 1554*," 314–37; Schulz-Buschhaus, "Der frühe Góngora und die italienische Lyrik," 219–38.

Oh gelosia, d'amanti orribil freno,
Ch'in un punto mi volgi e tien sí forte;
Oh sorella dell'empia amara Morte,
Che con tua vista turbi il ciel sereno;
    Oh serpente nascosto in dolce seno
Di lieti fior, che mie speranze hai morte;
Tra prosperi successi avversa sorte;
Tra soavi vivande aspro veneno;
    Da qual valle infernal nel mondo uscisti,
Oh crudel mostro, oh peste de' mortali,
Che fai li giorni miei sí oscuri e tristi?
    Tórnati giú, non raddoppiar miei mali.
Infelice paura, a che venisti?
Or non bastava Amor con li suoi strali?[20]

Góngora does not make use of his models in a rigid manner, but rather develops them into a very original poem:

1–4. Oh fog of the most serene state, infernal fury, wicked snake! Oh venomous viper hiding in the sweet-smelling hollow of a green meadow!
5–8. Oh mortal poison in the nectar of Love, in a crystal glass you take away life! Oh sword hanging over me by a hair, harsh rein to the spur of love.
9–11. Oh jealousy, eternal hangman of favor! Return to the sad place where you were found, or to the Kingdom (if you fit there) of fear.
12–14. But you will not fit there, because for so long you've been eating yourself up, and you never end, you must be greater than hell itself.

(Ô niebla del estado más sereno,   1
Furia infernal, serpiente mal nacida!
Ô ponçoñosa viuora escondida
De verde prado en oloroso seno!
    Ô entre el nectar de Amor mortal veneno,   5
Que en vaso de crystal quitas la vida!
Ô espada sobre mi de vn pelo assida,

20. Jacopo Sannazaro, Sonnet 23, *Opere di Iacopo Sannazaro* (quoted in Cipli-jauskaité, ed., *Sonetos completos,* by Góngora, 243), preceded by my translation. Citations of this sonnet will be made parenthetically in the text by line number using the title Sonnet 23. I have not provided Garcilaso's sonnet since it is so similar to Sannazaro's, but I do make references to its peculiarities in the text.

De la amorosa espuela duro freno.
    Ô zelo del fauor verdugo eterno!   9
Vueluete al lugar triste donde estabas,
O al Reino (si allà cabes) del espanto.
    Mas no cabràs allà, que pues ha tanto
Que comes de ti mesmo, I no te acabas,   13
Maior debes de ser que el mismo infierno.)²¹

The poem is an invective apostrophe to jealousy that describes the terrible evil of the emotion. In the first line, jealousy is addressed (without name) as the "fog of the most serene state." This image dealing with disturbed serenity originates in the fourth line of Sannazaro's sonnet, "with your gaze you upset the serene sky," though the metaphorical conclusion that jealousy is fog (*niebla*) (because it disturbs the sky's serenity) seems to be a conceit of Góngora's (what exactly disturbs the sky is not made explicit in Sannazaro's sonnet— that is, it could be "fog," "clouds," or another natural phenomenon). Although at first glance these two images seem very similar, it is noteworthy that in Góngora's, the action that occurs in nature is transferred to the human realm ("the most serene state" is psychological), while in Sannazaro's the action remains within the domain of nature (it is the sky that is affected, though of course this represents the jealous person's mind). Góngora plays with the metaphorical value and makes it such that the "niebla" (natural phenomenon) interferes directly in the "serene state" of the jealous subject, which in turn more accurately describes the subjective mental confusion produced by the emotion.

More metaphors follow: jealousy is "infernal fury, wicked snake" (Furia infernal, serpiente mal nacida, Sonnet 65, 2). The adjectivized noun *furia infernal* is the first indication in the poem that it might be an imitation of Garcilaso de la Vega's poem. In Sannazaro's sonnet, the closest line is the ninth: "From which infernal valley of the world did you exit" (Da qual valle infernal nel mondo uscisti); the same line in Garcilaso's sonnet reads "From which infernal fury did you exit here . . . ?" (¿De quál furia infernal acá saliste . . . ?),²² a reference to the three chthonic furies who relentlessly persecute those accused of

21. Luis de Góngora, "O niebla del estado más sereno," Sonnet 65 in Ciplijauskaité, ed., *Sonetos completos,* by Góngora, 243. Citations of Sonnet 65 will be made parenthetically in the text by line number.
22. Garcilaso de la Vega, Sonnet 39, in *Obras completas con comentario.* Subsequent citations will be made parenthetically in the text by line number.

blood crimes and release evil into the world; hence Garcilaso introduces Greek mythology into the poem, a tendency that Góngora follows. The choice of *furia* in lieu of *valle* in Garcilaso's sonnet cannot
be explained by metrical requirements alone: both nouns are paroxytones that end in vowels permitting the synalepha with *infernal*.

In Garcilaso's model, the serpent is literally "born" (*nacida*), but
it is Góngora who writes "mal nacida" (Sonnet 65, 2), contributing
further to the semantic field of "evil" (*maldad*), and, in contrast to
his models, Góngora doubles the image of the serpent to elaborate it
further: "Oh venomous viper hiding in the sweet-smelling hollow of
a green meadow!" (O ponçoñosa vibora escondida / De verde prado
en oloroso seno, Sonnet 65, 3–4). These lines introduce the Virgilian
theme of evil lurking behind beauty, which is found in lines 5 and 6
of Sannazaro's sonnet. Góngora emphasizes the "green meadow" instead of Sannazaro's flowers (*fior*), evoking more closely the original
source, Virgil's "snake lurking in the grass" (latet anguis in herba),[23]
at the same time that he elicits the flowers without naming them
through the olfactory reference "sweet-smelling" (*oloroso*).

The second quatrain provides a duplicate example of lurking evil,
once again of exactly two lines: "Oh mortal poison in the nectar of
Love, in a crystal glass you take away life!" (O entre el nectar de
Amor mortal veneno, / Que en vaso de crystal quitas la vida! Sonnet
65, 5–6). The image of "poison" or "venom" (*veneno*) exists in Sannazaro's eighth line (aspro veneno), where, as in Garcilaso's, it is in
the food (*vivande; manjar*). Góngora transfers the poison to a liquid,
hidden in Love's nectar and twice as beautiful for it is contained in a
crystal glass. Thus, the poet implies that love (the nectar of love) is
accompanied by jealousy (poison/venom).[24] The liquid-poison image
agrees better with the other symbolism of the poem, and in particular with the serpent metaphors—in comparison with Sannazaro's
and Garcilaso's solid-poison images—since the venom of these animals flows in liquid form.

The seventh line, "Oh sword hanging over me by a hair" (O espada
sobre mi de vn pelo assida, Sonnet 65), is a vivid and intense image
not found in the precursor poems. The fatal danger and the volatile

23. Virgil, *Eclogues,* 3.93.
24. The hidden poison of love (in this case jealousy) is a common theme in
Góngora's lyric, evoked also in the famous sonnet "La dulce boca que a gustar
convida" (The sweet mouth which invites to taste [1584]), which shares lexical
similarities with the sonnet on jealousy.

threshold of the jealous male lover's suspicion, leading potentially to tremendous violence, are well described here, in this evocation of the sword of Damocles,[25] in which beautiful life and gruesome death are separated by the strength of a mere horse hair. The eighth line, "harsh rein to the spur of love" (De la amorosa espuela duro freno, Sonnet 65), is close to being a translation of Sannazaro's first; however, its subtle differences make it more similar to Garcilaso's first line. While the rein (*freno*) puts brakes on the lovers (*amanti*) in the Italian sonnet, in Garcilaso's, it puts an end to love: "Oh jealousy, terrible reins of love" (Oh çelos, de amor terrible freno, Sonnet 39). Góngora's "spur of love" (amorosa espuela) has more in common with *amor* in the abstract sense than with *amanti,* the human instantiation of lovers, that is, the real beings who experience love. In Garcilaso's poem, the semantic choice of abstract over particular may owe something to metrical concerns: his translated line requires a bisyllabic word, and thus *amantes* (the literal translation of the particular *amanti*) would have one too many syllables. But Góngora's new line is more dynamic than either: it puts in motion an agonistic force against the "rein" of jealousy; love is animated as a "spur" on a horse that fights a losing battle against jealousy, the reins that bring the galloping animal to a full stop. The passion of jealousy becomes an extremely powerful Thanatos image, for the running horse is a symbol of life's natural instincts—according to Jung—and is associated with the power of the gods Apollo, Poseidon, and Mars. The Greeks considered it the most beautiful animal.[26] Additionally, the galloping horse recalls the presence of that animal's hair in the allusion, in line 7, to the sword of Damocles.

In the first of the tercets, the poem's addressee is named, strangely, in the singular: "Oh jealousy [*zelo*]" (Sonnet 65, 9). This marks the first explicit mention of the central theme, in contrast to Sannazaro's and Garcilaso's sonnets, which begin, respectively, "Oh gelosia" and "Oh çelos." The first edition of the early-eighteenth-century *Diccionario de Autoridades* (Dictionary of Authorities) makes a point of reporting that the word *zelo* (or *celo,* with modern orthography) did not have the meaning of *zelos* in the plural. The entry for the plural *zelos*—jealousy—begins with the caveat "Always used in the plural" (Usado siempre en plural). Thus the poet's singular usage is

25. Ciplijauskaité, ed., *Sonetos,* by Góngora, 128n7.
26. J. A. Pérez-Rioja, *Diccionario de símbolos y mitos,* 103–4.

apparently strange. It can probably be explained by Góngora's desire to maintain grammatical agreement between the singular subject (*zelo*) and the singular metaphors (*niebla, furia, serpiente*) for the purpose of creating a more forceful overall hyperbole in the sonnet. Since the word for jealousy is singular in Italian, this is not an issue in Sannazaro's sonnet. In the first tercet, for instance, Sannazaro addresses *gelosia* in apostrophe, with the verb *uscisti* in the second-person singular. However, Garcilaso employs the normal Spanish plural for jealousy, *çelos,* in line 1, which in line 9 creates a hermeneutic problem that ends up debilitating his overall hyperbolic effect. Where the Italian poet wrote *uscisti,* Garcilaso writes *saliste,* a translation of *uscisti,* and thus he is also addressing a singular "you" (*tú*) in apostrophe; and again in line 12, he uses the second-person singular in the command "Go back to hell" (Tórnate al infierno). Grammatically, however, this verb does not agree with *çelos,* which would obviously require a plural verbal form. To whom, then, is Garcilaso addressing himself? To the singular metaphors themselves, individually (*serpiente, veneno, monstruo,* and so forth). In this manner, the metaphors gain a certain power over that which they symbolize; hence *jealousy* loses its autonomy, and its hyperbolic stature is weakened. This, I would argue, is most likely why Góngora, in his efforts to create the greatest of all hyperboles—anticipating in 1582 both Cervantes's "most jealous man in the world" (1613) and Lope's Sonnet 56 (1602)—used the singular *zelo* instead of *zelos.*

Góngora's metaphor "eternal hangman" (verdugo eterno, Sonnet 65, 9) agrees in number and gender with *zelo* and evokes Satan, the hangman of eternal life, according to the Christian tradition. Here the *verdugo* is of the beloved's "favor," and refers to the social negativity of jealousy: it is not attractive, for it debases not only the lover but also the beloved by calling the latter's virtue into question (the problem that Periandro seems to have overcome in the *Persiles*).

His next two lines duplicate the image of Sannazaro's last tercet, "Go back, do not double my ills" (Sonnet 23, 12) and incorporate the adjective *sad* (*tristi*) from Sannazaro's line 11, with an important nuance. The emphasis on the "Kingdom . . . of fear" (Reino . . . del espanto) (which Gonzalo Sobejano has shown to be a periphrasis of hell created originally by Garcilaso in Sonnet 15)[27] follows Garcilaso's "Tórnate al infierno" (Sonnet 39, 12) more closely than it does San-

---

27. Gonzalo Sobejano, "Reinos del espanto," 259.

nazaro's "valle infernal" (Sonnet 23, 9). In the three sonnets, there is a progression from Sannazaro's adjective *infernal* to Garcilaso's noun *infierno* to Góngora's hellish metaphor *Reino del espanto*. In its original formulation, Garcilaso's periphrasis was the plural "kingdoms of hell" (reinos del espanto) and was used in reference to Orpheus's descent into Hades, a mythological reference absent from Góngora's line.[28] Góngora's metaphor includes an important parenthesis that leads to a radical progression in his poem, in which he deviates completely from his precursors. This parenthesis, "if you fit there" (si allá cabes, Sonnet 65, 11), is a sublime reference to that which cannot be named and that which cannot be contained, according to Kant's view of the sublime. In the *Critique of Judgement,* Kant refers to the "Jewish Law" against graven images as the most "sublime passage":

> We have no reason to fear that the feeling of the sublime will suffer from an abstract mode of presentation like this, which is altogether negative as to what is sensuous. For though the imagination, no doubt, finds nothing beyond the sensible world to which it can lay hold, still this thrusting aside of the sensible barriers gives it a feeling of being unbounded; and that removal is thus a presentation of the infinite. As such *it can never be anything more than a negative presentation*—but still it expands the soul. Perhaps there is no more sublime passage in the Jewish Law than the commandment: Thou shalt not make unto thee any graven image, or any likeness of any thing that is in heaven or on earth, or under the earth, &c.[29]

That thing that cannot be represented is beyond discursive and conceptual possibilities, and therefore the subject reacts to it by expe-

---

28. Ibid. Sobejano convincingly argues that in Quevedo's use of the image in line 14 of the sonnet "En los claustros del alma" (In the cloisters of my soul)—a line that reads "my heart is kingdom of fear" (mi corazón es reino del espanto)—it loses the artificiality inherent in its mythological overtones, becoming instead "a true saying, a few true words" representing the psychological state of the poet (Sobejano, "Reinos del espanto," 267). It is, thus, furthest away from its mythological origins, with Góngora's a close second, in contrast to the other poets who employ the periphrasis. Sobejano examines sixteen other examples, all of which are largely steeped in its mythological usage.

29. Kant, *Critique of Judgement,* 127 (Ak. 5:274), emphasis added. It is interesting to note that what Kant calls the most "sublime passage" is an example of God's ontological jealousy. Jealousy is a theme that lends itself to expressions of the sublime.

riencing the sublime. The same move is operating in Góngora's sonnet. Whereas the model sonnets use the noun *hell* and the adjective *hellish* (*infierno* and *infernal*) to represent the evil thing described, as well as the nouns for *monster* (*mostro* or *monstruo*, line 10 in both sonnets), giving these a conceptual basis in language, "Kingdom . . . of fear" defies such one-to-one concept-bearing, particularly with the added caveat "if you fit there," which evokes a magnitude that cannot be captured. In Greco-Roman mythology, and especially in the Christian tradition, the concept of hell is an imaginative repository of the worst possible outcomes. For Góngora, jealousy is not simply worse than hell. Its horror is inconceivable and can only be represented by what it is not, by "a negative presentation," thus exemplifying the mathematical sublime in Kantian terms.

While at this point in the sonnet Sannazaro pauses reflectively, asking a rhetorical question in a first-personal Petrarchan turn ("Oh unhappy fear, why did you come? Wasn't Love enough with his arrows?" [Infelice paura, a che venisti? / Or non bastava Amor con li suoi strali? Sonnet 23, 13–14]),[30] the progression of increasing hyperboles continues in Góngora's poem, extending the conditional if-clause of the *Reino del espanto* metaphor, which remains conditional no longer but is emphatically asserted in the final tercet:

> But you will not fit there, because for so long you've been eating yourself up, and you never end, you must be greater than hell itself.

> (Mas no cabràs allà, que pues ha tanto
> Que comes de ti mesmo, I no te acabas,
> Maior debes de ser que el mismo infierno. Sonnet 65, 12–14)

Góngora's jealousy is not a mere constituent that can return to an "infernal valley" (which is but a small part of the world [*nel mondo*]) or even to *infierno* itself; rather, it is "greater" (*maior*). This image of a jealousy that continually consumes itself evokes infinity (no te acabas) and recalls the gnostic symbol of the Ourobouros, a serpent

---

30. Góngora's move away from the typical Petrarchan first-personal suffering voice is what Schulz-Buschhaus views as the most important way in which Góngora distinguishes his aesthetics from the Italian imitators of Petrarch, such as Sannazaro (Schulz-Buschhaus, "Der frühe Góngora und die italienische Lyrik," 231).

(or dragon) eating its own tail that represents self-fertilization, self-sufficient nature, and eternal return.[31] Góngora combines this with the other images to intensify the creation of evil in the poem. Furthermore, through this symbol he revives once again the serpent and liquid-venom metaphors (of lines 2–3 and 4–5, respectively), bringing unity to the poem, in great crescendo, amidst the diversity.

In this sonnet, Baroque hyperbole is key. Góngora's jealousy, like Kant's experience of the sublime, defies conceptualization. It is eternal (no te acabas) and spatially inconceivable (larger than hell). In moral terms—which is the type of transference that the metaphor begs of the reader, since the enormity obviously relates to the metonymical malevolence of *infierno*—the evil is beyond a concept: even Lucifer resides in hell (for example, Dante's is limited to the ninth circle), as do Pluto (in "the Kingdoms of fear" of Garcilaso's Sonnet 15) and Sannazaro's jealous "monster" (who lives in an "infernal valley of the world"). Yet *zelo* in Góngora's sonnet defies the concept of space. This is the greatest evil precisely because it is the evil that cannot even be conceived of, and therefore it is truly sublime in the Kantian sense. Góngora has utilized hyperbole to its fullest, defying concepts in evoking the worst evil of all. Jealousy is sublime and especially Baroque precisely because of its opposition to the beauty of love (alluded to in lines 8 and 9 of Góngora's sonnet). As in Kant's phenomenological account, the sublime experience is more powerful than one of beauty:

> For the beautiful is directly attended with a feeling of the furtherance of life, and is thus compatible with charms and a playful imagination. On the other hand, the feeling of the sublime is a pleasure that only arises indirectly, being brought about by the feeling of a momentary check to the vital forces followed at once by a discharge all the more powerful, and so it is an emotion that seems to be no sport, but dead earnest in the affairs of the imagination.[32]

This is exemplified *avant-la-lettre* in "Oh fog of the most serene state" as jealousy obliterates love. Thus, as was seen in line 8, the beautiful galloping horse of love is overpowered by the rein of jealousy.

31. J. E. Cirlot, *A Dictionary of Symbols,* 246–47.
32. Kant, *Critique of Judgement,* 91 (Ak. 5:245).

Whereas love, for its perfect harmony, is beautiful according to Renaissance aesthetic notions as exemplified by Ficino's *Commentary on Plato's "Symposium,"* jealousy becomes the perfect theme by which to express the sublime in the Baroque, the power that can conquer or destroy the greatest of goods: Beauty and Love.

This sonnet is an aesthetic creation consisting of the artful manipulation and surpassing of two precursor poems, leading Jammes to proclaim that "it gives us a good idea of the role that Italian poetry plays in Góngora's development, and also shows how the poet always strives to surpass his model."[33] Góngora's sonnet works toward the creation of a single hyperbole, building a gradual crescendo from beginning to end; starting with a "disturbed serenity" and finishing with "greater than hell," it expresses the mathematical sublime by avoiding conceptualization. Jealousy is greater than hell, but, after all, what is it? Bringing his evocation of this emotion beyond the bounds of representation, Góngora offers the reader a glimpse of the sublime.

Dynamically Sublime Jealousy: *The Fable of Polyphemus and Galatea*

The sonnet "To Jealousy" was Góngora's first exploration of what modern aestheticians would later call the sublime. His interest in investigating the onslaught of jealousy as a force beyond concept was renewed in *The Fable of Polyphemus and Galatea* (1613), in which he created the supreme example—*avant-la-lettre*—of Kant's dynamic sublime as he set in motion the diabolical, mathematically sublime jealousy evoked earlier, in the sonnet.

As he did in the sonnet, the poet sets up in the *Polifemo* the representation of jealousy as the antithesis of love. Indeed, the emotive value of love is much more pronounced in his *Polifemo* than in earlier versions of the Polyphemus myth, for the love the Cyclops feels engenders the poet's compassion and affection for him. In my reading of this poem, I will compare it primarily to Ovid's version of the tale in *Metamorphoses*—which Alonso has shown was the principal base for Góngora's *imitatio*—and to poems by Theocritus and Virgil, which have been established as precursors of Ovid's.[34]

As antithetical to jealousy, the treatment of love in the poem must

33. Jammes, *Etudes,* 370.
34. Alonso, ed., *Góngora y el "Polifemo,"* 3:186–207.

first be examined. The first mention of the Cyclops's love is connected to the hyperbolic description of Galatea, in the first half of stanza 13:

> He adores a nymph, the most beautiful daughter of Doris seen by the kingdom of foam. Galatea is her name, and sweetly Venus unites in her the triad of the Graces.

> (Ninfa, de Doris hija, la más bella,
> adora, que vio el reino de la espuma.
> Galatea es su nombre, y dulce en ella
> el terno Venus de sus Gracias suma.)[35]

Since his love is unrequited, the suffering of this Polyphemus is like that of Ovid's Cyclops in book 13 of the *Metamorphoses,* in which Galatea also loved only Acis. This is gathered, as Jammes elucidates, from the moment in which Polyphemus enumerates his riches and thinks of his own greatness, in stanzas 49 and 52. These are motifs that are already present in the precursor versions of the poem (Theocritus's Idyll 11 and Ovid's tale), but with a marked difference. Here, the lover is not just bragging, but as Jammes eloquently puts it, "[T]he Cyclops' innumerable flocks remind him of his suffering, and if he's able to touch the sky with his finger, it's only to write there the immensity of his love."[36] In Góngora's poem, Polyphemus's old way of being is recalled as a "horror" and is elaborated in the first half of stanza 9:

> Trinacria [Sicily] in its mountains has never armed a beast with ferocity or shod it with the wind to fiercely redeem or swiftly save its skin, marked with a hundred colors. . . . (*RBPS,* 9.1–4)

> (No la Trinacria en sus montañas, fiera
> armó de crüeldad, calzó de viento,
> que redima feroz, salve ligera,
> su piel manchada de colores ciento . . . *FPG,* 9.1–4)

---

35. Góngora, *The Fable of Polyphemus and Galatea,* in *Renaissance and Baroque Poetry of Spain,* trans. and ed. Elías L. Rivers; Góngora, *Fábula de Polifemo y Galatea,* ed. Alexander A. Parker, 13.1–4. All quotes in Spanish of the *Polifemo* are to the edition edited by Parker, and the prose translations provided are from this Rivers anthology. Subsequent citations will be made parenthetically in the text by stanza and line number using the abbreviations *FPG* and *RBPS.*
36. Jammes, *Etudes,* 542.

In his own song, the Cyclops recalls his former custom of murdering all those who passed by his cave. This he no longer does, he explains, "because of you" (por tu causa), speaking in apostrophe to Galatea, as he recounts the case of the shipwrecked man to whom he granted refuge instead of killing him (*FPG*, 54.5–8), in stark contrast to the treatment he gave the poor men of Odysseus, who, though never mentioned in the text, are present implicitly since Homer's is the earliest known version of this myth.[37] By means of the hyperbolic initial description of gigantism and past brutality, Góngora portrays Polyphemus as a real monster. But his song, strangely enough, does not sound correspondingly monstrous to the reader. Rather, it is *beautiful* (in contrast with the same motif in the versions of Theocritus and Ovid, in which the Cyclops's songs are unpolished and base), owing to the effects of his incredible love for Galatea. The lines are instilled with great musicality, as Jammes explains: "The song to Galatea is imbued with moving resignation, and under the effects of love, this voice which made the mountains tremble becomes astonishingly soft-spoken and touching."[38]

Polyphemus's voice sings out in great contrast to the horrific music of his panpipes (*albogue*), which once led to chaos in the world and inspired fear in all, as described in a series of hyperboles:

> The forest is confounded, the sea is disturbed, Triton breaks his twisted conch, deafened flees the ship by sail and oar: such is the music of Polyphemus! (*RBPS*, 12.5–8)

> (La selva se confunde, el mar se altera
> rompe Tritón su caracol torcido,
> sordo huye el bajel a vela y remo:
> ¡tal la música es de Polifemo! *FPG*, 12.5–8)

But later, in stanza 55, Polyphemus tells us that his music has served as a "yoke" (*yugo*) to calm the sea. This change reflects the effects of love in his soul. With love, the chaos is replaced by harmonious beauty, in a Neoplatonic vein, evoking the idea of Pythagoras and the Platonists, who believed that music expressed the harmony or disharmony of the soul, a concept elaborated by Ficino and other

37. Homer, *The Odyssey*, bk. 9.
38. Jammes, *Etudes*, 541.

Neoplatonists.[39] In the *Polifemo,* this ordered soul points to the presence of a moral love, of *agape.* Jammes insists correctly on Polyphemus's "humanization" through love in Góngora's poem. Clearly, a
love that can induce such change in a horrific monster is truly hyperbolic and worthy of the Renaissance Neoplatonic-Christian tradition,
which posited love as the greatest good.

Apart from the effects that it has on the one-eyed giant, love has
two other important associations in the poem. First, there is the
praise of the Nereid, whose beauty has enamored the entire island
and subsequently led to the neglect of the sheep flocks by the shepherds. In stanza 19, the exaggeration of Galatea's beauty and the
shepherds' adoration of her continues:

> For all those who reap gold, shear snow, or store in casks the
> pressed-out purple, either because of religion or because of love,
> Galatea, though temple-less, is a deity. (*RBPS,* 19.5–8)

> (De cuantos siegan oro, esquilan nieve,
> o en pipas guardan la exprimida grana,
> bien sea por religión, bien amor sea,
> deidad, aunque sin templo, es Galatea. *FPG,* 19.5–8)

In stanza 21, "the youth are burning" with love (Arde la juventud,
FPG, 21.1) and the animals are left "without a shepherd to whistle
at them" (sin pastor que los silbe, *FPG,* 21.5).

Last, the most beautiful love in the poem is the requited love described in the *locus amoenus* in which Galatea and Acis first fall
in love with each other. After a delicate description of their mutual
falling in love, they consummate their desire in absolute harmony
with the stream, the laurel trees, and the nightingales, in a scene of
extreme beauty and sensuality (stanzas 23–45). A Renaissance ideal
of beauty is emphasized in the harmonious world described here,
recalling Ficino's ideas on orderliness. This first meeting between
Acis and Galatea—in which their love is almost palpably felt by the
reader because of the use of present-tense narration—is not told in
any of the precursor versions of the poem. Góngora has radically
changed Ovid's version, in which Galatea narrates her past love,
which cannot create such an emotive effect in the reader—because

---

39. Roger Scruton, *The Aesthetics of Music,* ix.

of the greater distance it creates between text and reader—as can the use of the present tense.[40]

Polyphemus's Sublime Jealousy

In this mythological poem, there is only one thing stronger than love, one force that can blind the love-struck Cyclops, and that is jealousy, the passion that is hyperbolized in Góngora's *Polifemo* to a much greater extent than in its intertexts. In Theocritus's *Idylls,* jealousy is lacking: there is no rival, only a Cyclops who suffers unrequited love. Virgil's *Second Eclogue* (based on Theocritus's Idyll 11) depicts a shepherd in love whose jealousy is only insinuated without details. The denouement of Góngora's *Polifemo* has most in common with book 13 of Ovid's *Metamorphoses.* In both cases, there is an explosion of violence accompanying jealousy. Since Ovid's giant never attains much humanity—he is described throughout the tale with such words as *ferocious* and *beast*—it is not surprising that he would burst out in violence and murder Acis. But when the violence does erupt, it is not as powerful in Ovid's poem as it is in Góngora's. In the Latin poem, the jealous monster resents Galatea's preference for Acis and threatens to kill him even before he sees them together, ever conscious of the relationship between the two of them, which is, for him, already a fait accompli:

> But to repulse the Cyclops, and prefer
> The Love of Acis, (Heav'ns) I cannot bear.
> But let the Stripling please himself; nay more,
> Please you, tho that's the thing I most abhor;
> The Boy shall find, if e'er we cope in Fight,
> These Giant Limbs endu'd with Giant Might.
> His living Bowels, from his Belly torn,
> And scatter'd Limbs shall on the Flood be born. . . .

> (. . . sed sur Cyclope repulso
> Acin amas praefersque meis conplexibus Acin?

---

40. The relevant sections for comparison here are stanzas 23–45 of Góngora's *Polifemo* and 13.750–58 of Ovid's *Metamorphoses.* Since he was strong in Latin, Góngora probably read Ovid in the original, which is why I have decided to provide quotes from Ovid in Latin. However, he might also have been familiar with one of the popular Spanish translations of the *Metamorphoses,* such as Pedro Sánchez de Viana's.

ille tamen placeatque sibi placeatque licebit,
quod nollem, Galatea, tibi: modo copia detur,
sentiet esse mihi tanto pro corpore vires!
viscera viva traham divisaque membra per agros
perque tuas spargam—sic se tibi misceat!—undas . . .)

Ovid's Cyclops compares his jealous fury to Sicily's famous volcano:

For Oh! I burn with Love, and thy Disdain
Augments at once my Passion, and my Pain.
Translated Aetna flames within my Heart,
And thou, Inhuman, wilt not ease my Smart.

(uror enim, laesusque exaestuat acrius ignis,
cumque suis videor translatam viribus Aetnam
pectore ferre meo nec tu, Galatea, moveris . . .)[41]

When he finally sees them in each other's arms, in a moment of evidential jealousy, he cries out: "a bellowing Cry he cast, / I see, I
see; but this shall be your last" (video que exclamat et ista / ultima
sit, faciam, Veneris concordia vestrae), which sounds neither ferocious nor volcanic.[42] Nonetheless, Galatea does report that his voice
was as great as befitting a furious Cyclops; it was so strong that the
volcano shook with the noise (13.876–77). Certainly, his jealousy is
hyperbolic.

Stylistically, the Cyclops's jealous rage is so much more condensed
in Góngora's version that it seems much more powerful than in
Ovid's (in which the reader is told—not shown—how horrible it is).
In a poem of 504 hendecasyllables, the jealousy is conceived, experienced, and released in eight lines near the very end. The relevant
passage begins in stanza 61, though the actual representation of jealousy begins only at the end of the stanza. In this passage, Góngora
creates a tremendous hyperbole by having the voice of the jealous

41. Latin quotes are from Ovid, *Metamorphosen,* 13.860–66, 867–69; English
translations are from Garth, Dryden, et al., trans., *Metamorphoses,* bk. 13.
42. Garth, Dryden, et al., trans., *Metamorphoses,* bk. 13; Ovid, *Metamorphosen,* 13.874–75. This translation makes it sound less prosaic than it does in Latin;
an even closer translation of 13.875 would be "I see you and this shall be your
last love union."

giant sound like the "horn of thunder" (trompa del trueno), which sets in motion a group of trees:

> The fierce giant, seeing the fugitive snow [Galatea] run with muted step toward the sea (for to such sharp vision the naked Libyan reveals the limited area of his shield) and, seeing the boy, stirs as many aged beechtrees as could be stirred by jealous thunder: thus before the dark cloud breaks, a blasting trumpet warns of the thunderbolt. (*RBPS*, 61.1–8)

> (Viendo el fiero jayán, con paso mudo
> correr al mar la fugitiva nieve
> [que a tanta vista el líbico desnudo
> registra el campo de su adarga breve]
> y al garzón viendo, cuantas mover pudo
> celoso trueno, antiguas hayas mueve;
> tal, antes que la opaca nube rompa
> previene rayo fulminante trompa. *FPG*, 61.1–8)

The poet delays letting out the word *jealous* (*celoso*), using the hyperbaton with *cuantas mover pudo* in line 485 to further postpone its mention. According to Antonio Vilanova, the image of "jealous thunder" (celoso trueno) is based on two passages in book 8 of Virgil's *Aeneid:* in one, the thunder is compared with the sound of the "Tyrrhenian horns"; in the other, thunder and lightning are caused by "the amorous ardor of Vulcan."[43] The hyperbolic nature of Polyphemus's jealousy is apparent through the comparison to the immortals: power over thunder and lightning lies in the hands of the gods. Furthermore, the implicit mythological relationship between Polyphemus and Vulcan (due to the tradition that has the Cyclops making Jupiter's lightning bolts in Vulcan's smithy) takes shape, as does the etymological relationship between the god *Vulcano* and the geological phenomenon known as *volcán* (both derived from the Latin names of the god Vulcan, *Volcanus* or *Vulcanus*). The power of thunder and lightning before the actual breaking of the cloud (antes que la opaca nube rompa, 7) creates a dynamic tension in the poem, and foreshadows the act of violence (metaphorically, the actual bursting of the cloud) that will result in Acis's death.

---

43. Antonio Vilanova, *Las fuentes y los temas del "Polifemo" de Góngora,* 2:729–31.

Polyphemus acts in the present—in contrast with the Ovidian version—and hence, the violence of this Cyclops explodes before the reader's eyes. Thus, jealousy here seems greater than that in the earlier versions and also more plausible. In the immediate present (*viendo*), the reader witnesses the very moment of evidential jealousy in which the evidence comes to be. Strengthening the hyperbole to an even greater extent is the concision used to describe jealousy: the entire psychological and physical complex of the emotional episode, from suspicious fear to evidential jealous fury, is reduced to a mere eight lines. First, Polyphemus sees Galatea and Acis leaving their first embrace as they flee naked into the sea, forewarned by the sounds of his song and the falling stones from the cliff. The incredible love that had been capable of transforming Homer's homophagous monster into a quasi-human being who sang beautifully and felt love and compassion can only be surpassed by a power greater than it, a sublime power: "With infinite violence he tore loose the greatest peak of the lofty rock" (*RBPS*, 62.1–2) (Con vïolencia desgajó infinita / la mayor punta de la excelsa roca, *FPG*, 62.1–2). Jealousy, with the *infinite violence* that accompanies it, is portrayed as supremely gigantic in the poem because not only must it extinguish the love between Acis and Galatea, but also it must cause the transformed Cyclops to revert to his primordial, barbaric being.

Jammes suggests that the *Polifemo* is really about the beautiful love of Acis and Galatea, and of Polyphemus, that Góngora only had him kill Acis because he could not change the ending (since Ovid's myth was known to all the readers). He contends, "Love does not just triumph over Galathea in a difficult battle, but it also triumphs over Polyphemus, whom he humanizes and civilizes. Apparently, it was not possible for Góngora to modify the tradition to the point of avoiding the bloody denouement."[44] Of course, his hypothesis is challenged by the fact that Góngora had no trouble modifying many other aspects of the tradition; for example, Góngora determines that Acis slyly seduces Galatea, and that all events take place on one short afternoon. And if he did feel constrained by the myth's traditional plot, he most certainly did not have to represent the ending, just as he chose not to retell Medoro's demise in the "Romance de Angélica y Medoro" (Ballad of Angélica and Medoro), where he focused only on earlier events. On the contrary, the *Fable of Polyphemus and Galatea*

44. Jammes, *Etudes*, 547.

is about the destruction of the love shared by Galatea and Acis and that felt by the Cyclops. It is about the sublime power that could annihilate a force so absolutely harmonious and beautiful, a power that strikes in an instant, like lightning, and devastates with the force of the gods—one that describes the new, violent zeitgeist of the Baroque, and overcomes the harmony of the Renaissance. That the destructive force of Polyphemus dominates in the experience of reading the poem is attested to indirectly by the fact that most readers shorten the poem's title to *Polifemo;* it is the jealous monster—not the beautiful lovers—who comes first to the mind of readers.

There is an interesting poetic postscript to the explosion of Polyphemus's jealousy, reflecting a stylistic corollary to the thematic release that supports my view. After the eruption, the poetic space so carefully and painstakingly created by Góngora is also destroyed. Nothing is left. The poem ends quickly, with a stanza dedicated to Acis's conversion into a river, in which the physical destruction of his body is at least as important as the metamorphosis. This is quite distinct from Ovid's version of the myth, in which Galatea expresses a measure of glee at her lover's triumphant conversion. As Ovid tells it,

> When, (wond'rous to behold) full in the Flood,
> Up starts a Youth, and Navel high he stood.
> Horns from his Temples rise; and either Horn
> Thick Wreaths of Reeds, (his Native Growth) adorn.
> Were not his Stature taller than before,
> His bulk augmented, and his Beauty more,
> His Colour blue; for Acis he might pass:
> And Acis chang'd into a Stream he was.
> But mine no more; he rowls along the Plains
> With rapid Motion, and his Name retains.

> (miraque res, subito media tenus exstitit alvo
> incinctus iuvenis flexis nova cornua cannis,
> qui, nisi quod maior, quod toto caerulus ore,
> Acis erat, sed sic quoque erat tamen Acis in amnem
> versus, et antiquum tenuerunt flumina nomen . . .)[45]

It should also be noted that the new figure of Acis is similar to the old one, except that he is now taller, more beautiful, and his face

45. Garth, Dryden, et al., trans., *Metamorphoses,* bk. 13; Ovid, *Metamorphosen,* 13.893–97.

"blue." In some way, the new Acis, for Ovid, is superior to the old. In contrast to this scene in the *Metamorphoses,* Góngora's Acis is little more than water. The destructive effects of jealousy are felt even at the formal level, given that the last stanza seems to stand out from the rest of the poem as more prosaic:

> Hardly were his limbs lamentably oppressed by the fatal rock when the feet of the biggest trees were shod in the liquid pearls of his veins. Finally, his white bones converted into flowing silver, lapping the flowers and silvering the sands, he reached Doris, who, with pitying tears, greeted him as a son-in-law, acclaimed him as a river. (*RBPS,* 63.1–8)

> (Sus miembros lastimosamente opresos
> del escollo fatal fueron apenas,
> que los pies de los árboles más gruesos
> calzó el líquido aljófar de sus venas.
> Corriente plata al fin sus blancos huesos,
> lamiendo flores y argentando arenas,
> a Doris llega, que con llanto pío
> yerno lo saludó, lo aclamó río. *FPG,* 63.1–8)

At a rhetorical level, the poetry of the first sixty-two stanzas has in large part disappeared. Along with the eruption of jealousy, not only Acis expires, but much of the musicality of the poetry dies as well. First of all, the syntactic order is only slightly altered in the last stanza: the powerful hyperbatons found throughout the poem are absent here (for example, this syntax can be compared to that of the beginning and end of the previous stanza, in which there are two strong hyperbatons). In addition, the last two verbs in the preterit, *greeted* (*saludó*) and *acclaimed* (*aclamó*), as well as the noun *son-in-law* (*yerno*), belong to a prosaic register. Certainly there are still poetic flourishes, such as the "liquid pearls" (líquido aljófar), "flowing silver" (corriente plata), and "lapping the flowers and silvering the sands" (lamiendo flores y argentando arenas). Nevertheless, this last stanza, unlike much of the poem, reads without much difficulty at all, that is, more like a prose epilogue. Such is the sublime jealousy of Polyphemus! It not only destroys a Renaissance-inspired harmonious beauty, but is self-annihilating. It is not a poem about love and jealousy, but about how the latter obliterates everything.

The jealousy of this poem is again "infinite," like that of the sonnet

"To Jealousy," but here, in Kant's terminology, it represents an experience of the dynamic sublime, since it portrays not just the enormity but the force of this terrifying power, in movement. Here the dynamically sublime jealousy is without concept; it is greater than love, the most beautiful, greatest good. The sublimity of jealousy destroys the beauty of love and poetry itself in this descriptive poetics calling attention to a new focus on the sublime.[46]

In Ovid's version, the fact that Galatea is indeed the narrator of the tale makes it necessary that she appear in the final scene, explaining what happened to Acis and reporting what the Cyclops did and said. In contrast, Góngora has her disappear, as if she, "the fugitive snow" (la fugitiva nieve), had melted in the sea, and along with her, love, Acis, Polyphemus, and poetry all vanished too. Everything becomes nothing.

The sonnet "To Jealousy" and the *Polifemo,* portray, respectively, the phenomena of the mathematical and the dynamic sublime. In the sonnet, jealousy is described in a kind of eternal stasis, while in the *Polifemo* it erupts in the action as one of the principal dramatic

---

46. Another example is the sonnet "Ya besando unas manos cristalinas" (Already kissing two crystalline hands), which presents possessive jealousy as dynamically sublime. This poem sensually describes the touching and kissing in which the poet-lover and his beloved are engaged under the cover of darkness. These are interrupted by the sun's coming out at dawn; the sun, of whose consciousness the reader never becomes aware, is described as "envious" (*invidioso*), as were the mountains in "What of the tall envious mountains," analyzed in Chapter 6. The lover wishes death upon the sun for its daring, evoked by the reference to Phaeton's tragic death; to this end, he calls on Jupiter (*el cielo*) to kill Apollo (the father of Phaeton [*tu hijo*]), just as the former had once killed Apollo's son. This poem is unique among Góngora's jealousy poems in that it contains an imaginary rival (in "What of the tall envious mountains," it turned out that the mountains were not the true rival, that there was indeed a husband of flesh and blood). That is, the sun is a threat only in the poet's imagination. This projection of the jealous contest as a cosmic battle to the death ("killed my delight" [mató mi gloria, 11], "may its rays kill you" [te den muerte, 14]), one in which the ontological reality of one of the participants is in question, recalls the Sartrian reflection that male jealousy is a means of "laying hold of the world." This possessive jealousy on the part of the lover pits human against divine, and imbues humans with a passion that, though perhaps only wishfully, gives them a power so great that they can challenge the gods. Moreover, given the importance of the sun to life on earth, it is surely a sublime desire to wish death upon this orb. Once again, in Kantian terms, there is a *negative* representation leading to sublimity. In this case, it is the inconceivable phenomenon of the lack of light and life on earth. Another kind of jealousy is again described in sublime terms. (Translations of "Already kissing two crystalline hands" in this note are by Alix Ingber, http://sonnets.Spanish.sbc.edu/Gongora_Sol.html.)

elements, in movement. These poems are not only hyperbolic; rather, they are sublime, describing that which goes beyond conceptualization. Góngora used jealousy as a way to express the sublime destructive power within humans. Employing passages in the *Polifemo* imbued with Renaissance Neoplatonic images of harmonious beauty, only to shatter them later, Góngora ushers in an infinite destructive force in this Baroque poem, describing—*avant-la-lettre*—a modern Kantian notion of the sublime.

While striving to proclaim a universal truth about humanity, Góngora is nevertheless describing male emotional experience quite exclusively. And while breaking intellectual and artistic bounds, he appears historically trapped in his own culture's assumption that only male jealousy is capable of sublimity. Like the women who experience it, female jealousy is simply beautiful.

Conclusion
A Culture of Jealousy

> **In everything I talk about jealousy is at stake.**
> **—Peggy Kamuf, *A Derrida Reader: Between the Blinds***

I began this book by stating my purpose of investigating a plurality of jealousies, some of which conflict, but all of which are evoked by a single word. Despite the different meanings of the word, jealousy is often conceived of as one thing; while it may evoke a whole range of nuances, it is usually assumed to be "bad" or "irrational." While some forms of jealousy, as I have shown, may be fully rational and justified, these are often associated with the negativity of the term *celos*. With Platonism and Christianity supporting it philosophically, love was conceived of in early modern Europe as the greatest good. Since certain kinds of jealousy are conceived of as the primary antagonist of love, through a process of conceptual contamination all forms of jealousy take on the characteristics of an evil force capable of destroying that which makes life most worth living. However, in some instances, it seems to be a necessary evil, one that, paradoxically, is really a good.

G. E. Lessing warned in his aesthetic treatise, *Laocoön*, that "nothing is more deceptive than the laying down of general laws for our emotions. Their texture is so delicate and intricate that even the most cautious speculation can hardly pick out a single thread and follow it through all its interlacing."[1] Since jealousy is an emotion in flux, the way a character experiences it tends to change over time, and yet at each moment, we may say that she or he is jealous, despite the fluctuating feeling, desire, and belief. With this one word

---

1. G. E. Lessing, *Laocoön*, 28.

we designate many shifting phenomena. While Lessing may ultimately be right that, for any given emotional experience, it may be
impossible to lay down a "law," analyzing emotions with contemporary philosophical criteria seems fruitful. In early modern Spain, the
kind of jealousy represented often reveals assumptions concerning
the nature of characters. The way they experience it, in many cases,
seems determined by their gender, social class, and race or ethnicity, in representations that lay down a different kind of "law," that of
the essentialization of constructed differences. Certain general features of the experience's literary description, which become manifest
through this type of analysis, help reveal these presuppositions.

The varied and contradictory representations of early modern jealousy in my study illustrate that these writers appreciated a concern
like Lessing's about the variety of kinds and the subtleties of each.
A taxonomy of the kinds of jealousy encountered in these chapters
helps demonstrate this: jealousy may be suspicious, possessive or
protective, angry or sad, rational or irrational, murderous or suici-
dal, female or male, productive or counterproductive, hyperbolic or
hypobolic, good or bad, beautiful or sublime. As such, the designator
of all these phenomena—the word *celos*—means both very little and
quite a lot at one and the same time. Occasionally, jealousy seems
banal and conventional, functioning as Hymen Alpern suggested, as
a mere plot device.[2] Frequently, however, as I hope these chapters
have shown, jealousy is integrated into the formal and ideological
makeup of these texts in a more profound way, in which rhetoric is
intricately linked to issues of race, class, gender, morality, epistemology, and aesthetics.

In the worldview of the three authors studied, tremendous power
is associated with the affective subject who experiences such a hyperbolic emotion, especially when this subject is male. The relationship of jealousy to the power of the gods is not a construct of
Sartre's, Girard's, or Derrida's. On the contrary, Lope de Vega, Cervantes, and Góngora each describe forms of jealousy that they compare with the divine, evoking the Greco-Roman or Judeo-Christian
gods through a plethora of rhetorical strategies. Even when jealousy
is not portrayed hyperbolically, it still imbricates questions of power
in a sociopolitical as well as an aesthetic vein. For one, typical hypobolic representations of jealousy tend to naturalize the weakness

2. Alpern, "Jealousy as a Dramatic Motive."

of lower-class women as a gender- and class-specific trait. The jealousy of these women is likened to trifles, their cares are deflated, their effective power shown to have profound limits that they do not challenge. Furthermore, when higher-class women seem to experience hyperbolic jealousy, this is almost always shown to be a partial illusion: their jealous threats are not realized into action, their passion is belittled, and the effective power of men is heightened. In showing themselves unsteady under the influence of a powerful emotion, women characters themselves are used to suggest a paternalizing rationale for continued patriarchal dominance, not only in the home but in the monarchy as well. Just as the alleged affective unsteadiness of Philip II's grandmother—Joan the Mad—was a rationalization used to keep her from her legitimate claim on the throne throughout her long life (she died only in 1555, just as her son Charles V was abdicating to his son, Philip), the portrayal of uncontrollable and irrational emotion of dramatic women in positions of authority—Duchess Diana, Queen Arminda—attempts to prove that women should not rule; in a sense, these plays serve as symbolic apologia for the historical fact of keeping one queen locked up in the Castle of Tordesillas and away from the throne.

Furthermore, in a culture that was anxious both about losing its hegemony in Europe as well as about keeping its internal borders "pure," jealousy was a perfect descriptor for national suspicion and possessiveness, which arose from the perceived threat of enemies from both without and within. Ultimately, the beloved whose protection Lope justifies with jealousy is Spain herself, as the Spanish monarchy and inquisitors perceived themselves as assaulted by engaño plots from water and land, by Jews, Muslims, conversos, Protestants, and other reformers. From the time he took the throne as paterfamilias of the Empire in 1556, Philip II saw his inherited territories under constant assault, and the chastity of Spain thus needed guarding. It was a culture of jealousy.

The mate-stealing occasioned by both men and women in plays like *The Dog in the Manger* and *Jealous Arminda* was based on the disloyalty and concomitant mistrust inspired by jealousy and served to promote these same values within the society, in a culture that José Antonio Maravall and J. H. Elliott describe as rife with strife between a variety of social groups, and among the members of each group. Thus, the representation of jealousy in mass theater further debilitated the bonds between and among classes, and promoted the alleged necessity of the king, who, at one extreme of the political spectrum, sanctioned specific violent outbursts of jealousy in plays such as *The Commanders of Cordoba* and *Peribáñez*. In both of these plays (and many others), vengeful male jealousy was made to be a formal aesthetic necessity, one that was coupled with the requirement that a monarch sanction the violent behavior. These dramas thus attempted to legitimize societal power structures, both in the household and at the court, in a further play on the association between paterfamilias as head of the family and as leader of nation and empire. In this way, Lope de Vega, as the most prominent practitioner of the popular drama, strengthened the direct link between the vassal and *his* king. The political ramifications of justified murder are even more specifically drawn out, in the equation of Peribáñez's actions and Enrique II's murder of Pedro I, a historical regicide with contemporaneous ramifications, since Philip III, in power at the time the play was written, was Enrique's descendant through Isabella the Catholic.[3] Just as Pedro I had to be murdered by his brother in the middle ages, Peribáñez had to be suspicious of his wife, and murder his rival.

In regards to aesthetic creation, jealousy is largely about the power of the poet who engages in a continual competition with other forms and other poets and artists. Cervantes, Góngora, and Lope, respectively, each elaborated an image of jealousy that he hoped would be the greatest hyperbole the world had seen: "the most jealous man in the world," "you never end, you must be greater than hell itself," and "far worse for a man to see another lover in the arms of his lady." While Lope de Vega propped up the powers that be with his aesthetic creation, Cervantes turned the emotion against the playwright, in an attempt to discredit the honor code that the comedia did so much to popularize. While all vied for the laurel intertextually, Góngora intuited another claim to power, which was to subdue the monstrous beast itself. Góngora harnessed his sublime creation, making himself a kind of god. Thus in singing not only Polifemo's sublime song of chaos, but also the sweet song of "honey," he fashioned himself as both Jove and the god of love.

3. Burke, "The Ritual Frame of *Peribáñez*."

Works Cited

Alfonso X. *Cantigas de Santa María.* Ed. Walter Mettman. 2 vols. Vigo: Edicións Xerais de Galicia, 1981.

Alonso, Dámaso. *En torno a Lope: Marino, Cervantes, Benavente, Góngora, Los Cardenios.* Madrid: Editorial Gredos, 1972.

Alonso, Dámaso, ed. *Góngora y el "Polifemo."* 6th ed., expanded. 3 vols. Madrid: Editorial Gredos, 1974.

Alpern, Hymen. "Jealousy as a Dramatic Motive in the Spanish *comedia.*" *Romanic Review* 14 (1923): 276–85.

American Psychiatric Association. *Diagnostic and Statistical Manual of Mental Disorders (DSM-IV TR).* 4th ed., text revision. Washington, DC: American Psychiatric Association, 2000.

Apuleius. *The Golden Ass.* Trans. Jack Lindsay. Bloomington, IN: Indiana University Press, 1960.

Ariosto, Ludovico. *Orlando furioso.* Ed. Cesare Segre. 2nd ed. Milan: A. Mondadori, 1987.

Aristotle. *Metaphysics. The Basic Works of Aristotle.* Ed. Richard McKeon. New York: Random House, 1941.

———. *Nicomachean Ethics.* Trans. Martin Ostwald. New York: Macmillan, 1962.

———. *On the Generation of Animals.* Trans. A. L. Peck. Loeb Classical Library. Cambridge: Harvard University Press, 1943.

———. *Poetics. The Basic Works of Aristotle.* Ed. Richard McKeon. New York: Random House, 1941.

———. *Rhetoric. The Basic Works of Aristotle.* Ed. Richard McKeon. New York: Random House, 1941.

Armiño, Mauro, ed. *El perro del hortelano,* by Lope de Vega. Madrid: Cátedra, 1996.

Armstrong, Nancy. "Some Call It Fiction: On the Politics of Domesticity." In *Literary Theory: An Anthology,* ed. Julie Rivkin and Michael Ryan. 2nd ed. Oxford: Blackwell, 2004.

Aulnoy, Madame d' [Marie-Catherine]. *La cour et la ville de Madrid vers la fin du XVIIe siècle: relation du voyage d'Espagne.* 1691. Ed. B. Carey. Paris, 1874.

Avalle-Arce, Juan Bautista. *"El celoso extremeño* de Cervantes." In *Homenaje a Ana María Barrenechea,* ed. Lía Schwartz Lerner and Isaias Lerner, 199–205. Madrid: Castalia, 1984.

————, ed. *Los trabajos de Persiles y Sigismunda,* by Miguel de Cervantes. Madrid: Castalia, 1969.

Baader, Horst. "Eifersucht in der Spanischen *Comedia* des Goldenen Zeitalters." *Romanische Forschungen* 74.3–4 (1962): 318–44.

Babb, Lawrence. *The Elizabethan Malady.* East Lansing: Michigan State College Press, 1951.

Bandello, Matteo. *Le novelle.* Ed. Delmo Maestri. Alessandria: Edizione dell'Orso, 1992.

Barthes, Roland. *A Lover's Discourse: Fragments.* Trans. Richard Howard. New York: Hill and Wang, 1978.

Bataillon, Marcel. *Erasmo y España.* 2nd ed. Mexico: FCE, 1966.

Benassar, Bartolomé. *Los españoles: actitudes y mentalidad.* Barcelona: Argos, 1978.

Bergmann, Emilie L. *Art Inscribed: Essays on Ekphrasis in Spanish Golden Age Poetry.* Cambridge: Harvard University Press, 1979.

La Biblia, que es, los Sacros libros del Vieio y Nuevo Testamento. 1569. Trans. Casiodoro de Reina. Facs. ed. Horeb: Guarro Casas, 1986.

Blecua, José Manuel, ed. *Obras poéticas de Lope de Vega.* 2nd ed. Barcelona: Planeta, 1974.

Boccaccio, Giovanni. *Decamerone.* Ed. Vittore Branca. 3rd rev. ed. Torino: Einaudi, 1987.

Boitani, Piero. *The Tragic and the Sublime in Medieval Literature.* Cambridge, UK: Cambridge University Press, 1989.

Brant, Sebastian. *The Ship of Fools.* Trans. Edwin H. Zeydel. New York: Dover, 1944.

Burke, James. "The Ritual Frame of *Peribáñez.*" In *The Centre and Its Compass: Studies in Medieval Literature in Honor of Professor John Leyerle,* ed. Robert A. Taylor, et al., 11–27. Studies in Medieval Culture 33. Kalamazoo: Western Michigan University, 1993.

Burton, Robert. *The Anatomy of Melancholy.* Ed. Thomas C. Faulkner, Nicolas K. Kiessling, and Rhonda R. Blair. 6 vols. Oxford: Clarendon, 1989–2000.

Cable, Mary. *El Escorial.* New York: Newsweek, 1971.

Calderón de la Barca, Pedro. *El mayor monstro, los celos.* Ed. Everett W. Hesse. Madison: University of Wisconsin Press, 1955.

————. *Obras completas.* 2nd ed. 3 vols. Madrid: Aguilar, 1991.

Callejo, A., and María Teresa Pajares. *"Fábula de Polifemo y Galatea" y "Las soledades": textos y concordancias.* Madison: Hispanic Seminary of Medieval Studies, 1985.

Capellanus, Andreas. *The Art of Courtly Love.* 12th cent. Trans. John Jay Parry. New York: Columbia University Press, 1960.

Carreira, Antonio, ed. *Antología poética: Polifemo, Soledad primera, Piramo y Tisbe y otros poemas,* by Luis de Góngora y Argote. 3rd ed. corr. Madrid: Castalia, 1990.

Casalduero, Joaquín. *Sentido y forma de las novelas ejemplares de Cervantes.* Madrid: Gredos, 1962.

———. *Sentido y forma del teatro de Cervantes.* Madrid: Gredos, 1966.

Castro, Américo. "Algunas observaciones acerca del concepto del honor en los siglos XVI y XVII." *Revista de Filología española* 3 (1916): 1–50, 357–86.

———. *De la edad conflictiva.* Madrid: Taurus, 1961.

———. *Hacia Cervantes.* 2nd ed. muy renovada. Madrid: Taurus, 1960.

———. *El pensamiento de Cervantes.* Ed. Julio Rodríguez-Puértolas. 2nd ed. Barcelona: Noguer, 1972.

Castro, Guillén de. *La tragedia por los celos.* In *Obras completas,* ed. Juan Oleza. Madrid: Fundación José Antonio de Castro, 1997.

Cervantes y Saavedra, Miguel de. *La casa de los celos.* Vol. 1 of *Obras completas (comedias y entremeses).* Ed. Rodolfo Schevill and Adolfo Bonilla. Madrid: Bernardo Rodríguez, 1915.

———. *El celoso extremeño* (Porras ms.). In vol. 12 of *Obras completas (Novelas ejemplares).* Ed. Rodolfo Schevill and Adolfo Bonilla. Madrid: Bernardo Rodríguez, 1922–1925.

———. *El celoso extremeño.* In *Novelas ejemplares.* Ed. Harry Sieber. 2 vols. Madrid: Cátedra, 1987.

———. *Exemplary Stories.* Trans. and ed. Lesley Lipson. Oxford: Oxford University Press, 1998.

———. *La fuerza de la sangre.* In *Novelas ejemplares.* Ed. Harry Sieber. 2 vols. Madrid: Cátedra, 1987.

———. *La Galatea.* Ed. Juan Bautista Avalle-Arce. Madrid: Espasa-Calpe, 1987.

———. *El ingenioso hidalgo don Quijote de la Mancha.* Ed. Luis Murillo. 5th ed. 2 vols. Madrid: Castalia, 1978.

———. *El juez de los divorcios.* In *Los entremeses de Cervantes,* ed. Nicholas Spadaccini. 9th ed. Madrid: Cátedra, 1992.

————. "Romance de los celos." In *Poesía lírica del Siglo de Oro,* ed. Elías L. Rivers. 7th ed. Madrid: Cátedra, 1985.

————. *Los trabajos de Persiles y Sigismunda.* Ed. Juan Bautista Avalle-Arce. Madrid: Castalia, 1969.

————. *The Trials of Persiles and Sigismunda, A Northern Story.* Trans. Celia Richmond Weller and Clark A. Colahan. Berkeley: University of California Press, 1989.

————. *Viaje del Parnaso.* Critical ed. Intro. and notes by Vicente Gaos. Madrid: Castalia, 1974.

————. *El viejo celoso.* In *Los entremeses de Cervantes,* ed. Nicholas Spadaccini. 9th ed. Madrid: Cátedra, 1992.

Checa, Fernando. *El Real Alcázar de Madrid.* Madrid: Nerea, 1994.

Chevalier, Maxime. *L'Arioste en Espagne (1530–1650).* Bordeaux: L'Université de Bordeaux, 1966.

Ciplijauskaité, Biruté, ed. *Sonetos completos,* by Luis de Góngora. Madison: Hispanic Seminary of Medieval Studies, 1981.

Cirlot, J. E. *A Dictionary of Symbols.* Trans. Jack Sage. 2nd ed. New York: Dorset, 1971.

Cirot, Georges. *"El celoso extremeño* et *L'Histoire de Floire et Blance-flor."* *Bulletin Hispanique* 31 (1929): 138–43.

Colie, Rosalie L. *The Resources of Kind: Genre-Theory in the Renaissance.* Ed. Barbara K. Lewalski. Berkeley: University of California Press, 1973.

Collins, Marsha S. *The "Soledades," Góngora's Masque of the Imagination.* Columbia and London: University of Missouri Press, 2002.

Combet, Louis. *Cervantès ou les incertitudes du désir: Une approche psychostructurale de l'œuvre de Cervantès.* Lyon: Presses Universitaires de Lyon, 1980.

Cotarelo y Mori, Emilio. Prólogo. *Obras de Lope de Vega Publicadas por la Real Academia Española.* New ed. Vol. 3. Madrid: Real Academia Española, 1916.

Covarrubias, Sebastián de. *Tesoro de la lengua española o castellana.* 1611. Ed. Felipe C. R. Maldonado. Madrid: Castalia, 1994.

Crawford, J. P. W. "Italian Sources of Góngora's Poetry." *Romanic Review* 20 (1929): 122–30.

————. "Notes on the Poetry of Hernando de Acuña; Notes on the Sonnets in the Spanish *Cancionero General de 1554." Romanic Review* 7 (1916): 314–37.

Damasio, Antonio. *Descartes' Error: Emotion, Reason and the Human Brain.* New York: Avon, 1995.

D'Antuono, Nancy L. "Lope de Vega y la *commedia dell'arte:* Temas y figuras." In *Actas del I Congreso internacional sobre Lope de Vega,* ed. Criado de Val. Madrid: EDI-6, 1981.

de Armas, Frederick A. *Cervantes, Raphael and the Classics.* Cambridge Studies in Latin American and Iberian Literature. Cambridge, UK: Cambridge University Press, 1998.

———. "La estructura mítica de *Los comendadores de Córdoba.*" *Actas del X Congreso de la Asociación Internacional de Hispanistas.* 1:763–71. Barcelona: PPU, 1992.

de Armas, Frederick A., ed. *A Star-Crossed Golden Age.* Lewisburg, PA: Bucknell University Press, 1998.

de Armas Wilson, Diana. *Allegories of Love: Cervantes' "Persiles and Sigismunda."* Princeton: Princeton University Press, 1991.

Descartes, René. *Meditations on First Philosophy.* Ed. Stanley Tweyman. New York: Routledge, 1993.

———. *The Passions of the Soul.* Trans. and ed. Stephen Voss. Indianapolis: Hackett, 1989.

de Sousa, Ronald. *The Rationality of Emotion.* Cambridge: MIT Press, 1987.

Díaz de Rivas, Pedro. *Discursos apologéticos por el estylo del Poliphemo y Soledades. Documentos gongorinos: los Discursos apologéticos de Pedro Díaz de Rivas; el Antidoto de Juan Juaregui.* Ed. E. J. Gates. Mexico: Colegio de México, 1960.

Diccionario de Autoridades. 1726. Facs. ed. 3 vols. Madrid: Real Academia Española, 1976.

Diccionario de la Real Academia Española. 21st ed. 2 vols. Madrid: Real Academia Española, 1992.

Díez Borque, José María. *Sociología de la comedia española del siglo XVII.* Madrid: Cátedra, 1976.

Duncan-Irvin, Hayden. "Three Faces of Diana, Two Facets of Honor: Myth and the Honor Code in Lope de Vega's *El perro del hortelano.*" In *A Star-Crossed Golden Age,* ed. Frederick A. de Armas, 137–49. Lewisburg, PA: Bucknell University Press, 1998.

Elliott, J. H. *Imperial Spain: 1469–1716.* New York: St. Martin's, 1963.

El Saffar, Ruth. *Novel to Romance: A Study of Cervantes' "Novelas ejemplares."* Baltimore: Johns Hopkins University Press, 1974.

Equicola, Mario. *De natura d'amore, Libro quarto.* Ed. Enrico Musacchio and Graziella Del Ciuco. Bologna: Capelli editore, 1989.

Erasmus, Desiderius. *The Education of a Christian Prince.* Trans. and ed. Lester K. Born. New York: Columbia University Press, 1936.

Ferguson, Margaret W., Maureen Quilligan, and Nancy J. Vickers, eds. *Rewriting the Renaissance: The Discourses of Sexual Difference in Early Modern Europe.* Chicago: University of Chicago Press, 1986.

Ferraté, Juan. "Ficción y realidad en la poesía de Góngora." In *Dinámica de la poesía (Ensayos de explicación, 1952–1966),* 297–334. Barcelona: Seix Barral, 1968.

Ficino, Marsilio. *Commentary on Plato's "Symposium."* Ed. and trans. Sears Reynolds Jayne. University of Missouri Studies 19:1. Columbia: University of Missouri, 1944.

Forcione, Alban K. *Cervantes and the Humanist Vision: A Study of Four Exemplary Novels.* Princeton: Princeton University Press, 1982.

———. *Cervantes' Christian Romance: A Study of "Persiles y Sigismunda."* Princeton: Princeton University Press, 1972.

Foucault, Michel. *Discipline and Punish: The Birth of the Prison.* Trans. Alan Sheridan. 2nd ed. New York: Vintage, 1995.

Fox, Everett, trans. and ed. *The Five Books of Moses: Genesis, Exodus, Leviticus, Numbers, Deuteronomy.* Vol. 1 of *Schocken Bible.* New York: Schocken Books, 1995.

Fraker, Charles F., Jr. "Judaism in the *Cancionero de Baena.*" In *Studies on the "Cancionero de Baena,"* 9–62. Chapel Hill: University of North Carolina Press, 1966.

Freud, Sigmund. *The Interpretation of Dreams.* Trans. James Strachey. New York: Avon, 1980.

———. "Some Neurotic Mechanisms in Jealousy, Paranoia and Homosexuality." In vol. 18 of *The Standard Edition of the Complete Psychological Works,* trans. James Strachey, 223–32. London: Hogarth and the Institute for Psychoanalysis, 1955.

Frye, Northrop. *Anatomy of Criticism: Four Essays.* 1957. Princeton: Princeton University Press, 1971.

García Lorca, Federico. *La casa de Bernarda Alba.* Ed. Allen Josephs and Juan Caballero. 25th ed. Madrid: Cátedra, 1998.

Garcilaso de la Vega. *Obras completas con comentario.* Ed. Elías L. Rivers. Columbus: Ohio State University Press, 1974.

Garrot, Juan Carlos. "Sinagoga abandonada: Celos a lo divino en algunos autos calderonianos." In *Relations entre hommes et femmes en Espagne aux XVI et XVII siècles,* ed. Augustín Redondo, 199–206. Paris: La Sorbonne, 1995.

Gilman, Sander. *The Jew's Body.* New York: Routledge, 1991.

Girard, René. *Deceit, Desire and the Novel: Self and Other in Literary Structure.* Trans. Yvonne Freccero. Baltimore: Johns Hopkins University Press, 1965.

Goldie, Peter. *The Emotions: A Philosophical Exploration.* Oxford: Oxford University Press, 1999.

———, ed. *Understanding Emotions: Mind and Morals.* Ashgate Epistemology and Mind. Aldershot, England: Ashgate, 2002.

Góngora y Argote, Luis de. *Antología poética: "Polifemo," "Soledad primera," "Piramo y Tisbe" y otros poemas.* Ed. Antonio Carreira. 3rd ed. Madrid: Castalia, 1990.

———. *Fábula de Polifemo y Galatea.* Ed. with an intro. by Alexander A. Parker. Trans. Genoveva Ruiz-Ramón. 4th ed. Madrid: Cátedra, 1990.

———. *Obras poéticas.* Ed. R. Foulché-Delbosc. 2 vols. New York: Hispanic Society of America, 1921.

———. "Qué de invidiosos montes levantados" (1600). In *Canciones y otros poemas en arte mayor: Edición crítica,* ed. José María Micó. Madrid: Espasa-Calpe, 1990.

———. *Sonetos completos.* Ed. Biruté Ciplijauskaité. Madison: Hispanic Seminary of Medieval Studies, 1981.

González Amezúa, Agustín. *Cervantes creador de la novela corta.* 2 vols. Madrid: Consejo Superior de Investigaciones Científicas, 1956.

González Echevarría, Roberto. "Lezama, Góngora y la poética del mal gusto." *Hispania* 84 (2001): 428–40.

González Palencia, Ángel, ed. *Romancero general (1600, 1604, 1605).* Vols. 3 and 4 of *Clásicos españoles.* Madrid: Consejo Superior de Investigaciones Científicas, 1947.

Gracián, Baltasar. *The Critick.* Trans. Paul Rycaut. London: Printed by T. N. for Henry Brome, 1681.

———. *Obras completas.* Ed. Arturo del Hoyo. 3rd ed. Madrid: Aguilar, 1967.

Green, Otis. "El ingenioso hidalgo." *Hispanic Review* 25.3 (1957): 175–93.

———. *Spain and the Western Tradition: The Castilian Mind in Literature from "El Cid" to Calderón.* 4 vols. Madison: University of Wisconsin Press, 1963–1966.

Grieve, Patricia E. *Desire and Death in the Spanish Sentimental Romance (1440–1550).* Newark, DE: Juan de la Cuesta, 1987.

Griffith, Paul E. *What Emotions Really Are.* Chicago: University of Chicago Press, 1997.

Grzywacz, Margot. *"Eifersucht" in den romanischen Sprachen.* Bochum-Langendreer, Germany: H. Pöppinghaus, 1937.

Guyer, Paul. *Kant and the Experience of Freedom.* Cambridge, UK: Cambridge University Press, 1993.

Hansen, Gary L. "Jealousy: Its Conceptualization, Measurement, and Integration with Family Stress Theory." In *The Psychology of Jealousy and Envy,* ed. P. Salovey, 211–30. New York: Guilford, 1991.

Heidegger, Martin. *Being and Time.* Trans. John Macquarrie and Edward Robinson. San Francisco: Harper, 1962.

Heliodorus of Emesa. *Ethiopian Story (Aethiopica).* Trans. Sir Walter Lamb. New York: Dutton, 1961.

Hesiod. *Theogony.* Trans. Norman O. Brown. New York: MacMillan, 1953.

Holland, Henry Richard, Lord. *Some Account of the Lives and Writings of Lope de Vega and Guillén de Castro.* 2 vols. London: Longman, 1817.

Homer. *The Odyssey.* Trans. and ed. Richmond Lattimore. New York: Perennial-Harper, 1991.

Huet, Marie-Hélène. *Monstrous Imagination.* Cambridge: Harvard University Press, 1993.

Hupka, Ralph B. "The Motive for the Arousal of Romantic Jealousy." In *The Psychology of Jealousy and Envy,* ed. P. Salovey, 252–70. New York: Guilford, 1991.

Hutcheson, Gregory S. *Marginality and Empowerment in Baena's "Cancionero."* PhD diss., Harvard University, 1993.

Illades Aguiar, Gustavo. "Dos pacientes virtuales del médico Francisco de Villalobos: Anselmo y Carrizales." *Cervantes* 19.2 (1999): 101–12.

Iriarte, Mauricio de. *El doctor Huarte de San Juan y su Examen de ingenios. Contribución a la historia de la psicología diferencial.* 3rd ed. corr. Madrid: Consejo Superior de Investigaciones Científicas, 1948.

Jammes, Robert. *Etudes sur l'oeuvre poétique de don Luis de Góngora.* Bordeaux: Institut D'Etudes Ibériques et Ibéro-américaines de Bordeaux, 1967.

Jankowski, Theodora A. *Women in Power in the Early Modern Drama.* Urbana: University of Illinois Press, 1992.

Jones, R. O., ed. *Poems of Góngora,* by Luis de Góngora. Cambridge, UK: Cambridge University Press, 1966.

Kamen, Henry. *The Spanish Inquisition: A Historical Revision.* New Haven: Yale University Press, 1997.

Kamuf, Peggy, ed. *A Derrida Reader: Between the Blinds,* by Jacques Derrida. New York: Columbia University Press, 1991.

Kant, Immanuel. *Critique of Judgement.* Trans. James Creed Meredith. Oxford: Clarendon, 1991.

———. *Kant's Werke: Akademie-Textausgabe.* 9 vols. Berlin: W. de Gruyter, 1968.

Keller, John Esten, ed. *Libro de los enxemplos por A. B. C.* Madrid: CSIC, 1961.

King, Margaret L., and Albert Rabil Jr. "Introduction to the Series." In *The Education of a Christian Woman,* by Juan Luis Vives, ed. and trans. Charles Fantazzi, ix–xxviii. The Other Voice in Early Modern Europe. Chicago: University of Chicago Press, 2000.

Kossof, David, ed. *El castigo sin venganza,* by Lope de Vega. Madrid: Castalia, 1970.

Lacan, Jacques. *Écrits.* Trans. Alan Sheridan. New York: Norton, 1977.

La Rochefoucauld, F. *Maxims.* 1678. Harmondsworth, England: Penguin, 1959.

Larson, Donald. *The Honor Plays of Lope de Vega.* Cambridge: Harvard University Press, 1977.

Lazar, Moshe. "Fin'amor." In *A Handbook of the Troubadours,* ed. F. R. P. Akehurst and Judith M. Davis, 61–100. Berkeley: University of California Press, 1995.

Lehrer, Melinda Eve. *Classical Myth and the "Polifemo" of Góngora.* Potomac, MD: Scripta Humanistica, 1989.

Lessing, G. E. *Laocoön.* Trans. Edward Allen McCormick. Baltimore: Johns Hopkins University Press, 1984.

Lloyd, Rosemary. *Closer and Closer Apart: Jealousy in Literature.* Ithaca: Cornell University Press, 1995.

Longinus. *On the Sublime.* Trans. and ed. James A. Arieti and John Crossett. New York: E. Mellen, 1985.

Maravall, José Antonio. *La cultura del Barroco: Análisis de una estructura histórica.* 2nd ed. Barcelona: Ariel, 1980.

Marino, Giambattista. *Poesie varie.* Ed. Benedetto Croce. Vol. 51 of *Scrittori D'Italia.* Bari: Laterza, 1913.

Márquez Villanueva, Francisco. "Jewish 'Fools' of the Fifteenth Century *Cancioneros.*" *Hispanic Review* 50.4 (1985): 385–409.

Martínez-Bonati, Félix. *"Don Quixote" and the Poetics of the Novel.* Trans. Dian Fox. Ithaca: Cornell University Press, 1992.

Mathes, Eugene W. "A Cognitive Theory of Jealousy." In *The Psychology of Jealousy and Envy,* ed. P. Salovey, 52–78. New York: Guilford, 1991.

May, T. E. *Wit of the Golden Age: Essays on Spanish Literature.* Kassel: Ediciones Reichenberger, 1986.

McCaw, R. John. "Turning a Blind Eye: Sexual Competition, Self-Contradiction, and the Impotence of Pastoral in Góngora's *Fábula de Polifemo y Galatea.*" *Hispanófila* 127 (1999): 27–35.

McKendrick, Melveena. "Celebration or Subversion?: *Los comendadores de Córdoba* Reconsidered." *BHS* 61.3 (1984): 352–60.

———. *Woman and Society in the Spanish Drama of the Golden Age: A Study of the* Mujer Varonil. Cambridge, UK: Cambridge University Press, 1974.

Menéndez Pelayo, Marcelino. "Observaciones preliminares a las comedias mitológicas." In *Obras de Lope de Vega,* vol. 13, 203–331. Biblioteca de Autores Españoles 188. Madrid: Atlas, 1965.

Menéndez Pidal, Ramón. *De Cervantes a Lope de Vega.* Buenos Aires: Espasa-Calpe, 1943.

Micó, José María. "La superación del petrarquismo." In *El fragua de las "Soledades,"* 59–102. Barcelona: Sirmio, 1990.

Molière. *Dom Juan ou le festin de pierre.* Ed. W. D. Howarth. Oxford: B. Blackwell, 1975.

Moore, Leslie E. *Beautiful Sublime: The Making of "Paradise Lost" 1701–1734.* Stanford: Stanford University Press, 1990.

More, Thomas. *Utopia.* Trans. Robert M. Adams. New York: Norton, 1975.

Morley, S. Griswold, and Courtney Bruerton. *Cronología de las comedias de Lope de Vega.* Madrid: Gredos, 1968.

Mozart, Wolfgang Amadeus, and Lorenzo da Ponte. *Three Mozart Libretti: Complete in Italian and English.* Trans. Robert Pack and Marjorie Lelash. New York: Dover, 1993.

Mujica, Barbara. "Violence in the Pastoral Novel from Sannazaro to Cervantes." *Hispano-Italic Studies* 1 (1976).

Mulcahy, Rosemarie. *The Decoration of the Royal Basilica of El Escorial.* Cambridge, UK: Cambridge University Press, 1994.

Nietzsche, Friedrich. *On the Genealogy of Morals.* Trans. Walter Kaufmann. New York: Vintage Books, 1989.

Nochlin, Linda. *Women, Art, and Power, and Other Essays*. New York: Icon-Harper, 1988.

Noreña, Carlos G. *Juan Luis Vives and the Emotions*. Carbondale and Edwardsville: Southern Illinois University Press, 1989.

Nozick, Robert. *The Nature of Rationality*. Princeton: Princeton University Press, 1993.

Nussbaum, Martha C. *Poetic Justice*. Boston: Beacon, 1995.

———. *Upheavals of Thought: The Intelligence of Emotions*. New York: Cambridge University Press, 2001.

Ovid [P. Ovidius Naso]. "The Art of Love," in *The Art of Love and Other Poems*. Trans. J. H. Mozley. Ed. G. P. Goold. 2nd ed. Loeb Classical Library. Cambridge: Harvard University Press, 1979.

———. *Las metamorfosis*. Trans. Pedro Sánchez de Viana. Ed. Juan Francisco Alcina. Barcelona: Planeta, 1990.

———. *Metamorphosen*. Ed. M. Haupt, O. Korn, R. Ehwald. 2 vols. Zurich: Weidmann, 1966.

———. *Metamorphoses*. Trans. Sir Samuel Garth, John Dryden, et al. Amsterdam, 1732. Reprint, New York and London: Garland Publishing, 1976.

Panofsky, Erwin. *Studies in Iconology: Humanistic Themes in the Art of the Renaissance*. New York: Icon-Harper, 1972.

Pariente, Angel. *Góngora*. Madrid: Júcar, 1982.

Parker, Alexander A. *The Approach to the Spanish Drama of the Golden Age*. London: Hispanic and Luso-Brazilian Councils, 1957.

———, ed. Introduction to *Fábula de Polifemo y Galatea,* by Luis de Góngora, trans. Genoveva Ruiz Ramón. 4th ed. Madrid: Cátedra, 1990.

———, ed. *Polyphemus and Galatea: A Study in the Interpretation of a Baroque Poem by Luis de Góngora*. Trans. Gilbert F. Cunningham. Edinburgh: University Press of Edinburgh, 1977.

Parrott, W. Gerrod. "The Emotional Experience of Envy and Jealousy." In *The Psychology of Jealousy and Envy,* ed. P. Salovey, 3–30. New York: Guilford, 1991.

Pérez-Rioja, J. A. *Diccionario de símbolos y mitos*. 3rd ed. Madrid: Tecnos, 1988.

Petrarca, Francesco. *Rime*. Ed. Ugo Dotti. 2 vols. Rome: Donzelli, 1996.

Plato. *The Republic*. Trans. G. M. A. Grube. Ed. C. D. C. Reeve. Indianapolis: Hackett, 1992.

————. *Symposium*. Trans. and intro. by Alexander Nehamas and Paul Woodruff. Indianapolis: Hackett, 1989.

Poggi, Giulia. "*Exclusus amator* e *poeta ausente:* alcune note ad una canzone gongorina." *Linguistica e Letteratura* 8 (1983): 189–222.

Quevedo, Francisco de. "Comparación con el significado de los colores." In vol. 3 of *Obras de don Francisco de Quevedo,* 490–91. Biblioteca de Autores Españoles 69. Madrid: Atlas, 1953.

————. *Poesía original completa.* Ed. José Manuel Blecua. 3rd ed. Barcelona: Planeta, 1990.

Reed, Cory A. "Harems and Eunuchs: Ottoman-Islamic Motifs of Captivity in *El celoso extremeño.*" *BHS* 76 (1999): 199–214.

Ricapito, Joseph. *Formalistic Aspects of Cervantes' "Novelas ejemplares."* Medieval and Romance Studies 17. Lewiston, NY: E. Mellen, 1997.

Rivers, Elías L. *Garcilaso de la Vega, Poems: A Critical Guide.* London: Grant, 1980.

Rivers, Elías L., ed. *Renaissance and Baroque Poetry of Spain: With English Prose Translations.* Long Grove, IL: Waveland Press, 1988.

Roberts, Helen. *Encyclopedia of Comparative Iconography.* Chicago: Fitzroy Dearborn, 1998.

Rorty, Amélie, ed. *Explaining Emotions.* Berkeley: University of California Press, 1980.

Rosales, Luis. *Cervantes y la libertad.* 2nd ed. 2 vols. Madrid: Edición Cultural Hispánica, 1985.

Rose, Stanley E. "Anti-Semitism in the *Cancioneros* of the 15th Century: The Accusation of Sexual Indiscretions." *Hispanófila* 78 (May 1983): 1–10.

Rosher, W. H., ed. *Ausfürliches Lexicon der griechischen und römischen Mythologie.* 5 vols. Leipzig, 1884–1924.

Rougemont, Denis de. *Love in the Western World.* Trans. Montgomery Belgion. Rev. ed. Princeton: Princeton University Press, 1983.

Ruiz Ramón, Francisco. *Historia del teatro español.* Madrid: Alianza Editorial, 1967.

Salcedo Coronel, García de, ed. *Segundo tomo de las obras de don Luis de Góngora,* by Luis de Góngora. Madrid, 1648.

Sannazaro, Jacopo. *Opere di Iacopo Sannazaro.* Torino: Unions tipografico editrice torinese, 1952.

Sartre, Jean-Paul. *Being and Nothingness: An Essay on Phenomenological Ontology.* Trans. Hazel Barnes. New York: Philosophical Library, 1956.

————. *Sketch for a Theory of the Emotions*. London: Routledge, 2002.

Schack, Adolf Friedrich von. *Geschichte der dramatischen Literatur und Kunst in Spanien*. 3 vols. Berlin: Duncker und Humblot, 1845–1846.

Schulz-Buschhaus, Ulrich. "Der frühe Góngora und die italienische Lyrik." *Romanisches Jahrbuch* 20 (1969): 219–38.

Schwartz, Lía. "Figuras del Orco y el infierno interior en Quevedo." In *Hommage à Robert Jammes,* ed. Francis Cerdan, vol. 3, 1079–88. Toulouse: Presses Universitaires du Mirail, 1994.

Scruton, Roger. *The Aesthetics of Music*. Oxford: Oxford University Press, 1997.

Sears, Theresa Ann. "Sacrificial Lambs and Domestic Goddesses, or, Did Cervantes Write Chick Lit? (Being a Meditation on Women and Free Will)." *Cervantes* 20.1 (2000): 47–68.

Shakespeare, William. *Othello*. Ed. M. R. Ridley. London and New York: Arden-Routledge, 1965.

Sobejano, Gonzalo. "'En los claustros de l'alma.' Apuntaciones sobre la lengua poética de Quevedo." In *Sprache und Geschichte,* ed. Eugenio Coseriu and Wolf-Dieter Stempel, 459–92. *Festschrift für Harri Meier zum 65. Geburstag*. Munich: Wilhelm Fink, 1971.

————. "'Reinos del espanto': Garcilaso, Góngora, Quevedo y otros." In *Busquemos otros montes y otros ríos: Estudios de literatura española del Siglo de Oro dedicados a Elías L. Rivers,* ed. Brian Dutton and Victoriano Roncero López, 253–67. Madrid: Castalia, 1992.

Spitzer, Leo. *Estilo y estructura en la literatura española*. Barcelona: Crítica, 1980.

Stendhal. *On Love*. Trans. Gilbert and Suzanne Sale. New York: Penguin, 1975.

Stroud, Matthew. *Fatal Union: A Pluralistic Approach to the Wife-Murder Comedias*. Lewisburg, PA: Bucknell University Press, 1990.

Tasso, Torquato. *Delle rime et prose*. Vol. 4. Venetia, 1586.

Taylor, Gabrielle. "Envy and Jealousy: Emotions and Vices." *Midwest Studies in Philosophy* 13 (1988): 233–49.

Theocritus. *The Poems of Theocritus*. Trans. and ed. Anna Rist. Chapel Hill: University of North Carolina Press, 1978.

Tirso de Molina [Fray Gabriel Téllez]. *El burlador de Sevilla y convidado de piedra*. Ed. Mercedes Sánchez Sánchez. Madrid: Castalia, 1997.

Tripp, Edward. *The Meridian Handbook of Classical Mythology.* New York: Penguin-Meridian, 1974.

Trueblood, Alan S. *Experience and Artistic Expression in Lope de Vega: The Making of "La Dorotea."* Cambridge: Harvard University Press, 1974.

Urraro, Laurie L. "El travestismo y sus aportaciones cómicas en dos comedias del Siglo de Oro." *Selected Proceedings of the Pennsylvania Foreign Language Conference,* 219–28. Pittsburgh, PA: Duquesne Modern Language Dept., 2003.

Vega Carpio, Félix Lope de. *Adonis y Venus.* In *Obras de Lope de Vega,* vol. 13, ed. Marcelino Menéndez Pelayo, 335–73. Biblioteca de Autores Españoles 188. Madrid: Atlas, 1965.

———. *Arminda celosa.* In *Obras de Lope de Vega Publicadas por la Real Academia Española,* intro. Emilio Cotarelo y Mori, 693–711. New ed. Vol. 1. Madrid: Real Academia Española, 1916.

———. *Arte nuevo de hacer comedias en este tiempo. La discreta enamorada.* 5th ed. Madrid: Espasa-Calpe, 1991.

———. *Belardo el furioso.* In *Obras de Lope de Vega,* vol. 13, ed. Marcelino Menéndez Pelayo, 61–115. Biblioteca de Autores Españoles 188. Madrid: Atlas, 1965.

———. *El caballero de Olmedo.* Ed. Francisco Rico. 9th ed. Madrid: Cátedra, 1989.

———. *El castigo sin venganza.* Ed. C. A. Jones. Oxford: Pergamon Press, 1966.

———. *Los comendadores de Córdoba.* Ed. Federico Carlos Sainz de Robles. In *Obras escogidas,* vol. 3, 1233–66. 3rd ed. 2nd reprinting. Madrid: Aguilar, 1987.

———. *La discreta enamorada,* in *Arte nuevo de hacer comedias.* 5th ed. Madrid: Espasa-Calpe, 1981.

———. *La Dorotea.* Trans. and ed. Alan S. Trueblood and Edwin Honig. Cambridge: Harvard University Press, 1985.

———. *La Dorotea.* Ed. E. S. Morby. Madrid: Castalia, 1987.

———. *Epistolario de Lope de Vega (Lope de Vega en sus cartas).* Ed. Agustin González Amezúa. 4 vols. Madrid: RAE, 1935–1943.

———. *Obras escogidas.* Ed. Federico Carlos Sainz de Robles. 3 vols. Madrid: Aguilar, 1964–1974.

———. *Obras poéticas: Rimas; Rimas sacras; La Filomena; La Circe; Rimas humanas y divinas del licenciado Tomé de Burguillos.* Ed. José Manuel Blecua. 2nd ed. Vol. 1. Barcelona: Planeta, 1974.

———. *Peribáñez y el comendador de Ocaña.* 14th ed. Ed. Juan María Marín. Madrid: Cátedra, 1994.

———. *El perro del hortelano.* Ed. Mauro Armiño. Madrid: Cátedra, 1996.

———. *La reina Juana de Nápoles.* In *Obras de Lope de Vega,* vol. 15, ed. Marcelino Menéndez Pelayo, 227–80. Biblioteca de Autores Españoles 191. Madrid: Atlas, 1966.

Vilanova, Antonio. *Las fuentes y los temas del "Polifemo" de Góngora.* 2nd ed. 2 vols. Barcelona: PPU, 1992.

Virgil. *Aeneid.* Trans. Robert Fitzgerald. New York: Random House, 1990.

———. *Eclogues.* Trans. Barbara Hughes Fowler. Chapel Hill: University of North Carolina Press, 1997.

Vives, Juan Luis. *The Education of a Christian Woman,* ed. and trans. Charles Fantazzi. The Other Voice in Early Modern Europe. Chicago: University of Chicago Press, 2000.

———. *The Passions of the Soul.* Bk. 3 of *De Anima et Vita.* Trans. Carlos G. Noreña. Lewiston, NY: E. Mellen Press, 1990.

Vossler, Karl. *Lope de Vega y su tiempo.* Trans. R. de la Serna. 2nd ed. Madrid: Revista de Occidente, 1940.

Wardropper, Bruce W. *Siglos de Oro: Barroco.* Vol. 3 of *Historia y crítica de la literatura española.* Ed. Francisco Rico. Barcelona: Crítica, 1983.

Weber, Alison. "Tragic Reparation in Cervantes' *El celoso extremeño.*" *Cervantes: Bulletin of the Cervantes Society of America* 4.1 (1984): 35–51.

Weimer, Christopher. "The Politics of Husband Murder: Gender, Supplementarity and Sacrifice in Lope de Vega's *La reina Juana de Nápoles.*" *Hispanic Review* 68 (2001): 32–52.

Weinberg, Bernard. *A History of Literary Criticism in the Italian Renaissance.* 2 vols. Chicago: University of Chicago Press, 1961.

Wellek, René. "The Concept of Baroque in Literary Scholarship" with "Postscript 1962." In *Concepts of Criticism,* ed. Stephen G. Nichols Jr., 69–127. New Haven: Yale University Press, 1963.

Welles, Marcia L. *Arachne's Tapestry: The Transformation of Myth in Seventeenth-Century Spain.* San Antonio, TX: Trinity University Press, 1981.

Williamsen-Cerón, Amy. "The Comic Function of Two Mothers: Belisa and Angela." *Bulletin of the Comediantes* 36.2 (1984): 167–74.

Wistrich, Robert S. *Antisemitism: The Longest Hatred.* New York: Pantheon, 1991.

Wölfflin, Heinrich. *Principles of Art History: The Problem of the Development of Style in Later Art.* Trans. M. D. Hottinger. New York: Dover, 1950.

———. *Renaissance and Baroque.* Trans. Kathrin Simon. Ithaca: Cornell University Press, 1984.

Xenophon of Athens. *Kyrou paideia or The Institution and Life of Cyrus the Great.* Trans. Francis Digby and John Norris. London, 1685.

Yarbo-Bejarano, Yvonne. *Feminism and the Honor Plays of Lope de Vega.* Purdue Studies in Romance Literature. West Lafayette, IN: Purdue University Press, 1994.

Yerushalmi, Yosef Hayim. *Assimilation and Racial Antisemitism: The Iberian and the German Models.* Leo Baeck Memorial Lecture 26. New York: Leo Baeck Institute, 1982.

Zimic, Stanislav. *El teatro de Cervantes.* Madrid: Castalia, 1992.

———. "La tragedia de Carrizales, *El celoso extremeño.*" *Acta Neophilologica* 24 (1991): 23–48.

Zorrilla, José. *Don Juan Tenorio.* Ed. Aniano Peña. Madrid: Cátedra, 1987.

Index